THE NORTHERN CONQUEST

Katherine Holman

THE NORTERN CONQUEST

VIKINGS IN BRITAIN AND IRELAND

Signal

First published in 2007
This edition published in 2017 by
Signal Books Limited
36 Minster Road
Oxford
OX4 1LY
www.signalbooks.co.uk

This edition prepared for print by
Andrews UK Limited
www.andrewsuk.com

A catalogue record for this book is available from the British Library

ISBN 978-1-909930-55-1 Paper

Cover Design: Baseline Arts
Cover Images: © Crown Copyright, 2006, Historic Scotland Images;
Auckland War Memorial Museum; AndrzejTokarski/istockphoto;
Ray Roper/istockphoto; Alfio Ferlito/istockphoto

CONTENTS

LiST OF iLLUSTRATiONS

Map 1: The British Isles, showing key places mentioned in the text

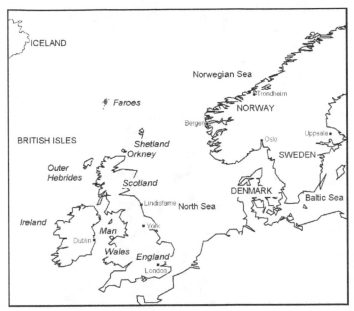

Map 2: The North Sea world

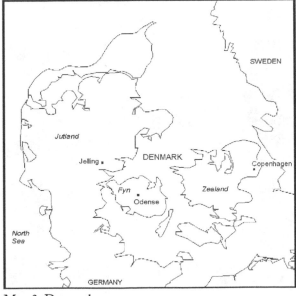

Map 3: Denmark

INTRODUCTION

Most of us need no introduction to the Vikings and their activities in the British Isles. They were brutal barbarians who sailed to Britain and Ireland from their bleak and barren Scandinavian homelands to loot monasteries, burn down villages and towns, slaughter whoever in their way, and generally make life miserable for the God-fearing Christian inhabitants of these islands. At least, that was the traditional picture that people of my generation were brought up with in our history books and at school. Today, schoolchildren are presented with a more balanced, if considerably less dramatic, picture of the Vikings and Viking Age that is built upon new archaeological evidence from Scandinavia and the British Isles. And even *The Vicious Vikings*, part of the Horrible Histories series for children that prides itself on the fact that 'the nasty bits [are] left in', has to concede that 'Not all the Vikings were vicious … and the ones who were, weren't vicious all the time … the Vikings were no more vicious than the rest of the world at that time.'[1]

Vicious or not, who were these Vikings? The word 'Viking' is often used in a general sense for those people from the modern Scandinavian countries of Denmark, Norway, and Sweden, during the historical period 800-1100. Yet, strictly speaking, a 'Viking' was not just a person living in medieval Scandinavia: the word has a more specific meaning. The word 'Viking' is first found in an Old English biblical poem, *Exodus*, dating to the eighth century, where the *wicingas* were seagoing sons of Reuben. Here the word seems to be derived from Old English *wic* 'port', and so the Vikings in this context were those people who frequented ports. 'Vikings' therefore were associated with the sea, and during the following centuries it was Scandinavian raiders and traders who proved themselves as masters of the sea. These Scandinavians, usually men, who sailed west across the North Sea also journeyed across the North Atlantic to Iceland, Greenland and even North America; they voyaged south and east through the Baltic, and down the Russian rivers into the Black Sea and beyond, trading and settling as well as raiding. The people who stayed at home in Scandinavia were, technically, not Vikings in the true sense of the word, although it is often hard to distinguish between the two groups of population clearly, as people who had lived peacefully at home all winter may well have turned to Viking activities in the summer.

The precise meaning and origin of the word 'Viking' is, however, uncertain. It may be connected to the place-name Viken, the name for the area around Oslofjord in Norway, which is derived from an Old Norse word for inlet or fjord (*vík*). So the first Vikings were perhaps those men who hailed from Viken or, more generally, the fjords of Norway and maybe Denmark too. However, given that the word 'Viking' first appears in Old English, it is possible that the term may even originate in the English word *wic* (settlement), commonly found in place-names such as Norwich (*Norðwic*) and York (*Eoforwicceaster*), and sometimes also used to describe camps or temporary fortifications of the kind that the Vikings built. Whatever its origins, though, it is important to realize that the word was only really popularized during the nineteenth century, and that contemporaries of the Vikings usually called them other names. In the Christian West they were often called 'heathen', and in the Muslim regions, such as Spain, they were called *majus*, a word that originally meant 'heathen' too, but which was later also associated with fire-worship and incest.

Most common, however, were the geographical terms 'Northmen' and 'Danes' that were usually used irrespective of which part of Scandinavia the raiders came from.

It is also necessary at this point to discuss the meaning of the word Scandinavia, as there is often some confusion over which north European countries this includes. Scandinavians use this word to refer to the three present-day countries of Denmark, Norway and Sweden and this is the definition that I have followed in this book; in other words, both Iceland and Finland are not considered to be part of Scandinavia. There are a number of good reasons for this: certainly Finland was and indeed is ethnically and linguistically quite distinct from Denmark, Iceland, Norway and Sweden, which during the Viking Age spoke a common language, sometimes called the *dönsk tunga*, 'the Danish tongue'. While the remote North Atlantic island of Iceland, inhabited by a handful of Irish hermits, was not part of the Scandinavian world at the beginning of the Viking Age, it was colonized by a Scandinavian-speaking population in the ninth century. Ethnically and linguistically part of the Scandinavian world, Iceland maintained close contacts with Norway in particular. Nevertheless, there are significant differences that place it outside the Scandinavian mainstream: politically, it was not a monarchy at least not until it acknowledged the Norwegian king, Hákon Hákonarson, as its king in 1262; ethnically, there appears to have been a small but significant Celtic strand in the Icelandic population, following the settlement of some Scandinavian families who had previously spent time in parts of the British Isles; economically, it lacked its own towns during the Viking Age and was instead dependent on trade with Scandinavia; and geographically, Iceland was, of course, a considerable distance from Denmark, Norway and Sweden.

Although there is a huge literature, scholarly and popular, on the Vikings and their impact on the British Isles, much of this follows the present-day borders of England, Scotland, Wales, and Ireland — or focuses instead on particular regions, such as the Danelaw or the Northern Isles. This approach is very necessary for amassing the wealth of information about the Vikings in those places and for discussing it in detail, but it is also important to step back occasionally and look at the evidence from a wider perspective. This too can improve our understanding of the impact of Viking raids and settlement, particularly as many of the armies that campaigned in Britain and Ireland did not limit their activities to one country — they appear to have moved around the British and Irish coasts indiscriminately, seeking wealth (in the form of loot or business), conquest, or new land on which to settle wherever they could find it.

Readers looking for a survey of Viking activity in the British Isles have two main choices at present (2007): *The Vikings in Britain* was written by the distinguished professor of Anglo-Saxon history, Henry Loyn, in the 1970s, and was partially revised and condensed for a new edition in 1994; *Blood of the Vikings* was written by the archaeologist, Julian Richards, in 2001 in conjunction with a BBC television series of the same name. The visual contrast between the two books could hardly be sharper: while Richards' book is large and lavishly illustrated in colour, Loyn's 1994 book is a slim paperback volume of rather densely-packed text, enlivened only by the occasional black-and-white map. In terms of their content, although Richards' and Loyn's approaches are as different as you would expect from an archaeologist writing for a television audience and an academic historian of the old school, both books spend a considerable amount of time detailing the Viking raids — what happened, when it happened, who was involved — in chronological order, as well as discussing what conditions were like in the Scandinavian homelands of Denmark, Norway, and Sweden. The chief difference in the scope, rather than the approach, of these books lies in their analysis of 'the

Viking legacy' (the title of Richards' final chapter). Richards' account is ten pages long and concludes with a brief summary of the genetic contribution the Vikings made to the British Isles, a project that was at the very heart of the BBC series and a theme that therefore runs throughout Richards' book. Loyn's is a much weightier, traditional discussion of the still unresolved historical debates that surround the Vikings' contribution to the culture and history of the British Isles, focusing primarily on the linguistic evidence, and this discussion accounts for a quarter of the total length of the book.

It is hoped that *The Northern Conquest* will provide readers with something that lies in between Richards' and Loyn's histories: something that will provide a relatively short insight into these people and this period of history for those seeking an introduction to the subject, but which also summarizes the most important debates and has references for those readers wanting to find more information on particular topics elsewhere. Most of the book focuses on themes and controversies relating to the Viking experience in the British Isles rather than outlining details of Viking attacks, but there is a list of key dates at the end of the book outlining the main sequence of events. The penultimate chapter, 'After the Norman Conquest', also introduces a theme that is not really discussed by either Richards or Loyn: that of the continued importance of contact with Scandinavia and Scandinavians after the Viking Age that is traditionally regarded to have come to an end. This will come as no surprise to those familiar with Viking activity in Scotland, Ireland, and the islands around their coasts: the Scottish islands and the Isle of Man retained close links with Norway long after England fell into Norman hands: Man and the Hebrides were not sold off to Scotland until 1266, and Shetland and Orkney were only pawned to the Scottish king in 1468-69. However, it is considerably less well known that even in England, contacts with the Scandinavian world flourished after the Norman

Conquest, in the form of trade, diplomacy, and religious links. I hope to show that events in the years that followed William the Conqueror's victory at Hastings are a necessary part of the historical movement that began with the first Viking raids on monasteries at the end of the eighth century.

Hull, January 2007   Katherine Holman

1
Uncovering the Viking Past

'Truth and fact may be related, but they are more often opposed, and a collection of facts, no matter how conscientious, does not constitute truth unless by accident' (Gavin Maxwell).[1]

How do we know what we know about the Vikings and the Viking Age? Reconstructing the past is something like putting together a jigsaw, a jigsaw where you do not know what the final picture is going to look like: each different piece of information about that past — whether it be a brooch or a book — needs to be slotted into the right place for the complete picture to emerge. Of course, when it comes to reconstructing a picture that lies some thousand years in the past, the jigsaw is, unavoidably and frustratingly, bound to be missing several key pieces. However, the jigsaw or, more accurately, the jigsaws that tell us about life in the British Isles at the time of the Viking invasions and settlements are particularly intriguing and exciting. Here we have a time of great change and, to judge from historical writings that have survived from the Viking Age, violent and sudden change at that. For example, the *Anglo-Saxon Chronicle* account of events in the year 866 provides some indication of the tumultuous realities of life in York, England's second city:

In this year the raiding-army went from East Anglia over the mouth of the Humber to York in Northumbria; and there was great discord among the people of York; and they had rejected their king Osberht and accepted Ælla, an 'unnatural' king; and it was late in the year when they turned to making war against the raiding-army, nevertheless they gathered a great army and sought out the raiding-army in York and broke into the city, and some of them got inside; and an immense slaughter was made of the Northumbrians there, some inside, some outside, and both the kings were killed, and the survivors made peace with the raiding-army.[2]

This brief entry in the *Chronicle* raises all sorts of questions: how big was the raiding army of the Vikings? How long did it take for them to travel from East Anglia to York? What did the fleet look like sailing along the Humber and up into York? How high did the Roman walls of York stand? Where were the people of York living, and in what conditions, before the raiders broke into their city? What was the reason for their rejection of Osberht? How long did they fight with the Viking occupiers of their city before making peace? How were Osberht and Ælla killed? How did the peace negotiations take place? With the help of a translator or sign-language? Could the Vikings and Northumbrians understand each other's language? What happened to the people of York after this Scandinavian takeover? Was there much hostility and conflict?

Unfortunately, many of these questions must simply go unanswered or remain the object of historical speculation, but asking the questions is, all the same, a useful exercise, because it brings to life the terse words of the Chronicler. These are not simply words written down on a page over a thousand years ago: real people, like you and me, were there experiencing the Viking takeover of York. If we saw this reported on the evening news, what sort of images would we expect to see and what sort of questions would we want answered? The news of 886 must have spread in shock waves through the British Isles, and beyond, leaving people wary and fearful of what might come next.

Despite their reputation as destructive barbarians, surprisingly the Vikings are also still regarded as heroic figures, great and loyal warriors, intrepid explorers who crossed oceans and colonized new lands. Or as Winston Churchill put it in his distinctive prose style:

> When we reflect upon the brutal vices of these salt-water bandits, pirates as shameful as any whom the sea has borne, or recoil from their villainous destruction and cruel deeds, we must also remember the discipline, the fortitude, the comradeship and martial virtues which made them at this period beyond all challenge the most formidable and daring race in the world.[3]

The 'romance' of the Viking Age was especially emphasized and embellished in the literature and art of the nineteenth century, a cultural expression of Germanic nationalism that turned its back on the Classical inheritance of the Roman Empire. During this time there was a new enthusiasm among scholars for Old English, Old Norse and other vernacular languages that had long been overshadowed by Latin. Artists, such as the pre-Raphaelites, increasingly sought their inspiration in the folk tales and mythology of medieval northern Europe rather than Greek and Roman myths. The nineteenth century was also a time when the political rights of the individual, as well as of the individual nation, were starting to be asserted. Icelandic sagas provided many inspiring examples of free and heroic individuals who rejected the rule of power-hungry kings and left their homes in Norway to found the Icelandic commonwealth and its 'parliament', which was lauded as the oldest democratic institution in Europe. Scandinavian poems, sagas and histories were translated into English for the first time, providing historians with the raw material that they needed to examine Viking society and values, to try and understand the reasons behind the expeditions and attacks of the Viking Age.

That the Vikings did good and bad things is, in itself, hardly surprising, but it is unusual for both sides of their reputation to have survived in popular legends and tales of the Viking Age: the Huns were evil, Robin Hood was good, but the Vikings defy such easy labelling. This means that when we look at the Viking Age, we are faced with conflicting images and pieces of information. Writing a book like this, a historian of course needs to try to separate fact from fiction, legend from history, and flesh out the caricature Viking warrior with horned helmet into a more rounded picture of the Vikings and their legacy. But it is equally important to realize that there simply is no such thing as objective history: people do not write it now and they did not write it then. No one person can record every event that takes place, and the very process of selecting what information to write down and what to discard is imposing values and views on the reader. Even the meaning of archaeological evidence — artefacts such as coins, combs, and clothes — is affected by our own imperfect understanding of the past. But this does not make our source material worthless — there is often a tendency to regard 'biased' sources as wrong, but instead they help us understand some of the opinions and ideas that were circulating at the time. As long as we do not see these ideas as the only valid view of history, we can use this evidence. Indeed, the historian of the Viking Age really has very little choice in the matter: there are so few shreds of information that we simply *must* use all the available evidence.

In attempting a survey of the Viking history of the British Isles, the historian faces a further complication: the geographical spread of primary sources (those sources created at the time) is very uneven. While there is a fair amount of written material for Ireland and southern England, there is much less for the central and northern areas of mainland Britain, and the remote islands of Scotland are almost entirely lacking in written sources during the period in which we are interested. Nevertheless, there is some compensation in the rich archaeological heritage of these areas that has been uncovered in recent years, and this is continually adding to our knowledge of life there in the Viking and medieval periods. Of course, archaeological evidence offers a rather different perspective on history than written evidence: we have only to think about what historians and archaeologists might make of our own society if they found, on the one hand, a newspaper and, on the other, the contents of a dustbin. While a newspaper would tell them about things that were happening at the time and values that were important to readers, the dustbin would reveal details about the food we ate and the items we used and discarded.

Written sources, such as the *Annals of Ulster* and the *Anglo-Saxon Chronicle*, are the stuff of conventional history, focusing on the key events and prominent people of the past, and through their selection of material and their comments presenting a particular viewpoint or interpretation of history. Although some of these texts were written during the Viking Age, most of them only survive in copies that were made later — and there is therefore the possibility, indeed the probability, that the people who copied them down made additions, alterations, omissions, or straightforward mistakes. However, an author is likely to have known more concerning the events and people about which he was writing if he was writing at the time when they were happening. Writing with the advantage of hindsight changes, reorders and eliminates 'facts'. And, in an age dominated by orality rather than literacy, by the spoken not the written word, there were few or no documents or histories to consult for the prospective historian writing more than a generation or two after the event. Imagine trying to write a history of the Victorian period if you had virtually no written evidence to consult — no newspapers, perhaps one or two biographies, a couple of wills, and a few letters — remembering all

11

the time that the authors of your scant source material may well have had their own particular axe to grind and are likely to have pruned the 'facts' to fit their purpose. Trying to work out what this purpose was, who the author and the audience were, is a crucial part in trying to make sense of historical source material. In the simplest terms, a Scandinavian author writing for a Scandinavian audience is likely to put quite a different slant on a Viking raid from a British author writing for a British audience. Scandinavians naturally saw their actions a little differently from those outraged monastic historians who were attacked by Vikings and from other writers who had never even been to the remote North, on the very edges of the known world.

Unfortunately, during the Viking Age, Scandinavians only seem to have used their runic script to carve short memorial texts on monuments to the dead, so we have no contemporary histories or chronicles. The famous sagas were produced, mainly in Iceland, some four or five hundred years after the Viking Age had begun, and by Christian authors for a Christian audience. Geographically, chronologically, religiously, culturally, these people were remote from their Viking-Age forebears. For example, the majority of the sagas were written after the independent commonwealth of Iceland had been incorporated into the kingdom of Norway; the founding fathers of the Icelandic republic, who had fled from the tyranny of the Norwegian king, must have therefore seemed particularly inspiring and heroic to contemporaries — indeed, the men who wrote down the sagas may well have exaggerated their achievements or even invented episodes in order to appeal to their audiences and perhaps to make a political point.

But these sagas do contain nuggets of contemporary skaldic poetry. Its name was derived from the Old Norse word *skald* meaning 'poet', and this was essentially praise poetry, usually composed by known authors in the service of Scandinavian kings, princes, and earls. Skaldic poetry was composed orally and recited in front of its subject in public performances. Most of the known skalds appear to be Icelanders, such as Egil Skallagrimsson, whose famous *Head Ransom Poem* was composed and recited in York before its king, Erik Blood-Axe. Full of praise for Erik's skills as a warrior and his generosity, Egil's poem managed to placate his arch-enemy and the skald escaped from York with his life. A number of surviving skaldic poems concern the activities of Scandinavian rulers in the British Isles. These shed some light on the campaigns of, for example, Olaf Haraldsson in England in the early eleventh century, Harald Hard-Ruler's battle against the English at Stamford Bridge in 1066, and Magnus Bare-Foot in the Western Isles and Wales at the end of the eleventh century.

Skaldic poetry was normally composed in stanzas of eight lines, and is often quite difficult for modern readers as it has a complex structure and cryptic vocabulary, derived from myths and legends, some of which are now lost. A variety of different metres could also be used, but *dróttkvætt* 'court metre' is the best-known of the skaldic metres. Typically, a *dróttkvætt* verse will consist of eight lines, with a total of 48 syllables. We owe much of our knowledge and under-standing of skaldic poetry to the Icelandic writer Snorri Sturluson. His *Edda*, sometimes called *Prose Edda*, is effectively a manual for those wishing to compose skaldic poetry — its rules of composition, its mythological background, and also a record of some pieces of skaldic poetry. Although believed to have been composed in the Viking Age, most skaldic poetry is preserved in medieval manuscripts, especially those containing sagas about Norway's Viking-Age kings, where they are used to lend authority to the prose text. Indeed, in his prologue to *Heimskringla* (a collection of kings' sagas), Snorri states that skaldic poetry was an important historical source because, although it was praise poetry, to recite false praise in front of an audience would be 'mockery, not praise'. Very few poems are quoted in full — usually a verse or two would be given to support the prose. The late preservation of this poetry has led to much discussion about its authenticity and reliability. It is generally argued that the complex rhythmical and alliterative rules helped the poems to retain their original form, in spite of the problems normally associated with oral transmission of texts.

Domesday Book is perhaps the single most important historical document in English history, providing the first historical record of the majority of English towns and villages twenty years after the Norman Conquest, in 1086. It has also been a key document for historians studying the impact of Scandinavian settlement, primarily because its picture of society in northern and eastern England looks quite different from that found in other parts of the country. The place-names of the settlements in these areas also clearly demonstrate the linguistic repercussions of Scandinavian colonization, repercussions that are echoed in many English texts produced in the post-Conquest period. The very scarcity of sources from the Viking Age naturally invites closer scrutiny of the more numerous written texts that have survived from the years after 1066, particularly as many of these so-called Middle English texts come from the areas that were settled by Scandinavians.[4] This is in stark contrast to the sources we have for the Viking Age, which were nearly all produced in southern England and which were therefore written in dialects untouched by the Scandinavian languages. However, these later sources raise considerable problems for historians interested in the impact of Scandinavian settlement — the debate is discussed in more detail in Chapter 3 — because of the 200-year interlude between the settlements and the written evidence. Are we really looking at changes the Vikings caused, or at developments that took place long after the Vikings ceased to be a recognizable part of the English population?

14

Nevertheless, the evidence of these late works cannot be ignored, even if we have to treat them with considerable caution.

This lack of written information for the Viking Age is at least partially offset by archaeological and linguistic evidence, which offer important insights into the cultures and structures of the places where they are found, and may, in the final analysis, provide us with more real understanding of the Viking impact than our written sources. One enormous advantage that archaeological artefacts have over most written sources is that they date from the Viking period, and were therefore used by real, live Vikings. To think that we can touch the shoes that Viking children wore and the swords that were once carried overseas in longships and wielded in war provides us with an incredibly direct link to those long dead people and times. Unlike the chronicles and histories penned in monasteries and royal courts, archaeological finds reveal a wealth of detail about normal people's diet, their way of life and death, rather than the political events they lived through, and they therefore fill a crucially important gap in our knowledge. However, there are still pitfalls for the unwary, for although archaeology may seem to offer a reliable and uncontroversial insight into daily life during the Viking Age, it is nevertheless important to remember that our understanding of archaeological evidence is very likely to be affected and impaired by our preconceptions or our inability to think or see things like a Viking-Age man or woman. Archaeologists may not be able to identify the purpose of some objects, particularly if they are only poorly preserved. Even when considering a recognizable object such as a comb, we simply cannot know, for example, how often people combed their hair, if everyone did it for themselves or if one person in the household combed everyone's hair.

There is also the not inconsiderable problem of dating archaeological finds. How does an archaeologist, who has just discovered a skeleton buried in the earth with some personal effects, actually go about finding out whether or not this was a Viking burial? There are three main ways to answer this question: first, by dating the bones and any other organic material ritually deposited in the grave; secondly, by seeing whether the artefacts with the skeleton are Scandinavian in their manufacture or design, and whether they are like other pieces from the Viking Age; and, thirdly, by seeing whether the overall form of the burial is like other known Viking burials. Scientific dating of objects such as bones is not usually precise, and is based upon the amount of C14 (an isotope of carbon found in all organic matter) in an object. Radiocarbon dating involves comparing the levels of C14 in the object with the levels of concentration found in all living things. On death, the proportion of C14 decreases at a known rate and so an approximate date for the time of death can be calculated. This will generally produce a date range of 50-150 years either side of a given point in time (e.g. 867 + or − 100 years). Alternatively, if there are any wooden artefacts, it might be possible to obtain a dendrochronological date by examining the pattern of the tree rings and matching them to known sequences: the cut-off point will give you the year in which the tree was felled. This is the most accurate form of dating currently available, but the wood needs to be well preserved and to have a sequence of tree-rings, the longer the better, in order to match it conclusively with a locally established pattern. However, for many non-organic objects archaeologists have to look at the way the object has been made and the style of the object, and try to date it with reference to similar objects — this is known as a relative typology — and again this provides only an approximate date. Similarly, the way the person is buried and the way the objects have been made may conform to a pattern found in Scandinavia, and therefore suggest that the burial was of a Scandinavian. But in the context of the British Isles, it may be that the person had adopted Scandinavian fashions, particularly if they had married into a Scandinavian family: it is not possible to say conclusively that a skeleton is Scandinavian because bones and artefacts cannot tell us about a person's ethnic origin. So while archaeology is a science, and certainly newer techniques are being continually developed, it is also important to remember that archaeological dating and identification are often not as precise as we would ideally like.

Archaeologists and historians seeking dates or fixed references upon which to pin their reconstructions of Viking life have a further crucially important source of help: numismatic evidence, that is, coins. During much of the Viking Age, Scandinavian kings did not mint their own coins, nor did most of the rulers of the British Isles, but England had a silver currency that was recalled and melted down at frequent intervals, while a new coinage was struck and issued. This treasure was carried by Scandinavians across the Viking world. Even though the coins did not have a date stamped on them, they can be easily and accurately dated because of the different issues produced in any one king's reign. In addition to this, it is also possible to work out where the coins were produced as most of them have the name of the mint and the moneyer (the person who made the coin) stamped on them. If a coin is found in a burial, it provides archaeologists with a date (known as *terminus post quem*) after which the burial must have been made: the burial cannot have been sealed before the coin was minted. As well as being occasionally found in graves, many coins, such as the enormous treasure found at Cuerdale in Lancashire, have been uncovered as part of hoards, collections of coins and silver objects such as arm rings and brooches that were buried and were never retrieved by the people who buried them. These hoards tell us about the Vikings in a number of ways, but how is it possible to identify a Viking hoard? How can you tell from the hoards who deposited them for safekeeping in the ground? What was unusual about the

Vikings, or what differentiated them from the Anglo-Saxons, was that for much of the Viking Age they did not use coins as a form of currency in the way that we do today. For example, if you melted down a ten-pence piece, it would not be worth anything like ten-pence — ten-pence is its face value, and the Bank of England and ultimately the government will guarantee that you are paid ten-pence for your ten-pence piece. For the Vikings, however, the value of the coin was not in its face value but in the actual amount of silver that made it up — they worked out all their deals by actual weights of silver. This means that Viking hoards can usually be identified by the fact that they often contain other silver objects, not just coins. In particular, they frequently contain chopped-up bits of silver, known as hack-silver, which measure a standard weight, as well as silver arm rings that again have a standard weight. Another characteristic of Viking coin hoards is that they often contain coins that had gone out of circulation and coins from a variety of places, reflecting the far-flung activities of the men who had won this booty and their thirst for silver.

Linguistic evidence, and in particular place-names, provide another crucial link between the present day and the Viking past. Indeed, in the areas of the British Isles where no written sources for the period have survived, they provided the earliest clues that the Vikings had settled in the region: 'The extent of Scandinavian place-names throughout Scotland is the surest indication of Scandinavian influence and provides us with the map of Scandinavian Scotland' and, for the Western Isles, 'we rely almost totally on place-names for evidence about Norse influence.'[5] This picture is changing as new archaeological finds are discovered and add to our knowledge of these remote areas. However, place-names remain absolutely vital indicators of the regions that were colonized by Scandinavians, and are central to the ongoing debates about the scale and intensity of this colonization and to understanding the relationship between the Vikings and local people across the British Isles.

The spread of Scandinavian place-names is uneven across the British Isles: in the Northern Isles and parts of north-eastern Scotland, virtually all names are Scandinavian; large numbers of Scandinavian names can be found in the Western Isles and along the western coast of Scotland; in parts of the English Danelaw as many as a third to a half of place-names are Scandinavian; while in Ireland, such names are largely confined to the few coastal towns, such as Wexford and Waterford, that were founded by the Vikings, as well as coastal landmarks that lay on the important sea-routes sailed so frequently by Scandinavians between the years 800 and 1200. On the other side of the Irish Sea, there are a few Scandinavian names from mainland Wales, probably established by settlers from England after the Norman Conquest, although the Welsh coast has many landmarks and islands that still have Scandinavian names: the Skerries, Milford Haven and Anglesey, as well as Lundy, Flat Holm and Steep Holm in the Severn estuary.

Scandinavian place-names are frequently divided into two main types: those called topographical names by place-name scholars, which describe features of the landscape; and those called habitative names, which were given to settlements. In the past, scholars believed that these two groups of names provided quite different evidence about the nature of the Scandinavian presence in the areas where they are found: the topographical names along the coast were created and used by Vikings sailing past them in their ships, suggesting that the Scandinavian presence in the area was transitory. This was in sharp contrast to the habitative names that, by their very nature, indicated a settled Scandinavian population in the region. However, recent work by Arne Kruse on the topographical names of Scotland's west coast has highlighted important problems with this traditional picture: the names of sailors and fishermen very rarely replace the words that local inhabitants must have had for the landscape around them. In order for a Scandinavian name to replace a local name, the Scandinavian language must have become, even if only for a very short time, the dominant language in the region.[6] By the time the Scandinavian language fell out of use, the new names were sufficiently well established for non-Scandinavian speakers to use them. Indeed, an important point to remember is that Scandinavian place-names do not simply show where Scandinavians settled, because even if a Viking called Olaf decided to name his farm 'Olaf's farm', in order for the name to stick and to outlive him it would have to be used by other people in the area. If the local population was English-speaking or Gaelic-speaking, they would not be likely to use the Scandinavian word for 'farm' when they had perfectly good English or Gaelic words for 'farm'. However, if the name was long-established they would adopt it wholesale, even if they did not know what it originally meant, simply because it had always been so. Sometimes this leads to hybrid names such as Breedon-on-the-Hill in Leicestershire, a name that means 'hill hill on-the-hill'! Here, the original British word for the hill, *bre*, was clearly known by Anglo-Saxon settlers who adopted it but, not understanding its meaning, they added their own word for hill, *dun*; later English speakers, not understanding either *bre* or *dun*, then added 'on-the-hill'.

One overarching problem that applies to all kinds of written and non-written evidence is that it may not give an accurate or representative historical picture: much evidence must have been lost, but we can never really know what has been lost, only what has survived. The picture that we have is undoubtedly skewed towards the better-off in Viking society in all forms of evidence — literacy was extremely limited and so only the cream of society is likely to have been able to read and write; and expensive artefacts and structures, such as stone buildings and large burial mounds or lavishly furnished graves, are much more likely to survive than their cheaper alternatives: wattle-and-daub houses, unmarked graves or unaccompanied burials (burials where the body was not accompanied by jewellery, possessions and other finery). However, in spite of all these difficulties, we are still able to create a partial jigsaw of life in the British Isles during the Viking Age, a tantalizing glimpse of events and people from some thousand years ago.

2
RAIDERS FROM
THE NORTH

'Never before has such a terror appeared in Britain as we have just suf-
fered from a pagan people, nor was it thought possible that an incursion of
this kind could be made' (Alcuin, an Anglo-Saxon monk, writing to King
Æthelred of Northumbria in the aftermath of the Viking attack on the
monastery at Lindisfarne in 793).

When did the Viking raids on the British Isles begin? Thanks to the
Anglo-Saxon Chronicle and the *Annals of Ulster*, this question seems
quite easy to answer: during the 790s, when a series of raids on the
coastal monasteries of present-day England, Scotland and Ireland
are recorded. The monastery of Lindisfarne was looted in 793, the
Annals of Ulster mention the 'devastation of all the islands of Britain
by the gentiles' in 794 and, in the following year, Iona, Skye, Rechru
(almost certainly Rathlin Island), Inismurray, Inisboffin, and St
Patrick's Island all suffered at the hands of the Vikings. The location
of these targets, around the coasts of northern Britain and Ireland,
suggests that their attackers hailed from Norway rather than Denmark. With a good wind, travel from the west coast of Norway to
the Shetland islands took perhaps as little as two days in longships
like that uncovered from the burial mound at Gokstad in southern
Norway (see Fig. 2), and from Shetland it was relatively easy to

travel south along the eastern coast of Scotland and England, or west through the Hebrides into the Irish Sea.

The frequency of attacks recorded in the 790s suggests that Viking raiders may already have established temporary bases on Orkney and Shetland at this early date, although unfortunately we have no written records from these northern outposts of the British Isles to confirm our suspicions. Indeed, without documentary evidence we would find it nearly impossible to describe the earliest phases of the Viking Age, for hit-and-run raids leave little definitive archaeological trace. Unless there is a localized pattern of damage, evidence of burning and destruction is often hard to date precisely and may just as well be the result of a domestic accident or local crime as of the depredations of marauding Vikings. Occasionally, there may be several coin hoards buried in an area, suggesting that people feared for the safety of their valuables and were also unable to recover them. This may indicate that Viking bands were looting in the area, but it may also have been because of some other long forgotten threat to local stability.

Nevertheless, ninth- and tenth-century Norwegian graves, many of which contain richly ornamented pieces of religious metalwork that originated in the monasteries and churches of Britain and Ireland, may offer some archaeological proof of the looting that chroniclers describe. For example, a man's grave from the now remote Romfohjellen in Sunndal on Norway's west coast, contained a rectangular mount of gilt bronze, amber and glass that had probably started life at the beginning of the ninth century in either western Scotland or Ireland, adorning a religious book. This is just one example of over three hundred similar finds from settlements all along the western coast of Norway right up to the Arctic Circle, and from the population centre around present-day Oslo. It seems, by way of contrast, that fairly few such objects from Britain and Ireland have found their way into Danish graves. This may be due to the fact that most ninth-century burials in Denmark appear to have been rather simple affairs, with few or no grave-goods, although recent metal detector finds have added some reused Anglo-Saxon book mounts and fittings for Irish reliquaries to the Danish finds. Yet, while these finds may seem to offer fairly clear-cut proof of Viking looting in the British Isles, it is impossible to know for certain exactly how these objects reached Scandinavia — might they have been traded rather than looted?

In the last twenty years or so there has been a lot of discussion about the real significance of the Lindisfarne raid and the other attacks that took place in the British Isles at the end of the eighth century. The extract from Alcuin's letter, quoted at the beginning of this chapter, gives the misleading impression that this was the first real meeting of Anglo-Saxon Christians with Scandinavian pagans. In fact, in the same letter Alcuin goes on to show how well Anglo-Saxons knew their Scandinavian neighbours:

> *Consider the dress, the hairstyle, and the luxurious habits of the [Scandinavian] princes and people. Look at the hairstyle, how you have wished to imitate the pagans in your beards and hair. Does not the terror now threaten of those whose hairstyle you wished to have?*

The finds of precious objects from the British Isles in Norwegian graves could, at least in part, be the result of peaceful trading across the North Sea. One British expert, John Hines, concludes that what changed with the attack on Lindisfarne was that the Vikings were acting not only as traders, but also as raiders, signalling a shift in political relationships between western Europe and Scandinavia.[1] The Norwegian archaeologist, Bjørn Myhre, supports Hines's conclusions, pointing to the evidence for considerable trade between Norway and the British Isles in the eighth century and, more tentatively, the possibility of Scandinavian settlement on the islands around the coast of Britain at this early date: '... the starting point for the Viking

25

Period could be fixed at any of several points along a timescale running from AD 700 to 800.'[2]

Why?

So why, at the end of the eighth century, did the Vikings launch these attacks on their neighbours? At the time, Churchmen were convinced that the Vikings were sent by God to punish the sinful. Indeed, given the rash of Viking attacks on the religious communities of western Christendom, it might well have appeared as though they were deliberately defiling and destroying these holy places out of pagan antipathy to Christianity. To the monks and the people of the British Isles, the arrival of the Vikings seemed ominously to confirm the words of the prophet Jeremiah: 'Out of the north shall an evil break forth upon all the inhabitants of the land.' There must have been a very real feeling among people in Britain and Ireland that they were being punished by God for their failure to observe Christian morals and teachings. Indeed, the brothers at Lindisfarne (in English Northumbria) were comforted following the devastation of their monastery in 793 with the words: 'This indeed has not happened by chance; it is a sign that someone has well deserved it [...] Do not be cut to the heart by this terrible plight. God chasteneth every son whom he receiveth. You he chastened more severely since he loved you more deeply.'[3] However, it is important to remember that these monasteries were valuable treasure houses, often poorly defended and located on vulnerable and isolated sites: the Vikings were opportunists intent on making money rather than pagans determined to desecrate Christian churches. In northern Britain and Ireland, monasteries were centres of wealth in an otherwise thinly populated area; in other parts of Britain (and Europe) market places and towns were targeted as well. Soon, however, the raiders raised their sights beyond the silver and precious objects of monasteries and towns alike: their new goals were land and political power.

Another explanation of Viking activity that can be found as early as the eleventh century is that overpopulation in parts of Scandinavia drove young men abroad in search of land and in order to make a living. Writing about Norway, Adam of Bremen comments, 'Poverty has forced them thus to go all over the world and from piratical raids they bring home in great abundance the riches of the lands. In this way they bear up under the unfruitfulness of their own country.'[4] Other commentators have noted that the Scandinavian custom of partible inheritance — where land and money are divided between sons — meant that many men and their families did not have enough land with which to support themselves. Yet, in addition to these 'push' factors which prompted and perpetuated Viking activity, there are other possible explanations: the perfection of the longship made their raids possible and their technological superiority at sea meant that their European neighbours could do little to prevent the Viking armies from landing and launching lightning raids on their coasts; politically, there was need for strong and concerted action against the unprecedented mobility of the raiders, but this was not always forthcoming; religiously, culturally, and politically, there were no ties that bound the Scandinavians to keep the peace with their European neighbours — there was no complex network of agreements and promises between Scandinavian and European kings, binding them to mutually beneficial arrangements; finally, sheer opportunism must have played a part — if wealth could be got with such little effort, then why not take it? The lure of easy money must have been particularly strong during dark, cold winters.

But while contemporaries of the Vikings would have us believe that they were the innocent victims of pagan atrocities, it is important to realize that they may have played their part in triggering the

27

raids that devastated their towns and monasteries. Continental rulers attempted to conquer and convert their Scandinavian neighbours in Denmark during the eighth century, well before the traditional beginning of the Viking Age. The first recorded Christian mission to Scandinavia took place around 700, when St Willibrord visited the Danish king, Angantyr. According to the *Life of St Willibrord*, written by the Anglo-Saxon cleric Alcuin, the pagan king sold Willibrord some 30 Danish boys to be trained as priests, although little else is known about Willibrord's mission. Later on in the eighth century, pressure on Denmark from the south increased as Charlemagne, king of the Franks from 768 and emperor of the Frankish or Carolingian Empire from 800, initiated a period of territorial conquest. This brought his empire to the southern border of Denmark. Charlemagne waged war in the name of Christianity, wiping out paganism in Saxony, and encouraging church reform and learning from his court at Aachen in present-day Germany. His son and successor, Louis the Pious, sent another mission to Denmark (and Sweden) and actively interfered in Danish politics.

The career of the Danish king Harald Klak (*Heriold* in the *Royal Frankish Annals*) clearly illustrates the close involvement of the Franks in Danish affairs. Harald was king of Denmark for two separate periods (812-13 and 819-27). During 812-13, he seems to have shared power with his brother, Reginfred, and possibly his brother, Hemming, who paid homage to Charlemagne. According to the *Royal Frankish Annals*, the three brothers even campaigned against rebels in southern Norway, which was then apparently part of the Danish kingdom. However, this first brief period of rule in Denmark was brought to an end by the revolt of a rival faction led by a man called Horik. Despite Frankish support, Harald and his brothers failed to win back power in 814. On Charlemagne's death, both Harald and Hemming (Reginfred was dead by this time) entered the service of the new emperor, Louis the Pious, who negotiated peace between Harald and Horik, establishing their joint rule in 819. The *Royal Frankish Annals* report that Harald was back at Louis' court in 826, and that he and his household in exile were baptized by the Bishop of Mainz at Ingelheim in present-day Germany. Harald was then granted Frisia (the Low Countries) by Louis, and he returned to Denmark in 827 with a Christian mission under Ansgar. However, he was unable to hold on to power, nor, following a further visit to Louis' court, was he able to win back the Danish throne in 828. Bjørn Myhre suggests that the result of Frankish attempts to expand their empire was that '[a] military and ideological conflict developed between Scandinavian kingdoms and the Christian powers of the Continent and the British Isles',[5] and the beginnings of Viking activity in the west should be viewed with this in mind. Alcuin, an Anglo-Saxon monk in the service of the Carolingian emperor, clearly had political as well as religious reasons for presenting the raiders as frightening pagans who should be conquered and converted.

The Vikings and the English

At around the same time as the first recorded attacks on the monasteries and islands of the north and west, three ships of men from Hordaland (the region around Hardanger fjord in western Norway) arrived at Portland in Dorset. Beaduheard, the king's reeve (an important official responsible for protecting the king's financial interests) at nearby Dorchester, rode to meet them, presumably with the intention of making sure that any customs duties due to the king were paid. However, these Norwegians were clearly not there to trade and the reeve was killed. Interestingly, the assumption that the Scandinavians were there to trade suggests that the English were used to peaceful visitors from the north. The *Anglo-Saxon Chronicle* remarks portentously: 'Those were the first ships of the Danish men

29

which sought out the land of the English race' (*s.a.* 787), a comment that was clearly written with the advantage of hindsight, probably a hundred years later during the reign of King Alfred (871-99). By Alfred's time much of the country was under Danish rule and Alfred's kingdom of Wessex stood alone against the 'Great Army'. Realizing this helps to explain the *Chronicle*'s description of these Norwegians from Hordaland as 'Danish men', for the Viking armies that plagued England later on, during the ninth century, seem to have consisted mainly of men from Denmark (although English chroniclers apparently used the word 'Dane' as a generic term for Scandinavians).

The use of the phrase 'the land of the English race' (*anglecynnes lond*) in the *Chronicle* entry for 787 is also very interesting, for in 787 there was no England. It simply did not exist as a political entity. Instead, the country was very much a divided kingdom — Wessex, Mercia, East Anglia, and Northumbria were the most important political units with their own, independent rulers. At the time of the first Viking raids, Mercia was the most powerful of these kingdoms. However, in the century that followed Viking raids brought Mercia, East Anglia and Northumbria to their knees, leaving Wessex as the last outpost of 'Englishness'. It was only during the late ninth century that the word *Anglecynn* became common, appearing in various texts produced at Alfred's court and strongly linked with Alfred's attempt to unite his countrymen against the Danes. This term appears in the *Anglo-Saxon Chronicle* again in 866, when that the 'great heathen raiding-army' arrived on English shores, and is directly linked with Alfred in the entry for 886 when: 'King Alfred occupied London fort [recapturing the town from the Danes], and all the English race turned to him, except what was in captivity to Danish men.' In other words, these Viking raids contributed significantly to the establishment of the English nation. United against a common enemy, the inhabitants of the country became English — and they became English because of the work of Alfred and his successors. In the words of a recent book on Alfred the Great, he was 'the man who made England.'[6]

Clearly by the time Alfred fought and won a last-stand battle against the Danes at Edington in Wiltshire in 878, the Vikings were no longer pirates plaguing the coasts of the British Isles during the summer. Larger fleets, consisting of as many as thirty-five ships, had descended upon the Channel and East Anglian coasts from 835 — the reference to 350 ships mentioned in the year 851 can probably be discounted as exaggeration, especially as it is exactly ten times larger than the last fleet recorded by the *Chronicle*. Viking armies had overwintered on the Isle of Thanet in the Thames estuary as early as 851, and Scandinavian warriors, described variously as 'Danes', 'the heathen', and 'the army', marched across the country, attacking and looting town and countryside alike. From this time until well into the eleventh century, England was never entirely free of a Scandinavian presence. Led by Ivar the Boneless and Halfdan, the 'Great Army' that arrived in England in 865 launched an all-out offensive against the Northumbrian capital, York, in 866, killing two of its kings (the rivals Ælla and Osbeht) and occupying the remains of the Roman town. While the *Anglo-Saxon Chronicle* is characteristically brief in its summary of these events (see the quotation at the beginning of Chapter 1), many later and rather bloody legends concern the main players in this episode. Ivar the Boneless is said to be one of the sons of the legendary Ragnar Loðbrók ('Shaggy-Breeches'). Although Ragnar's sons are historical figures, there is no evidence that Ragnar himself ever lived, and he seems to be an amalgam of several different historical figures and pure literary invention. This Ragnar, whose nickname was derived from the trousers he wore in order to protect himself during a battle with two giant serpents, was supposedly killed by Ælla of York, who threw him into a snake pit. His sons Ivar the

Boneless, Björn Ironside, Halfdan, and Ubba are said to have invaded England and to have killed Ælla with the gory ritual of the blood-eagle to avenge their father's death. Although there is some variation in details, the classic, most lurid, version of the blood-eagle (Old Norse *blóðörn*) involved the ribs being torn from the spine and the lungs being pulled out through an eagle-shaped cut on the victim's back. The earliest surviving reference to this ritual killing, and the only Viking-Age evidence for the blood-eagle, is a half stanza of the skaldic poem *Knútsdrápa*, composed in Old Norse by the Icelander Sighvatr Þórðarson. This has been traditionally translated as: 'Ivar had Ælla's back incised with an eagle', but this may be a too literal interpretation of the poem, and it could be interpreted as Ælla's back was cut by an eagle, one of the carrion birds that circled battlefields; in other words, he was simply killed.

The king of East Anglia, Edmund, was also killed by Vikings, in 870 — some writers have claimed that he too was subject to the brutal blood-eagle ritual, although others record his death in battle and others his murder by bow-and-arrow wielding Vikings. Shortly afterwards, the two remaining Anglo-Saxon kingdoms lost their rulers: Æthelred, Alfred's brother and king of Wessex, died in 871 following an exhausting campaigning season that saw at least four confrontations with the Danes; and Burghred, king of Mercia, was driven from his kingdom in 874. The threat that the Vikings posed to England at this point can hardly be underestimated, but luckily for Wessex — and indeed England — there seems to have been some kind of dispute within the ranks of the Great Army. After spending the winter of 874 at Repton in Derbyshire, the Viking army split into two: one half, under Halfdan, went north into Northumbria, where they settled in 876; the other half, under its leader Guthrum, headed into Wessex. Following a surprise attack on his residence at Chippenham in 878, Alfred and a small force took refuge from continued Viking attacks in the marshes of Athelney, Somerset, where he built a fortification and waged a guerrilla war. According to later tradition, this period of exile was when he burnt the cakes a peasant woman had asked him to watch, and when he was visited by a vision of St Cuthbert, whose relics were kept by the monks that had now relocated from Lindisfarne to Norham-upon-Tweed in Northumbria. After rallying his army, Alfred won a great victory at Edington in 878 against Guthrum's army, which resulted in the establishment of a formal border between Wessex and Guthrum's kingdom in East Anglia. This agreement, known as the Treaty of Wedmore, also included the baptism of Guthrum and his Vikings, with Alfred standing as Guthrum's godfather.

Alfred used the time bought by the peace of Wedmore to fortify his kingdom against further Viking raids, establishing a series of strongholds (*burhs*) at key points in his kingdom, so that no place in Wessex was more than twenty miles from a *burh*; organizing a more effective militia; and developing a naval force. In 886, he drove the occupying Viking force out of London and received the submission of all the English people who were not under Danish control. His son-in-law, Æthelred of western Mercia, was put in control of the town, signalling a new and effective alliance between the two Anglo-Saxon kingdoms, which ultimately resulted in the emergence of a unified kingdom of England. In 892 a new Viking army, led by the formidable Hastein, landed in Kent. This Hastein had harried France and the Mediterranean since the middle of the ninth century and had famously declared his intention of sacking Rome — although a mistake in navigation meant that the northern Italian town of Luna rather than the Eternal City suffered at the hands of Hastein's Vikings. However, Alfred's defensive measures proved effective: Hastein and part of his army were defeated at Benfleet by Alfred and his levies in 893; the garrison at Chichester put an army to flight in 894; and in 895 the Danes were forced to abandon a fort on the Lea after a river blockade was effected by the London garrison. The Danish army dispersed in 896, with some soldiers settling in East Anglia and Northumbria while others sailed south to Frankia in search of fresh — and easier — conquests.

'Foreigners' in Ireland

The Scandinavians who harried the coastline of Ireland in the 790s found a superficially similar political situation to that which prevailed in England. The island of Ireland was also divided into many small kingdoms and tribal districts, although there were some larger political units such as the southern kingdom of Leinster and the western kingdom of Connaught. However, the similarities end there, for conflict between the rulers of these kingdoms was much more frequent and intensive than in England. For example, Irish monastic chronicles record 26 attacks by Vikings in the first 25 years of their operations, but during the same period 87 raids were carried out by different Irish factions. Another distinctive feature of Ireland at the time of the Viking raids was the political and economic, as well as religious, prominence of monasteries. The abbots of these monasteries were frequently important local leaders, and they controlled considerable resources in their role as significant landowners and employers. There were no towns in Ireland; instead markets were organized under the auspices of the great monastic houses. The abbots of the larger monasteries, such as Armagh, therefore wielded considerable economic power that could be used as a political weapon, and because of this, the destruction of monasteries was a fairly common occurrence in Irish warfare, even before the Vikings arrived.

After a series of coastal attacks that intensified during the 820s, Viking fleets started to travel inland along Ireland's rivers, extending the range of their raiding activities: the important and wealthy monastery at Armagh was attacked three times in one month during 832. The character of most of the raids was, nevertheless, still small hit-and-run attacks by the crews of a few ships that seldom strayed far from navigable water. However, after 836 the scale, frequency and destructiveness of the raids intensified — interestingly at exactly the same time as Viking activity in southern England became a real threat. In 837, for example, large fleets of sixty ships appeared on the rivers Boyne and Liffey and ravaged the surrounding areas. The Vikings also seem to have begun one of their most profitable trades in Ireland around this time: the slave trade, taking large numbers of captives during their raids and selling them on as slaves back in Scandinavia and in European market places. According to Irish annals, Scandinavian armies spent their first winter in Ireland at Lough Neagh as early as 840/1, although the pattern of raiding suggests that they may have started overwintering a few years earlier. Shortly afterwards, the first permanent Scandinavian settlements were established on the River Liffey at Dublin and on the River Boyne at Annagassan in Dundalk Bay. These settlements were known as *longphorts* or ship camps, and were followed by further settlements on the Shannon at Limerick, on the Barrow at Waterford, at Wexford, and at Cork. Of course, with a permanent foothold in Ireland, the Viking fleets could now carry on their attacks all year round, rather than being forced to return home during winter. This onslaught was so violent and so relentless that Ireland seemed to be in serious danger of being totally overrun by the Vikings, as was the case in England during the 870s. The Frankish *Annals of St Bertin* for 847 records: 'After they had been under attack from the Vikings for many years, the Irish were made tributaries to them; the Vikings have possessed themselves without opposition of all the islands round about and have settled them.'[7]

But the Irish were soon to receive a respite. The *Annals of Ulster* record that a new Viking fleet arrived in Ireland in 849: 'A sea-going expedition of 140 ships of the people of the king of the Foreigners came to exercise authority over the Foreigners who were in Ireland before them and they upset all Ireland afterwards.'[8] There was a clash between incoming Vikings and those already on the scene, and then yet another new Viking force, led by Amlaíb (the Irish spelling of the Scandinavian man's name Olaf), arrived in Ireland. The arrival of Olaf's army was arguably the single most significant development in the history of Ireland and Britain during the early Viking Age. Described as the son of the king of Lochlann (*Laithlinde*),[9] Olaf was recognized as king of all the Scandinavians in Ireland in 853, with his base in the Viking town of Dublin. His brother Ivar (*Ímar*), who has been identified with Ivar the Boneless, is said to have ruled Dublin with him, although he was also busy campaigning in English Northumbria and East Anglia in the years between 866 and 870. The two brothers, and another brother called *Auisle* by the Irish annals, seem also to have campaigned in Scotland and perhaps even Wales. However, after Ivar's death in 873 and Olaf's, probably in 874, there seems to have been a good deal of infighting between rival claimants to the Norse kingdom of Dublin, and Olaf's own son was killed in 875. Conflict weakened the kingdom and in 902 the Dublin Norse were expelled by an Irish alliance of the northern kingdom of Brega and the southern kingdom of Leinster: 'The pagans were driven from Ireland [...] and they abandoned a good number of their ships, and escaped half-dead after they had been wounded and broken.'[10] This expulsion was to have a knock-on effect across the whole of the British Isles, sending the Dublin Vikings in search of new conquests. The repercussions of the Viking defeat in Ireland in 902 clearly demonstrates an important aspect of Viking-Age history in the British Isles (and Europe) that is easy to overlook if we concentrate on individual countries: the successes and failures of the Vikings in one region invariably affected the neighbouring countries.

Scotland, the Hebrides and the Isle of Man

There is no surviving set of annals that record events in Scotland and on Man, such as there is for England and Ireland, so our understanding of events in the Highlands and Islands is very limited. Much of our scant knowledge about Viking-Age Scotland and Man comes from Irish sources, reflecting the cultural, religious, and political links across the Irish Sea. After the first recorded Viking raids on the monasteries on Iona and Skye in 795, raids around the Scottish coast appear to have continued more or less regularly into the 830s: in 798 the Hebrides were plundered by Scandinavians; Iona was revisited by Scandinavian pirates in 802, in 806 when 68 monks were killed, and in 825, when the monk Blathmac was killed for refusing to reveal the location of St Columba's relics. Perhaps unsurprisingly, Irish records suggest a particularly close link between Scandinavian activity in Ireland and western Scotland, and portray an extremely complex political and ethnic situation in the ninth century. Although there is no definite reference to raids on the Isle of Man at this time, it is unlikely that the raids recorded in the Irish Sea region at the beginning of the ninth century did not also affect Man, situated right in the very centre of this important seaway.[11]

Scotland at this time was not a single political unit, but a disparate collection of regional kingdoms inhabited by several different ethnic groups. Most of mainland Scotland, north of the Clyde-Forth line, along with the Outer Hebrides, Orkney, and Shetland was Pictish territory.[12] The Scottish kingdom of Dalriada included western Argyll and the Inner Hebrides as far north as Skye. The Scots were in fact, rather confusingly, an Irish Celtic tribe who had settled in Scotland in the fifth century. The British kingdom of Strathclyde, centred on Dumbarton Rock, lay to the south-west of the Clyde-Forth boundary. The Britons were another Celtic population, with close linguistic links to Wales, Cornwall and Brittany. Anglian (English) settlers had also moved into lowland Scotland from Northumbria, and more Irish settlers also inhabited the Rhins of Galloway. This political geography was radically altered, probably as a consequence of Scandinavian raids and settlements: the north-eastern part of mainland Scotland, Orkney, and Shetland became Norse territories, while the Picts who had once lived there disappeared. By the mid-ninth century the Scots, who were themselves under pressure from Scandinavians in the west, had taken advantage of Pictish weakness in the east and, led by their king, Kenneth mac Alpin, had won political control of Pictland. This episode acts as an important reminder that it was never simply a case of Norseman versus native in Scotland during the Viking Age, or indeed anywhere else in the British Isles. For example, as early as 836, a chieftain of apparently mixed Norse and Gaelic ancestry from northern Ireland, Guðifreyr mac Fergus, went to fight on the side of Kenneth mac Alpin in Dalriada. The political situation in the Hebrides, or the *Innsi Gall* 'Islands of the Foreigners' as they were known to the Irish in the ninth century, seems to have been particularly confused and stands very much outside national-based political histories: the islanders influenced and were influenced by neighbours in Scotland, Ireland, the Isle of Man, and Orkney at different times during the Viking Age and beyond. Ninth-century Irish annals mention *Gall–Gaedhil* who were involved in wars in Ireland: these 'Foreign Gael' appear to have been warriors of mixed blood based in the Hebrides, who had a reputation for being particularly ruthless. Later Icelandic sources credit the most famous Norse Hebridean, Ketill Flat-Nose, with considerable political power in the islands in the mid-ninth century. This Ketill has been identified with the Ketill *find* (White) described as leader of the Gall-Gaedhil in Irish annals, and although the identification cannot be proved, it seems reasonable enough. Ketill and his family certainly personify the cultural and ethnic mixture of Norse and native popula-

38

tions in the Isles that is suggested by other written sources, as well as by the place-name and archaeological evidence: one of his daughters, Aud the Deep-Minded, married Olaf the White of Dublin; another daughter, Thorunn, was married to Helgi the Lean, who was the son of a Swede and an Irish princess and who worshipped Christ and Thor. During the early tenth century, Ketill's family left the Hebrides to settle in Iceland, a move that may be linked to the fortunes of the Norse kings of Dublin.

The Collapse of Viking Power in Dublin

Only when the Irish kings united against the Scandinavians did they succeed in driving the Vikings out of Ireland, in 902. The expelled Scandinavians scattered, travelling to England (especially north-west England), Wales, Scotland, and even as far as Iceland and France, to try and find new land to settle on. This led to a new rash of Viking attacks, such as the raids on Dunkeld (903) and Fortriu (904) in eastern Scotland. In north-west England, the new arrivals met with hostility not only from the English under Alfred's son, Edward the Elder, and his daughter Æthelflæd 'Lady of the Mercians', but also from those Scandinavians who had settled in northern and eastern England in the last quarter of the ninth century. Nevertheless, according to the *Three Fragmentary Annals of Ireland*, Æthelflæd did grant land near Chester to the Viking leader Ingimund and his followers in the first decade of the tenth century, and although the settlers appear to have started in a more or less peaceful manner, they attacked Chester shortly afterwards. While the *Anglo-Saxon Chronicle* does not mention Ingimund, the version of events preserved in the irish annals is given some support by Æthelflæd's refortification of Chester that is recorded by the *Chronicle* in 907.

About fifteen years after their expulsion from Dublin, some of these Norsemen returned to Ireland, under the leadership of the grandsons of Ivar the Boneless, but others succeeded in winning control of York and English Northumbria. By the 920s, these grandsons controlled the whole of the Irish Sea region from their strongholds in York and Dublin: clear evidence, if it were needed, that Viking activity transcended modern national borders. The complexity of tenth-century politics is clearly illustrated by the Battle of Brunanburh, fought in 937 by Athelstan, king of England, against an alliance of Dublin Vikings, Scots and Strathclyde Britons that was led by Constantine II, king of Scotland, and Olaf Guthfrithsson of Dublin.[13] The *Anglo-Saxon Chronicle* entry for 937 records Athelstan's victory over 'seamen and Scots' in the form of a heroic poem, and Celtic writers refer to the battle as 'the great war'. Viking activity had clearly moved on considerably since the early raids on monasteries — it was no longer a case of us versus them (if indeed it ever had been). Indeed, while Athelstan was involved in conflict with Scandinavians in Dublin and York, he also enjoyed more amicable relations with other 'Vikings', such as Egil Skallagrimsson, the Icelandic poet who served with Athelstan and apparently fought at Brunanburh on the side of the English king,[14] and the Norwegian prince, Hákon (d. 960), nicknamed *Aðalsteinsfóstri* 'Athelstan's foster-son', who was fostered and brought up, as a Christian, at the court of Athelstan. When Hákon became king of Norway he invited Christian missionaries into his kingdom, such as the English bishop Sigefridus of Glastonbury.

It is important to remember that this phase of Viking history also very much muddied the already complex ethnic waters of northern England: the Danes who had settled there in the 870s definitely did not welcome their Scandinavian brothers. This is made very clear by an entry in the *Anglo-Saxon Chronicle* for 942, triumphantly hailing further West-Saxon victories over Scandinavian armies:

> *...Earlier the Danes were*
> *under Northmen, subjected by force*

in heathens' captive fetters,
for a long time until they were ransomed again,
to the honour of Edward's son,
protector of warriors, King Edmund.

Even though we might suspect the evidence of English chroniclers, who would want to present the new Viking kings of York as an unwelcome presence necessitating the intervention of King Edmund, the arrival of the Dublin Norse dynasty upset the political balance of the region, resulting in a prolonged and bewildering period of what has been called 'musical thrones' in York.[15] It is also interesting to note that although the population of the north is seen as Danish rather than English, the Danes were differentiated from the Northmen, who were described as 'heathens', and the Danes were clearly an accepted part of the political landscape and viewed as subjects of the English king. The result was that during the mid-tenth century York was almost constantly under attack in a tug-of-war for power involving English kings, Dublin Norse kings, Scottish kings and the Norwegian prince Erik Blood-Axe (half-brother of Hákon Aðalsteinsfóstri), all struggling to win and maintain their control of the north (see Chapter 4 for more details). At the same time, Dublin and other fortified towns in Ireland came under renewed pressure from the Irish. The camps at Annagassan, Strangford Lough and Carlingford Lough were all evacuated during this period. By the mid-tenth century, both the English and the Irish appeared to have gained the upper hand over the Scandinavians who had so severely threatened their authority and their kingdoms. York fell to the English king Edgar in 954 and remained in English hands thereafter. Many of the Vikings had hung up their swords and axes, and instead picked up the plough, the fishing net, or the merchant's scales. The Battle of Tara, fought to the north-west of Dublin, in 980 was a significant moment in the Scandinavian history of Ireland. In this battle, the

Irish king of the southern Uí Néill, Máel Sechnaill II, defeated an army of Scandinavians from Dublin and the Hebrides, under their king, Olaf Cúarán. This 'very great slaughter' resulted in the recognition of Máel Sechnaill as overlord of Dublin, although he initially ruled through Olaf's son, known by either the Irish name *Glún Iairn* or the Norse *Járnkné*, both of which mean 'Iron Knee'. The political independence of Dublin was never regained.

The 'Second' Viking Age

However, back in Scandinavia, a new generation of men sought wealth, land and power, and at the very end of the tenth century a new threat appeared from across the North Sea. During this so-called 'Second Viking Age', the army of the Danish king, Svein Forkbeard, was intent on accumulating previously unheard-of amounts of silver and, more ambitiously, the English throne. Svein was the son of the Danish king, Harald Blue-Tooth, and deposed his father in around 986 in what Adam of Bremen describes as a pagan backlash. However, there is no other evidence that Svein was a pagan, and it seems more likely that the rebellion against his father was prompted by the high taxes needed to finance Harald Blue-Tooth's ambitious building and military projects. Svein campaigned extensively in England during the late tenth and early eleventh century, appearing sometimes in alliance with Olaf Tryggvason, who later became king of Norway.

The first proper battle fought during this new wave of Viking attacks was at Maldon, on the River Blackwater in Essex, in 991. The English, under Ealdorman Byrhtnoth of Essex, fought against a Viking fleet commanded by Olaf Tryggvason on either 10 or 11 August. While the *Anglo-Saxon Chronicle* contains only a brief reference to the battle, a fragmentary Old English poem preserves a fuller and more famous account of the battle in 325 lines of verse. According to this poem, the battle saw the English literally snatching defeat from the jaws of victory after Byrthnoth's ill-advised decision to allow the Vikings to cross a narrow causeway across the river to meet the English army. The poem's main theme is loyalty, particularly the loyalty of those who fought heroically to avenge the death of their lord, Byrhtnoth, despite the inevitable loss of their own lives.

This defeat did not bode well for the English response to this new Viking threat, and the much-maligned king of England, Æthelred II the Unready, was heavily criticized in the *Anglo-Saxon Chronicle* for his failure to defend his country. Although his nickname 'Unready' seems to neatly sum up his and his kingdom's situation, it is in fact derived from Old English *unræd*, which means 'poor' or 'no counsel' and is a pun on the literal translation of his first name ('noble counsel'). Æthelred's sin was failing to take enough advice or to follow the advice of the most important men in the kingdom, and nowhere was his failure clearer than in his attempts to pay the Vikings off. After its brief mention of the Battle of Maldon, the *Anglo-Saxon Chronicle* adds that 'the first tribute was paid', a disastrous policy of paying the Vikings large amounts of silver in return for the promise that they would leave without further looting or destruction. These payments are generally known as Danegeld, although the *Anglo-Saxon Chronicle* actually calls them *gafol*, a word meaning 'tribute' or 'tax'. Payments, ranging in weight from 10,000 (991) to 48,000 pounds (1012) of silver, were made in the years 991, 994, 1002, 1007, 1008, and 1012. Several thousand coins of Æthelred II have been found in Scandinavia and many more must have been melted down or spent.

After raiding in England and accumulating considerable wealth, Svein Forkbeard was later strong enough to challenge his former ally, Olaf Tryggvason. Together with his stepson, Olof Skötkonung of Sweden, Svein defeated Olaf at the Battle of Svöld and restored Danish control of Norway. Svein's daughter, Gytha, was married to Erik, son of the powerful earl of Lade, Hákon Jarl, and his other daughter, Estrith, to the Anglo-Saxon noble, Wulfsige (in Danish tradition, Earl Ulf). Svein's sister, Gunnhild, and her husband, Pallig, also seem to have lived in England, and were probably killed in the St Brice's Day massacre of 1002. This massacre of 'all the Danish men who were among the English race' was ordered to take place on St Brice's day (13 November) by Æthelred II. According to the *Anglo-Saxon Chronicle*, the massacre was ordered because of the king's suspicions of a Danish plot to kill him and claim his kingdom. If so, it seems to have backfired because it is likely that Svein's campaigns in Wessex and East Anglia in 1003-4 were to avenge the deaths of his sister and brother-in-law. Although the *Anglo-Saxon Chronicle* records Danish raids in 1006-7 and 1009-12, these were led by Thorkell the Tall, and it was not until August 1013 that Svein is said to have returned to England. By this time Thorkell, with a fleet of 45 ships, had submitted to Æthelred and promised to protect England against other Viking forces in return for food and clothes. However, this ploy backfired on Æthelred. After sailing up the Humber and down the River Trent to Gainsborough, Svein received the submission of Northumbria, Lindsey (north Lincolnshire), the Five Boroughs, and 'all the raiding army to the north of Watling Street'. Moving south, he received the submission of Oxford, Winchester and the southwest, and finally London. At this point, both Svein and Thorkell were demanding payment and provisions for their armies, and to add insult to injury 'they raided as often as they wanted.' Finally, at Christmas 1013, King Æthelred II fled England to join his wife and children in exile in Normandy.

However, the victorious Svein died in Gainsborough, Lincolnshire, on 3 February 1014. He was initially buried in England, but later his body was taken to the church he had built at Roskilde in Denmark and reburied. His son, Cnut, was elected as king by the Danish army, but Æthelred II returned to England after Svein's death and Cnut was forced to fight once more for the throne so recently won by his father. His success was to have enormous repercussions across the British Isles and throughout Scandinavia. The leader of the Danish Vikings was to become the ruler of a vast North-Sea empire.

3
colonists

'...*Apart from their settlements and their influence on the language and consequently on names and on some of the terminology of law and administration, the Scandinavians do not seem to have made a distinctive mark on England*' (P. H. Sawyer).[1]

Three terse entries in the *Anglo-Saxon Chronicle* for the years 876, 877 and 880 are the only direct and contemporary written accounts we have for the Scandinavian settlement of northern and eastern England. These tell us that:

876: And that year Halfdan divided up the land of Northumbria; and they [the raiding-army] were ploughing and providing for themselves.

877: And then in harvest-time the raiding-army went into the land of Mercia, and some of it they divided up and some they granted to Ceolwulf.

880: Here the raiding-army went from Cirencester into East Anglia, and settled that land, and divided it up.

The Chronicler's neglect of details such as how many Scandinavians were involved in this settlement and whether their wives and children and other relatives settled in England with the members of the raiding armies has given historians, archaeologists and linguists much fuel for debate and controversy. Frustratingly, this state of affairs is not any better as regards elsewhere in the British Isles. Ireland is the only other place for which we have reliable written references to the activities of the Scandinavian armies. However, the *Annals of Ulster* merely refer to the establishment of raiding bases in 841: 'There was a naval camp at Linn Duachaill from which the peoples and churches of Tethba were plundered. There was a naval camp at Duiblinn from which the Laigin and the Uí Néill were plundered.'[2] Unlike England, there is no reference to ploughing and farming in Ireland — the naval camps, in some cases at least, developed into permanent trading centres and towns, but in Ireland the Vikings seem not to have given up their sea-faring habits in the same way as the members of the Great Army did in England. Elsewhere, in the Northern and Western Isles, mainland Scotland and the Isle of Man, place-names and archaeology clearly demonstrate that the Vikings were there, but the same questions remain, along another: exactly when did this settlement take place?

When?

Orkneyinga Saga, written down in thirteenth-century Iceland, records what had clearly become the traditional version of events that marked the beginning of Scandinavian settlement in the Northern and Western islands of Scotland:

> One summer Harald Fine-Hair sailed west over the North Sea in order to teach a lesson to certain vikings whose plunderings he could no longer tolerate. These vikings used to raid in Norway over summer and had Shetland and Orkney as their winter base. Harald conquered Shetland, Orkney and the Hebrides, then sailed all the way to the Isle of Man where he laid its settlements in ruins. During his campaign he fought a number of battles, winning himself territories further west than any King of Norway has done since. In one of these battles Earl Rognvald's son Ivar was killed. On his way back to Norway, King Harald gave Earl Rognvald Shetland and Orkney in compensation for his son, but Rognvald gave all the islands to his brother Sigurd, the forecastleman on King Harald's ship. When the king sailed back east he gave Sigurd the title of earl and Sigurd stayed on in the islands.[3]

Harald's western expedition is said to have taken place after his victory over a motley collection of Norwegian chieftains and kings in the Battle of Hafrsfjord, which took place some time around the year 890. This is rather a late date considering the archaeological evidence which certainly suggests that Scandinavians had been on the Orkney and Shetland islands since the early ninth century, around the same time that Irish annals refer to Viking raids on islands around the coast of northern Britain. Yet, as the saga tradition makes clear, Vikings were already on the islands before the Norwegian king attempted to bring them under his control, and it may be that the late ninth-century date found in Icelandic sources refers to a new phase in Scandinavian relations with the inhabitants of the Northern Isles and the Hebrides, and probably the Isle of Man too. Indeed, comparison with events in England and Ireland suggests that such a scenario is likely: there, an initial period of raiding was followed by the establishment of winter bases, allowing the armies to stay all year round, and finally, the armies colonized new land.

Whether or not King Harald's expedition ever actually took place is unclear, and it has been argued by Peter Sawyer that his position at home in Norway was simply not secure enough to permit such a long absence from his newly won kingdom. Indeed, the story of this expedition sounds remarkably like that of a later Norwegian king, Magnus Bare-Foot, who attempted to assert royal control over Norwegian colonies in the west at the end of the eleventh century (see Chapter 7), and the whole Harald episode may well have been modelled on this later campaign. But even if this expedition can be dismissed as a fiction, it is nevertheless clear from Irish sources and archaeological evidence that by the end of the ninth century the Vikings were a permanent presence in the Scottish islands and the Isle of Man.

Living with the Vikings in the British Isles

Although much historical writing is concerned with the important questions of how many settlers there were, their impact on the societies where they settled, and the creation of new communities across the British Isles, we also need to remember the practical and everyday details of immigration and settlement: what sort of houses did Vikings live in? What sort of settlements did they live in? And how did they make a living in their new homeland? Such questions are best answered by the archaeological evidence that the settlers left behind them.

The Vikings who settled in the British Isles must have built themselves houses in both the countryside and in towns, although it is nearly impossible to distinguish these from Anglo-Saxon buildings of the same period as generally they too built rectangular long-houses. The best example of Viking-Age settlement comes from York, where the remains of wood and mud houses were preserved in waterlogged conditions and can still be viewed in the town's outstanding Jorvik museum. But we simply cannot know if Viking settlers lived there, or Anglo-Saxons, or Anglo-Scandinavians. If definite traces of Viking settlers can be hard to find in urban Jorvik, the quest becomes near impossible in rural areas of England where settlement was less dense and where, most crucially, dateable artefacts are very few and far between. A handful of sites in northern England provide evidence of settlements that were certainly occupied during the Viking Age: Ribblehead (also known as Gauber High Pasture) in West Yorkshire, Simy Folds in County Durham, and Bryant's Gill in Cumbria. Ribblehead was the first such site to be identified by archaeologists. The farm buildings there consisted of a longhouse, bakery and smithy placed around a central courtyard in the classic Norse fashion, and the settlement is dated to the ninth century on the basis on coin finds, which include a bronze *stycaf* (a coin worth half a farthing)

50

of Archbishop Wulfhere of York from around 862. Very few other artefacts were found on site, and those that were, such as a bronze bell and quernstone, are not particularly Scandinavian in character. Ribblehead is therefore normally described as an Anglo-Scandinavian, rather than Viking, settlement site, although one archaeologist has concluded that this is 'the nearest we will get to seeing Viking period farmsteads in northern England.'[4]

In other areas of the British Isles, traces of Viking farms are easier to identify because of their obvious differences from local traditions of building. Celtic houses seem to have been circular rather than rectangular, although there are some exceptions to this that urge caution, such as the rectilinear buildings that have been discovered in Pictish levels at Skaill, Deerness, in Orkney. On Shetland, a classic Norse farmstead was discovered at Jarlshof on the southern tip of the mainland following violent storms at the end of the nineteenth century. The complex succession of Scandinavian-style longhouses and outbuildings found beneath the sand rubs shoulders with the remains of an Iron-Age *broch* (circular fort) and roundhouse settlement, providing a neat example of the contrast between native and new building styles. The primary longhouse and outbuildings appear to have been constructed at some time early in the ninth century, with a second longhouse being built shortly afterwards, and a third added in the tenth century. Modification, demolition, and construction on this site continued all the way down to the sixteenth century when the New Hall was built. Most of the Norse finds come from the primary longhouse, a structure over 93 feet in length, and they include combs, loom-weights, hone-stones, spindle whorls, bone pins, playing pieces, pottery, and more than a hundred stone fragments with incised scratches and motifs. It is not clear whether Picts were still living at Jarlshof when the first Scandinavian settlers arrived and built their homes, but the rectangular houses must have

51

looked starkly alien to the island's Pictish inhabitants. The close link between existing buildings and new Scandinavian constructions is also found at The Braaid on the Isle of Man, where two Scandinavian-style longhouses stand next to a traditional Manx roundhouse. It is even possible that the 'Scandinavian' and 'Manx' houses were occupied at the same time for a brief period, although the lack of distinctively Norse or Celtic artefacts unfortunately makes it impossible to know what sort of contact there was between the people living in these houses.

The settlement at Buckquoy on mainland Orkney, excavated in the 1970s, offers more clues for assessing the relationship between Vikings and Picts. Excavations revealed that rectangular buildings, dated to the Viking period, succeeded cellular and figure-of-eight 'Pictish' buildings. However, the clear break in house types is not reflected in the objects that were found in them, for native Pictish-style artefacts continued to be used by the people living in the 'Viking' house. It has therefore been argued that there was some degree of social interaction between the native population and the incoming Norse settlers in the early Viking Age. However, the possibility that the rectangular buildings at Buckquoy were occupied by Picts rather than Vikings has been raised by the discovery of rectilinear buildings that are dated to the Pictish period at Skaill in Deerness on Orkney, although these were not known when the finds from Buckquoy were published in 1974. Nevertheless, a similar picture to Buckquoy has emerged from other sites in the Bay of Birsay area on Orkney: no distinctively Norse artefacts and the survival of native Pictish items in the early Viking Age. Although this could be used to argue that the meeting between Viking and Pict was not so violent as is sometimes assumed, it is worth remembering that even if the Pictish population had been wiped out, the new settlers are unlikely to have thrown useful objects away.

Houses, Halls and Churches

As common sense suggests, the houses that the Vikings built and lived in varied across the Viking world, according to the climate, the available building materials, the purpose of the building and the wealth and lifestyle of the people who were to live in it. The most common kind of house in Scandinavia was a rectangular structure (often with curved side walls), known as a longhouse, which might measure between 5 and 7 metres in width and between 15 and 75 metres in length. The longhouse usually consisted of one main living room where all the inhabitants ate and slept, and where household tasks such as cooking and weaving were performed. The two long walls of this room were lined with wall benches, built up with earth and lined with wood, upon which people sat, ate, and slept. In rural communities, the longhouse may have been divided into two, with one room functioning as a cattle shed (although towards the end of the Viking Age, animal houses and living quarters were often in separate buildings). The longhouse was heated by a fire in the middle of the room, used also for cooking food, and the smoke from the fire escaped from a small hole in the roof of the longhouse. Lighting was also supplied by the fire, as well as oil lamps (using herring or seal oil) and, later on, wax candles. There were often no windows in the longhouse, although there might be some very small holes left in the walls, covered by a translucent material such as thin, scraped and stretched animal skin, letting in a little light. The two exterior doors were positioned so as to minimize draughts, depending on the direction of the prevailing winds. As well as the longhouse, there were often other smaller, separate buildings nearby, with specialized functions, such as a smithy, a dairy, servants' quarters, shelter for small animals and a bathhouse.

In Sweden and Norway, where timber was in plentiful supply, these longhouses were generally made from pine logs placed horizontally with overlapping corners and were roofed with birch-bark and turf. However, in Denmark, where the climate was milder and where there was less timber, the walls of houses were frequently of wattle construction — clay plaster put on to a framework of upright wooden (usually oak) posts — with a roof of reeds or thatch. A reconstruction of a wattle-and-daub house in Hedeby can be found at the Moesgård Museum, near Århus in Denmark, and the Viking settlers in York seem to have built the same kind of house for living and working in. As wood (and other organic material) is only preserved if the conditions are right — primarily if the soil is waterlogged — relatively few such structures are known from around the Viking world, although they were almost certainly the most common kind of house. In largely treeless Iceland — and Orkney and Shetland — where wood was in very short supply, houses were built from turf, earth and stone, often partially sunken for insulation, and with walls measuring a metre or more in thickness. The Stöng farmhouse, preserved in volcanic debris, is a good illustration of an Icelandic longhouse, and is probably similar to the Norse longhouses found at Jarlshof at the southern tip of mainland Shetland.

The Viking lords and kings who established themselves in the British Isles naturally built on a grander scale than the ordinary farmers, craftsmen and merchants who settled here. Their halls would need to house their personal retinues of servants, soldiers and guests, and provide enough space for feasting and entertaining in a suitably impressive fashion. Unfortunately, archaeologists have not yet uncovered the remains of any building that can be clearly identified as the hall of a Viking king in two of the most important seats of Viking power in the British Isles, York and Dublin. The hall of the Viking-Age kings of York is believed to have been located at King's Square, a name first recorded in the thirteenth century as *Kuningesgard* (from Old Norse *Konungsgarðr*), by one of the main gateways into the Roman fortress. This site was not used by the later earls of Northumbria or the Norman rulers of York, and according to the *Anglo-Saxon Chronicle* Earl Siward (d. 1055) was buried in the church of the Norwegian saint Olaf Haraldsson at *Galmanho* or *Earlsburgh* 'the earls' residence'.

However, archaeologists have had more luck in locating the residence of the earls of Orkney. *Orkneyinga Saga* relates how Earl Thorfinn the Mighty (d. 1065) 'had his permanent residence at Birsay, where he built and dedicated to Christ a fine minster, the seat of the first bishop of Orkney.'[5] Since the 1930s, there have been extensive archaeological excavations on the Brough of Birsay, a tidal island off the north-west coast of mainland Orkney. The Brough is an excellent defensive location, with sheer cliffs on its north, south and west sides, and a causeway to the mainland on the east side that could only be reached at low tide. Finds from the island show that the island was inhabited before the Vikings arrived in Orkney: an important bronze-working industry was based on the Brough in the late eighth century; three Pictish ogham inscriptions have been found there; and, most spectacularly, a unique symbol stone decorated with three warrior figures has also been recovered from the Brough. Is it possible that this now remote island was the centre of both political and ecclesiastical power in the Northern Isles during the late Viking Age? A complex of buildings, dated to the tenth and eleventh centuries, has been excavated on the landward side of the Brough. These are high-status constructions, with complex drainage and heating systems and skilful masonry. More conventional Norse longhouses, occupied from the ninth into the thirteenth or fourteenth century, have also been excavated on the island's slopes. The remains of what appears to be a Norse smithy, in use during the tenth and eleventh centuries, were also found on this site.

The ruins of a church, incorporating the fragments of six Scandinavian runic inscriptions, also stand on the Brough. This church was previously believed to be the remains of Earl Thorfinn the Mighty's Christchurch, although it is recorded as being dedicated to either St Peter or St Colme, not Christ. However, archaeologists now believe that this church was built in the early twelfth century, and so this identification seems unlikely. While excavations have revealed an earlier church and graveyard underlying the twelfth-century church on a slightly different alignment, these can unfortunately not be dated. Indeed, it is uncertain if Thorfinn's church was actually located on the Brough, as *Orkneyinga Saga* only records the earl's residence and church in the parish of *Byrgisherað* (Birsay), which might mean that Thorfinn was instead based in the present-day village of Birsay, opposite the Brough on the mainland. While the remains of an eleventh-century church have not yet been identified in the locality of the village, the remains of a large and impressive twelfth-century church have been excavated below the present parish church of St Magnus (a suggestive dedication given that the Orkney martyr, Magnus, was initially buried in Thorfinn's church). The sixteenth-century Stewart earls' palace and bishops' palace are also situated in the modern village of Birsay, and recent excavations have uncovered a substantial tenth-century hall and later buildings in the village area. It therefore seems quite likely that this, rather than the structures on the Brough, is the first seat of the earls of Orkney.

Orkneyinga Saga also contains a description of a later earl's hall at Orphir, overlooking Scapa Flow:

> *There was a great drinking hall at Orphir, with a door in the south wall near the eastern gable, and in front of the hall, just a few paces down from it, stood a fine church. On the left as you came into the hall was a large stone slab, with a lot of big ale vats behind it, and opposite the door was the living-room.*[6]

The remains of this church, dedicated to St Nicholas, can still be seen. Only the eastern apse remains, but the lines of the church's circular foundations are laid out in gravel. Circular churches became popular at the time of the Crusades, inspired by the Church of the Holy Sepulchre in Jerusalem, and Earl Hákon Paulsson's own pilgrimage to Jerusalem in the early twelfth century may provide a possible source for the inspiration behind Orphir's Round Kirk. Although he is not mentioned in connection with the site in *Orkneyinga Saga*, he inherited his father's share of the earldom, which included Orphir, and his son, Paul, is the first earl mentioned at Orphir.

Viking Towns: York and Dublin

Anyone interested in the Vikings will be well aware of their connection with York, the political, economic, and religious centre of northern England. Located on the River Ouse, the town could be reached by Viking ships sailing from the North Sea up the Humber estuary to the Ouse. The city's Viking connection was brought astonishingly to life by the Coppergate excavations in the city (begun in 1972) and the subsequent construction of the Jorvik centre. The excellent preservation conditions at 16-22 Coppergate in particular allowed the recovery of wood, textiles, and other organic matter, and excavations revealed traces of tenth-century buildings built on regular plots that are largely the same as present-day property boundaries in the area. Excavations at York Minster in 1967-73 also revealed a tenth- to eleventh-century graveyard, although the Viking-Age cathedral church was not found directly underneath the present Minster: the north-south alignment of the graves suggests that the earlier church most probably overlay the earlier Roman fortress.

York had certainly existed long before the first recorded attack on the city by the Viking Great Army in 866 — it was founded by Romans in the first century AD. So what was the Scandinavian contribution to the city's history and development? And, more importantly for our purpose, what does the town's archaeology tell us about the Vikings who settled in York? Perhaps the most important discovery is that the town's fortunes certainly appear to have been revived following the Scandinavian settlement of Northumbria. The Anglo-Scandinavian settlement was concentrated in the area to the south of the Roman fort, and by around 1000 the town probably had a population of around 10,000 to 15,000. The trading contacts of Viking York extended from Ireland to the Middle East, and it seems to have been an important centre of production too. Many of the street-names of York are derived from the various trading and craft activities that took place there. Coppergate itself is probably derived from Old Norse *koppari* 'cup-maker' and *gata*, which means 'street' rather than gate. Evidence of glass-making, textile manufacture, metalwork, amber- and jet-working, as well as wood-, bone-, leather-, and antler-working have been found in the extensive excavations undertaken in the town. Here we have clear evidence for the positive effects of the Viking settlement of England — something that is never mentioned in written sources such as the *Anglo-Saxon Chronicle* — new, profitable trading links that tied northern England to markets throughout the extensive Viking world, allowing York's inhabitants to specialize in the manufacture of many goods. The city thrived as traders came there to buy and sell, and the establishment of the joint kingdom of York and Dublin brought important political and religious visitors to the town, who would have enjoyed the hospitality of the royal court — bringing employment to the town, as well as the demand for food, drink and luxury goods. Of course, the turbulent politics associated with the attempts of the English to win this northern city back must have disrupted life in the town, but not enough to discourage commercial life permanently.

We are also fortunate that another centre of Scandinavian power in the British Isles has been exceptionally well preserved and uncovered by excavation in recent years. The *longphort* or fortified camp established on the banks of the River Liffey in 841 was one of the first permanent settlements established by the Vikings in Ireland. The site of this *longphort* has not yet been identified archaeologically, although Kilmainham on the outskirts of present-day Dublin is a strong possibility. The so-called Dublin Norse were expelled from this settlement by an Irish alliance in 902, and when the town was re-established in 917, it was at a slightly different location, underneath the present-day capital. Between 1961 and 1981, excavations in the Wood Quay area of Dublin, between the River Liffey and Christchurch cathedral, revealed successive phases of settlement on this site. As at York, regular plots, surrounded with earth banks, were systematically laid out. Interestingly, the houses that were built on these plots were not of characteristic Norse design and instead appear to represent an Irish Sea tradition of building. The archaeological finds from Dublin are varied and of high quality, reflecting the town's powerful economic position from the end of the tenth century. Dublin appears to have been a centre for the export of slaves, textiles and animal skins, while imports included silk, amber, walrus ivory, pottery, glass from England, the Continent, Scandinavia, and the East. A unique collection of some twelve runic inscriptions carved on everyday objects of wood, a comb, and pieces of bone and antler was also discovered during excavations. These have been dated to the period c. 950-1125, and were probably carved by Scandinavian craftsmen working in the town. Various crafts flourished in Viking-Age Dublin, including ship-building: the 95-foot-long Skuldelev 2 longship, sunk in Roskilde Fjord in Denmark, was probably built in the town in the last half of the eleventh century. Although this ship is badly preserved, it is the largest longship ever excavated and could carry a crew of at least forty or fifty men.

How 'Great' were the Viking Armies?

This brings us back to the question of numbers. Trying to assess the impact that Viking settlers had on their new homelands is a tricky business, and one of the key questions is just how many Scandinavians permanently relocated to the British Isles? If there were relatively few settlers, then we would not expect the results of this colonization to be too traumatic for most people already living in the area. But if there were thousands of newcomers, then we can imagine that many people would have been driven from their homes and land, and the Vikings would have dominated the region, perhaps bringing about the total Scandinavianization of its society and culture.

The question of numbers, of how many Vikings made their homes in the British Isles, is closely connected with two radically different schools of thought on the fundamental character of the Viking armies who later settled the lands they had once terrorized. Did these armies consist of relatively small numbers of soldiers, or were the 'great raiding armies' of the *Anglo-Saxon Chronicle* as 'great' as English propaganda would have us believe? Rather surprisingly, the starting-point for anyone wanting to answer this question is Domesday Book, produced in 1086 in the aftermath of quite a different kind of conquest and settlement of England. Domesday Book is the earliest surviving written record for most places in England, although the surveys of London, Durham and the surrounding shire of Northumberland, and several other towns were not transcribed, and most of north-west England was not even surveyed as it was not yet a part of England.[7] It records owners, landlords, tenants, population, land and taxation values, and a wealth of other social and economic data. Although produced some two hundred years after the Scandinavian settlement recorded by the *Anglo-Saxon Chronicle*, Domesday Book records a number of peculiarities in the social and economic structure of the counties which lie to the north of Watling Street, the traditional border between Danish and English England. The most important of these peculiarities, for the present debate, is the large numbers of freemen, or sokemen as they are also known, listed among the inhabitants of the Danelaw, as well as the many Scandinavian place-names and personal names. Sir Frank Stenton argued in a series of enormously influential publications, but most notably in his *Anglo-Saxon England* first published in 1943, that these Domesday freemen were the descendants of the free Viking warriors who had colonized this area. Essentially, Stenton believed that Domesday records the legacy of mass Scandinavian settlement in northern and eastern England during the ninth century, and that this settlement was undertaken by the rank and file of huge Viking armies which the *Anglo-Saxon Chronicle* recorded taking land in Northumbria, (eastern) Mercia, and East Anglia. His views are neatly summed up by Winston Churchill:

> *The Danish settlement in England was essentially military. They cut their way with their swords, and then planted themselves deeply in the soil.*[8]

Stenton's view of the Viking-Age history of north-east England was brought into serious question by Peter Sawyer's *The Age of Vikings*, published in 1962, resulting in a radical reassessment of Scandinavian settlement that is still ongoing. Sawyer rejected the idea of a massive settlement — principally because the Viking armies that attacked England in the ninth century are now generally believed to have consisted of hundreds rather than thousands of Scandinavians. Most Viking longships cannot have carried more than thirty-two men (which coincides with the number of oars and shields found on the Gokstad ship from Norway), particularly when provisions, other family members and even horses are added in to the total. And most of the fleets that the *Anglo-Saxon Chronicle* records in the ninth century consisted of fewer than 100 ships. Even the largest army, the so-called *micel here*, that is said to have arrived in England in 892, was likely to have been 'well under 1,000 men' and 'the probability is that most, if not all, the raiding bands were about three or four hundred men.'[9] Of course, if you take away the settlement of huge numbers of Scandinavian warriors, then how can the Domesday sokemen and the map of Scandinavian place-names really represent the consequences of a large-scale settlement?

Unfortunately, as we have no direct or reliable reference to the numbers of Vikings who made their homes in the British Isles, we have to turn to other forms of evidence. The distribution map of Scandinavian place-names found throughout the British Isles has proved the most important of these sources, mainly because it provides evidence for all the regions settled by Scandinavians, as well as a clear and striking picture of the variation between different areas. However, the real significance of these place-name distribution maps is not so straightforward as it may seem, and has given rise to considerable discussion of the question of numbers. Before considering this debate, we need to examine the place-name evidence in more detail.

Place-Names in Northern England

If you look at a distribution map of Scandinavian place-names in England (see Fig. 8), two things are immediately obvious: first, there are lots of them; and secondly, virtually all of them are found in northern and eastern England. There are, nevertheless, a few surprises: for example, there are a handful of Scandinavian place-names in Northamptonshire and Warwickshire, which were politically on the English side of Watling Street, the Roman road that became the border between English and Danish England. Within north-east England, there is also clearly quite a degree of difference in the density of Scandinavian place-names, with very few examples in County Durham, Northumberland, Cambridgeshire, Essex and Hertfordshire. The modern counties where Scandinavian influence on place-names is most marked are Lincolnshire and Yorkshire. Lincolnshire has the highest density of Scandinavian place-names in England, with approximately fifty per cent of village names in northern Lindsey being of Scandinavian origin. Remarkably, this degree of Norse influence is also apparent from the number of field names; indeed in some cases the proportion of Scandinavian names is even higher there, reflecting the language of the farmers who gave and used these names. In Yorkshire, nearly half (48 per cent) of all village names are of Scandinavian origin in the East Riding; the figure for the North Riding is similarly high at 46 per cent, while just under a third of names in the West Riding are Scandinavian. The term 'riding' is also a Scandinavian borrowing, from the Norse word *þriþing*, 'a third part'.

Most place-names in England consist of two, sometimes more, parts: for example, Anlaby (in East Yorkshire) is made up from two words *Anlafs* and *by*. The last part of the place-name in English place-names is normally the so-called generic element, most often a word for a type of settlement (in this case, *by* is the Scandinavian word for a village or farmstead); the word(s) before this generic is known as a specific, which distinguishes this particular settlement from others (in this case, the Scandinavian personal name *Anlafs*: this was Anlaf's village). Anlaby is typical of the most common type of Scandinavian place name in northern and eastern England: approximately 850 place-names ending in -*by* have been recorded in England, the majority in Lincolnshire, especially on the Wolds, and Yorkshire, concentrated in the Vale of York. Unlike the -*by* names in Denmark, many of the English place-names are combined with a personal name — normally Scandinavian. Another common Scandinavian place-name element in the Danelaw is -*thorp*, which appears to refer to secondary settlements, sometimes on marginal land, which are often smaller than the places that were given names in -*by*. As might be expected in the ethnic and linguistic melting pot of northern and eastern England, there are also many hybrid place-names, which combine English and Scandinavian words. Most common are compounds with a Scandinavian first element and an Anglo-Saxon second element. These are generally referred to as Grimston hybrids, after one of the most famous examples of this sort of hybrid place-name, Grimston. In their classic form, these hybrid place-names consist of a Scandinavian personal name, such as Grim, with the English word -*tun*, meaning village or settlement. Place-name experts interpret these hybrid names as representing existing settlements that were taken over by a person with a Scandinavian personal name: while the name of the new owner replaced that of the old one, the rest of the place-name was unchanged. Finally, Scandinavian influence can also be detected in some other English place-names, which have been affected by Scandinavian pronunciation: for example, the soft *sh*- of Old English became *sk*- under Scandinavian influence, changing Shipton into Skipton and Fisherton into Fiskerton; while Old English *ch*- became Scandinavian *k*-, so that Cheswick was transformed into Keswick.

As will be clear from the previous chapter, north-west England was never actually part of the Danelaw even though it was settled by Scandinavians in the early tenth century. The Scandinavian place-names that are found in this region are also in many respects different from those found in north-east England. In particular, there is a group of names known, rather grandly, as Hiberno-Norse inversion compounds. To put it simply, this type of place-name is usually made up of two Scandinavian words (a specific and generic), but the order of these words when put together to make the place-name is Celtic. A good example of a Hiberno-Norse inversion compound is the name Kirkbride, a Scandinavian name meaning 'The Church of St Bride', but following Celtic rather than Scandinavian name-forming rules, with the generic '*kirk*', meaning 'church', first and the specific 'Bride' second (incidentally, the 'correct' Scandinavian order is found in the north-west too, at Bridekirk). These names clearly reflect the fact that many of the Vikings who settled this area in the tenth century had been living in Dublin before they were driven out of the town by an alliance of Irish kings. The place-names of north-west England differ from those in north-east England in other ways too: in particular, there is more variation in the Scandinavian place-names of the north-west, and names ending in *-by* are much less common.[10] Instead, words like *-thwaite* ('clearing'), *-beck* ('small stream') and *-seter* ('hill farm') are more common, reflecting a different sort of settlement in a different sort of landscape. This place-name evidence is in fact the most important source for the Scandinavian settlement of Cumbria, which is not recorded in any contemporary source.

No-one disputes the fact that there are large numbers of Scandinavian place-names in northern and eastern England, but their value as a source for assessing the numbers of Vikings who settled there is highly controversial. What do place-names really tell us about the Scandinavian settlement of England? At the most basic level, they give us some idea about the distribution of Scandinavian settlement. However, it is important to realize that settlements with Scandinavian place-names were not necessarily inhabited by Scandinavians. For example, there are some Scandinavian place-names that suggest just the opposite: Ingleby is a Scandinavian place-name but it means 'village of the English'! To understand why this is so, we need to consider in more detail the way in which a settlement gets its name and how that name is used. I live in Hull, but if I were talking to someone else who lives in Hull, I would usually refer to Hull as 'town'. In other words, a place-name is most frequently used when its inhabitants talk to people from outside the settlement (particularly in the days when travel away from one's immediate area was uncommon) or, as is often the case, when people from outside the settlement talk to other people from outside it. Therefore, Scandinavian place-names simply show that the people in the area around the settlement used Scandinavian words to describe these settlements, and that these names stuck. Ingleby was inhabited by English people, but their neighbours were speakers of a Scandinavian language, and that is why the place-name is Scandinavian not English.

Nor do Scandinavian place-names necessarily mean that the settlement was founded by Scandinavians — as we have already seen with the case of Grimston, it may simply be that an existing settlement was partially renamed after someone with a Scandinavian name. We know of at least two examples of English names being totally replaced: Whitby ('white village') was known as *Streoneshalh* to the Anglo-Saxons before being renamed during the Viking Age, and Derby ('village where deer/animals were') was formerly *Northworthig*. So the map of Scandinavian place-names does not necessarily give any clues to the colonization of new land by Viking settlers. A further problem is that we cannot be sure when many of the place-names were given. Did the first generation of Scandinavian settlers give these places their names, or was it their descendants who continued to use some of the names and words of their parents and grandparents long after they stopped thinking of themselves as Scandinavians?

The Arguments against a Mass Migration

Sawyer argues that the Viking takeover was that of a relatively small number of men, who nevertheless wielded considerable political power in the region. The disruption of native traditions that followed the Scandinavian conquest resulted in the break-up of land into smaller parcels that were sold off in the tenth and eleventh centuries, when the Scandinavian language had had a significant enough impact on some dialects for Scandinavian names and words to be adopted by people who were essentially English. He points to the absence of Scandinavian place-names in Cambridgeshire and Essex, which were part of the Danelaw, but which were reconquered by the English relatively early on, in the first half of the tenth century. If the Scandinavian place-names in Domesday Book were linked to the ninth-century settlement of Vikings recorded by the *Anglo-Saxon Chronicle*, then we would expect more Scandinavian names in these areas. The sokemen recorded in Domesday were not the descendants of Scandinavians, but the Viking takeover had established different customs that affected the status of native farmers. Indeed, Sawyer — and others — have also argued that the differences between the Danelaw and the rest of England may even have been simply differences of terminology: elsewhere in England the sokemen may have been called something else, but in practice they enjoyed the same status at the Danelaw sokemen. And why, for example, are there large numbers of sokemen in some places in the Danelaw that have relatively few Scandinavian place-names? A final point that Sawyer raises is that while a Scandinavian place-name shows that there were enough people in the area who used the Scandinavian name for it to stick, it may not have been because they were numerically the dominant group, but because they were politically dominant.

The Arguments for a Mass Migration

The place-name scholar Gillian Fellows-Jensen agrees that a process of internal migration, dividing the land up into smaller parcels, did play some part in establishing the map of Scandinavian place-names, as the traditional pattern of landholding was reorganized

67

in the wake of the Vikings. In recent years, she has also outlined how some Scandinavian place-names may have been transplanted by later settlers and administrators at a relatively late date. However, she argues that despite the late evidence of Domesday Book, many of the Scandinavian place-names in England were probably coined fairly early on in the tenth century. To support her argument, she points to place-names that contain archaic forms of Scandinavian personal names (e.g. Thorketill rather than later Thorkell); anglicized forms of Scandinavian personal names, which were only given during the early years of settlement; and comparatively rare Scandinavian personal names. Finally, she draws attention to some place-names that show Scandinavian grammatical inflections, clearly indicating that the Scandinavian languages were spoken and understood by the people who used these names — they were not just Scandinavian loan-words adopted by English speakers. Indeed, there are still many scholars who, while rejecting Stenton's idea of a massive military settlement, also reject Sawyer's arguments that the Scandinavian settlement of north-east England was the work of a small number of Vikings. Their view is based not only on the evidence of place-names, but also on the sheer number and variety of Scandinavian loan-words incorporated into English — and their everyday character — which must reflect the fact that the Vikings and their Anglo-Saxon neighbours had extensive contact at a very basic level of daily life, rather than simply in court. This, they argue, cannot be the result of a small-scale aristocratic settlement. If, as is generally accepted, the Viking armies were smaller than Stenton believed, then the only explanation can be an unrecorded secondary colonization of Scandinavians after the initial settlement recorded in the *Anglo-Saxon Chronicle*. The linguistic evidence cannot be explained in any other way. Apart from settlement of some Viking soldiers following the attacks of 892-96, there is, however, no definite historical evidence for this. Clearly the evidence of Scandinavian loan-words in English must be very convincing to justify such a theory. Before we examine this, we need to take a brief look at the languages spoken by the Vikings and the inhabitants of England to try and understand what happened when they met in northern and eastern England during the ninth century.

Old English Meets Old Scandinavian[11]

The question of whether the Vikings and English could communicate without interpreters is one that has concerned historians for a long time. The two languages are certainly related: Old English, sometimes also called Anglo-Saxon, was a West-Germanic language, while the Scandinavian languages[11] form the North Germanic branch of the Germanic languages. Within England, there were four main dialects of Old English: Northumbrian in northern England and south-east Scotland; Mercian in central England; Kentish in south-east England; and West Saxon in southern and south-west England. Yet, our understanding of the relationship between these dialects and their development during the Viking Age is severely restricted by the fact that virtually all surviving Old English texts are written in the West Saxon dialect, and many of these are associated with King Alfred the Great's reign at the end of the ninth century, when he personally encouraged and initiated projects designed to make Latin learning and culture available in English for the first time. The king translated four works himself, and his preface to the translation of Pope Gregory the Great's *Pastoral Care* calls for a programme of education, in English, to alleviate the decline of England's fortunes and to bring wealth and wisdom to the country. Alfred also seems to have commissioned the immensely important *Anglo-Saxon Chronicle*, again written in English rather than Latin, the conventional language of learning. Ideally, we would like many more examples of the Northumbrian dialect, particularly from the tenth century and later,

69

in order to study the impact that the Scandinavian languages had in the districts where they settled.

Danes, Norwegians and Swedes could probably communicate with each other without difficulty (indeed, they still can) and thought of their language as one: 'the Danish tongue'. However, we do know that dialectal differences did emerge in Scandinavia during the Viking Age and led to a division between the more conservative West Scandinavian area (Norway and its colonies, especially Iceland) and the innovative East Scandinavian countries (Denmark and Sweden) in the medieval period. The only surviving written source for studying the language of the Vikings is the 2,500 or so runic inscriptions found across Scandinavia, most of which were written on memorial stones. Unfortunately, the content of these inscriptions is rather repetitive: the vast majority of inscriptions simply record that someone 'raised this stone in memory of' someone else. The evidence of the inscriptions is also heavily skewed towards eastern Sweden and towards the end of the Viking Age, which affects their usefulness as a source for understanding what happened when Danes and Norwegians met English people in ninth-century England.

Luckily for us, we have one account that records in some detail a meeting between Englishman and Norseman. Around 890, a Norwegian trader called Ohthere paid homage to King Alfred at his court, an event that is recorded in the Old English translation of Paulus Orosius's *Seven Books of History against the Pagans* that Alfred commissioned. The lack of information about the geography of northern Europe in the Latin original was made good by the addition of what seems to have been an interview that Alfred had with Ohthere. The Norwegian recounts several journeys he had made in order to gather tribute from Lappish and Finnish tribes in northern Norway, to sell his goods at the southern Scandinavian market towns of Hedeby and Sciringesheal, and to satisfy his own curiosity about what lands lay to the north of his own home in Halogaland. As well as details about sailing times, there is also information about the landscape, wildlife and way of life in the extreme north of Norway, including some things that were obviously alien to Anglo-Saxons: walruses, fjords (in modern English we still have to borrow the Norwegian word), and reindeer. This remarkable account is preserved in Old English, but how exactly did the Norwegian merchant communicate with King Alfred? Did he know some Old English? Did Alfred, or someone at his court, know enough Norse? Or could they each talk in their own language and understand the other? Christine Fell has suggested the latter, on the basis of 'occasional fumbling for words which hesitant communication would necessitate.'[12] Indeed, in his recent book, Matthew Townend highlights evidence from place-names and other texts which support the idea of mutual intelligibility between speakers of Old English and Norse, two Germanic languages that had probably only started to diverge from each other in the fifth century when the Anglo-Saxons arrived in England.[13] In many cases only the inflected endings of English and Scandinavian words differed, reflecting their different grammatical rules, while the root, or main part, of the word was identical. For example, the two languages share numerous nouns, including father, mother, brother (but not sister); man, wife; ground, land, tree, grass; summer, winter; cliff, dale. Many verbs were also virtually identical, such as bring, come, get, hear, meet, see, set, sit, spin, stand, and think. The adjectives full and wise were the same in both languages, as were the colours grey, green and white; the prepositions over and under; and the possessives mine and thine.

Scandinavian Loan-Words in English

The Scandinavian settlement of England nevertheless clearly resulted in a linguistic contribution to English. Old English sources suggest that this contribution was numerically small, about forty words, and limited to a few specific spheres, such as seafaring and administrative terminology. For example, there are several words that were originally used in the law-codes of the Danelaw, such as hold (a nobleman), wapentake (a name for a local administrative district), riding (another administrative district, but covering a larger area, equivalent to the modern county), and outlaw. Yet today there are about 900 fully convincing Scandinavian words in Standard English, and many more Scandinavian words are still part of everyday speech in north and east England. These loan-words are not just nouns, adjectives, and verbs, but include pronouns (he, she, they), prepositions (by, at), adverbs and even the verb 'to be'. It is extremely rare for these types of words to be transferred from one language to another, as they are such integral parts of people's vocabulary. The most common kind of loan-word is one that expresses a concept or describes an object that is entirely unknown or alien to the receiving language, such as the fjord or walrus that Ohthere talked about to King Alfred. However, many Scandinavian loan-words in English could not have supplied any real need or gap in English vocabulary: Old English had its own words for the nouns band, birth, bloom, crook, dirt, egg, gait, gap, girth, knife, loan, race, rift, root, score, seat, skill, sky, snare, thrift, and window; for the adjectives awkward, flat, happy, ill, loose, rotten, rugged, sly, tight, ugly, weak, and wrong; and for the verbs call, cast, clasp, clip, crave, die, droop, drown, flit, gape, gasp, glitter, life, rake, rid, scare, scowl, skulk, snub, sprint, thrive, thrust, and want. These lists of words demonstrate very clearly the everyday character of the Scandinavian loans into English, and stand in stark contrast to later loans from French, following the Norman Conquest, which are almost all linked to government and upper-class culture. These loan-words seem to suggest that contact between English and Scandinavian speakers took place at all levels of society on a regular basis.

As well as loan-words, the Scandinavian language affected English in other ways. As we have already seen with the place-names Skipton and Keswick, soft Old English sounds such as *sh*, *g*, and *ch* were hardened in Scandinavian speech to *sk*, hard *g*, and *k*. The meanings of some Old English words even changed as a result of Scandinavian influence: the modern English word 'bloom' meaning 'flower' could technically come from either Old English *bloma* or Old Norse *blom*. However, the Old English word means 'ingot of iron', while the Old Norse means 'flower'. Similarly, the modern sense of the English word 'plough' owes its origin to the Old Norse word for this important agricultural implement; speakers of Old English used the word to describe a measurement of land. It is harder to prove Scandinavian influence on grammar and syntax, but it has been argued that the simplification of Old English grammar was significantly accelerated by the Scandinavian settlements. It is generally recognized that when two languages meet, there is often a tendency to use only the root part of the word and drop the complicated inflections at the end that express, for example, the number and grammatical gender of nouns and their meaning within a sentence. Some idea of the complexity of Old Norse and Old English can be seen in the following tables:

Old Norse: the grammatical variations in the form of word 'this'

	Masculine	Feminine	Neuter	
Singular	sjá, þessi	sjá, þessi	þetta	**Nominative**[14]
	þenna	þessa	þetta	**Accusative**
	þessa	þessar	þessa	**Genitive**
	þessum	þessi	þessu	**Dative**
Plural	þessir	þessar	þessi	**Nominative**
	þessa	þessar	þessi	**Accusative**
	þessa	þessa	þessa	**Genitive**
	þessum	þessum	þessum	**Dative**

Old English: the grammatical variations in the form of word 'this'

	Masculine	Feminine	Neuter	
Singular	þes	þis	þeos	**Nominative**
	þisne	þis	þas	**Accusative**
	þisses	þisses	þisse	**Genitive**
	þissum	þissum	þisse	**Dative**
	þys	þys		**Instrumental**
Plural	þas	þas	þas	**Nominative**
	þas	þas	þas	**Accusative**
	þissa	þissa	þissa	**Genitive**
	þissum	þissum	þissum	**Dative**

In the linguistic melting-pot of northern and eastern England, this process of simplification must (thankfully!) have begun fairly quickly after the Vikings settled among the English, and particularly after they converted to Christianity and became an accepted part of the local community, attending church side-by-side with Anglo-Saxon neighbours.

Sources for the Linguistic Influence

As mentioned above, Old English sources provide relatively little evidence for the extensive linguistic impact of the Viking settlements, but this must, at least in part, reflect the fact that virtually all of the surviving documents in Old English come from southern and western England — Wessex, the only Anglo-Saxon kingdom that managed to escape conquest by the Scandinavian armies. We might have a very different picture if only we had more manuscripts from the north and east. Unfortunately, however, as with Scandinavian place-names, the vast majority of which are first recorded in Domesday Book, it is not until the post-Conquest period that we start to find substantial numbers of Scandinavian words in English documents. During the late eleventh century and the first half of the twelfth a further thirty-odd Scandinavian terms appear for the first time in vernacular manuscripts, but it is really from the middle of the twelfth century onwards that texts from the north and east become increasingly common — and at the same time so do Scandinavian words. Writing in the second half of the twelfth century, the Lincolnshire writer Orm (itself a Scandinavian name) uses around 200 Scandinavian loan-words in his *Ormulum*.[15] These include anger, awe, bloom, kid, and thrive, as well as many other words that have not passed into modern English, but which will be familiar to speakers of Scandinavian languages: *occ* 'and' (modern Danish *og*; Norwegian *ok*; and Swedish *och*); *gal* 'mad' (still *gal* in modern Danish, Norwegian and Swedish); *sum* 'as' (modern Danish, Norwegian and Swedish *som*); *allesaman* 'everybody' (modern Danish and Norwegian *allesammen*, modern Swedish *allesamman*). Laghamon's *Brut* composed in late twelfth-century Worcestershire has Scandinavian loans 'leg' and 'Thursday' instead of Old English 'shank' and 'Thundersday'. Even Chaucer in his fourteenth-century *Canterbury Tales* uses around 25 Scandinavian loan-words. However, some linguists argue that the real linguistic contribution of Scandinavian to English may have been even more extensive than these Middle English texts suggest. For example, the *Ormulum*, produced in an area of apparently heavy Scandinavian settlement, has around 200 loan-words in 20,000 lines of text, but we know that Orm was trying to standardize his language to make it intelligible to a wider audience. It is almost certain that there would be many more Scandinavian loan-words in the everyday spoken language of Lincolnshire farmers and their families. We know from our own experience in schools that when we write we are encouraged to leave out slang words and everyday phrases and adopt a more formal style. During the early medieval period, when most people could not even read or write, the gap between the written and spoken language must have been even wider. The local dialects that were rich in Scandinavian loans were not considered appropriate for proper literature. This was very much in contrast with later loans from Norman French, which were closely associated with the more literate upper classes and so were seen as prestigious.

How Long Did the Scandinavian Language Survive in England?

A further and final question which has much puzzled scholars is 'How long did the Scandinavian language survive in England?' Unfortunately, there is no anecdotal evidence for this, such as the well known example from the Scandinavian colony of Normandy, where in the 930s Richard Longsword, the son of the Duke of Normandy, had to be sent to Bayeux in the west of the duchy to learn Scandinavian because there was no-one in Rouen who could teach the boy the language of his forefathers.[16] Common sense suggests that the survival of Danish or Norwegian must have varied from place to place, depending on the density of Scandinavian settlement in the area — and the number of English-speakers living there too. Trade with Scandinavia — at least along England's east coast — must have played some part in keeping the language alive, while more isolated communities across northern England may have been able to preserve their own spoken language into the eleventh century and perhaps even later. The evidence of inscriptions — in both Scandinavian runes and the Roman alphabet used by the Anglo-Saxons (which we still use today) — suggests that, for the most part, there was a blending of language, and in many cases, what was spoken was probably neither classical Old English nor Old Norse, but something that can be called Anglo-Scandinavian. The inscription on the sundial at St Gregory's Minster in North Yorkshire, made between 1055 and 1065, provides a good example of this dialect. The 'correct' grammatical endings are missing from words and there is confusion of grammatical gender, although it must be concluded that even in this now isolated spot, English rather than Scandinavian predominates. Interestingly, the personal names Hawarð, Brand, Orm, and Gamal are all Scandinavian, and the word 'solmerca' is either a Norse loan or a hybrid English and Norse word.

+ ÞIS IS : DÆGES : SOLMERCA + ÆT ILCUM : TIDE +

This is the day's sun-marker for each hour

+ 7 HAWARÐ : ME WROHTE : 7 BRAND PREOST

And Hawarð made me, and Brand the priest

+ ORM : GAMAL : SVNA : BOHTE : SCS [SANCTUS] GREGORIVS : MINSTER : ÐONNE HIT : WES ÆL : TOBROCAN : 7 TOFALAN : 7 HE HIT : LET : MACAN : NEWAN : FROM GRVNDE : XPE [CHR(IST)E] : 7 SCS [SANCTUS] GREGORIVS : IN : EADWARD : DAGVM : CING 7 IN : TOSTI : DAGVM : EORL +

Orm the son of Gamal bought St Gregory's minster when it was utterly ruined and collapsed and he had it rebuilt from the foundations (in honour of) Christ and St Gregory in the days of King Edward and in the days of Earl Tosti.[17]

The problem with assessing the significance of this obviously extensive linguistic impact is that scholars still do not really know enough about the processes whereby one language influences another — did there really need to be a large number of Scandinavian speakers for the loans to have taken place, or could these changes have been made by a small but prestigious elite group of Viking settlers? How significant is the fact that Old English and Old Norse were both Germanic languages, with similarities in vocabulary and grammatical structure? Does the late date of most of the surviving evidence for the Scandinavian language in England exaggerate or distort the significance of these loan-words? Did Cnut's conquest of England at the beginning of the eleventh century bring a new wave of Scandinavian loan-words into England? These questions can probably never be entirely resolved, for there are simply too many unknowns about the social, political and economic factors surrounding the Viking colonization of northern and eastern England. But the nature of the loan-words in particular does demonstrate the way in which the Scandinavian settlement touched all aspects of English life. More than anything else, the language of the Vikings is their legacy in England.

The Celtic Languages

In the Gaelic-speaking areas of the British Isles — Ireland, Scotland and its Isles, and the Isle of Man — the linguistic situation is yet harder to trace, partly because many place-names are not recorded until well into the medieval period. But in addition the languages that the Vikings encountered in these areas were, in contrast to English, quite unlike their own, meaning that 'conscious and sustained effort had to be made by Celtic-speakers and Scandinavians alike in order to understand and be understood. There could be no slow folding together of language elements such as occurred in the Danelaw in England.'[18] We have already seen that the word-order in Celtic place-names is different from that found in English and the Scandinavian languages. In addition to this, the vocabulary of Gaelic was totally alien to the Vikings — again in contrast to the linguistic situation that they found in England, where many words were similar to those found in the Scandinavian languages. More fundamentally, the grammatical rules of Gaelic — affecting the way in which sentences were constructed and therefore the whole pattern of speech — bore no similarities to those of the Scandinavian languages. In this kind of linguistic situation, there was no chance of any complex communication without translation by a speaker of both languages or the use of a third language that was understood by both groups. As early as 850, the *Annals of Ulster* record a deal between an Irish king and the Vikings; for this agreement to have been reached, there must have been someone capable of conducting negotiations. Before moving on to look at the linguistic relationship between Scandinavian and the Celtic languages in the British Isles, we need first to examine more closely the different varieties of Gaelic that existed in these areas.

As the historical geography of Scotland and Ireland (see Chapter 2) suggests, the linguistic situation in these areas was complex even before the Vikings arrived. The Scots who left north-east Ireland and settled in western Scotland transplanted Irish Gaelic there in the fifth century. There appears to have been no serious divergence from the language of the Irish homeland until the tenth century, so the two languages were still mutually comprehensible at the beginning of the Viking Age. Even though Scottish and Irish Gaelic subsequently evolved along different lines, it has been argued that even as late as the end of the sixteenth century Ireland and the Highlands could still be regarded as a single linguistic province. In Scotland, the Irish settlers encountered the Picts, who also seem to have spoken a Celtic language, although this language has only survived in a few ogham inscriptions and astonishingly little is known about it. As well as the Picts, there were speakers of yet another Celtic language in south-west Scotland and Cumbria. These people spoke a language that was closer to Welsh than Irish, and generally known as Brythonic or British. The level of Scandinavian influence on these different versions of Gaelic varied, reflecting the social and political mix that followed the Scandinavian settlement of the British Isles. Indeed, Norse influence on both place-names and vocabulary is one of the main differences between East (Scottish and Manx) and West (Irish) Gaelic. While Irish Gaelic remained relatively unaffected by Scandinavian loans, reflecting the fact that most Scandinavian settlement was confined to a few towns along the east coast of Ireland, the Gaelic spoken by people living in the Western Isles and Scotland's west coast indicates a much closer relationship between Norseman and native. For example Scottish and Manx Gaelic include loans such as *dail* ('field'), *vidh* ('ford'), *strome* ('current'), *lagh* ('law'), *nabaidh* ('neighbour'), and *stailinn* ('steel') that are not found in Irish, and Eastern Gaelic underwent a process of vowel shortening that brought it closer to Old Norse.

The Scandinavian Language in Ireland

The surviving Old Norse contribution to Irish amounts to fewer than fifty words, many connected with shipping (*ancaire* 'anchor' from Norse *akkeri*; *bád* 'boat' from Norse *bátr*; *scód* 'sheet' from Norse *skaut*; *stíuir* 'rudder' from Norse *stýri*; *langa* 'ling' from Norse *langa*; *trosc* 'cod' from Norse *þorskr*) and trade (*margadh* 'market' from Norse *markaðr*; *pinginn* 'penny' from Norse *penningr*; *scilling* 'shilling' from Norse *skillingr*; *cnaipe* 'button' from Norse *knappr*; *bróg* 'shoe, earlier trousers' from Norse *brók*; *pónair* 'beans' from Norse *baunir*). As with English, some of these loans were not recorded until comparatively late, and a twelfth-century index reveals fewer than thirty words of Norse origin. The earliest known loan-word into Irish is *erell* from Old Norse *jarl* 'earl', recorded in the ninth century, a word that was also loaned into Old English.

Most of the Scandinavian place-names that resulted from settlement in Ireland are confined to the coasts, such as Dursey, Fastnet, Fota, and Waterford (Old Norse *Veðrafjörðr*) on the south coast, and Wexford (Old Norse *Veigsfjörðr*), Wicklow (Old Norse *Vikingaló*), Lambay, Skerries, Carlingford, and Strangford on the east coast. Outside Dublin, just four runic inscriptions have been found in Ireland: at Greenmount (County Louth), Killaloe (County Clare),

Beginish (County Kerry), and (just one rune from) Roosky (County Donegal). Although written in Old Norse and Scandinavian runes, both Greenmount and Killaloe demonstrate to some extent the mixing of Norse and Irish cultures in Ireland, the former in the Irish personal name *Domnall* and the latter in the ogham inscription that accompanies the runes. Some Irish surnames preserve Scandinavian personal names too: MacManus 'son of Magnus' and MacAulay 'son of Olaf'. Nevertheless, despite cultural, social, and political interaction, it does appear that the Scandinavian towns of Ireland may have continued to be distinct Norse-speaking communities, distinct from the surrounding area, until as late as the twelfth or perhaps even the thirteenth century.

While the Scandinavian language did not affect Irish very much in terms of loan-words or place-names, there is some evidence that the presence of Vikings in Ireland caused social and cultural changes in Ireland that contributed to the shift to from Old Irish to Middle Irish. As in England, where a grammatically simpler form of English emerged in the period after the Norman Conquest, the heavily-inflected and highly complex Old Irish also underwent considerable simplification that may well have been the result of the need to communicate between native and newcomer.

What Was the Relationship between Scandinavians and Picts in the Northern Isles?

At the other end of the spectrum from Ireland, the influence of Scandinavian speakers on the language of the Northern Isles is enormous. Place-names and the survival of the Norse language, Norn, into the eighteenth century clearly demonstrate the thorough Scandinavianization of the Orkney and Shetland islands. Indeed, the islands are so thoroughly 'Viking' in character that historians once argued that they must have been uninhabited at the end of the eighth century. There are very few Celtic place-names surviving on the islands and there was no resurgence of the Gaelic language as happened elsewhere in Scotland and the Western Isles. Yet excavations have demonstrated that the native Picts were still living on Orkney and Shetland when the Vikings first arrived. What happened to them? Did Norseman and Pict live side by side, before the two communities gradually integrated, leaving no trace of Pictish culture? Was there bitter fighting which wiped out the native population, either through violence or emigration? Or was there some other kind of relationship? In the absence of written sources, the answer to this mystery hinges upon archaeological evidence. However, as we have already seen, the archaeological picture is itself far from simple. Evidence from a number of sites hints at some kind of continuity from the Pictish period through to the early Viking Age, as Pictish type artefacts have been found in Norse-style houses and settlements. While this might be explained by a degree of social integration between the Pictish and Norse populations on Orkney in the ninth and perhaps the tenth century, the artefacts could equally well be the work of Picts whom the Vikings had forced into slavery, objects left behind by fleeing or even murdered Picts, or items that were traded between the two populations.

On Shetland too, there are some suggestions of continuity from the pre-Norse period. Carved stones in the Christian Pictish tradition continued to be produced in Shetland after Norse raids and settlement had commenced, although the custom disappeared from Orkney at the end of the eighth century. The most significant of these slabs is that from Culbinsgarth, Bressay, off the coast of east Shetland, which has been dated to the tenth century. Hooded figures with croziers and satchels, interpreted as monks, are depicted alongside animal figures, and each face of the slab bears a circular cross-head with interlace. The two narrow edges are inscribed with a late Pictish ogham inscription, but the word-dividers seem to be modelled on those used in Norse runic inscriptions. Ritchie suggests that the continuing production of sculpture on Shetland and the lack of such sculpture on Orkney '...must reflect a difference in the intensity of early Norse settlement, the larger number of colonists being attracted by Orkney, both for its fertile land and for its proximity to the rest of the British Isles.'[19]

While the archaeological evidence is therefore patchy and far from conclusive, it is certain that incoming Scandinavian settlers had more or less obliterated the culture of the pre-existing Pictish population of the Northern Isles by the end of the tenth century. It seems reasonable to deduce from this that the relationship between the two populations on the islands was not an equal one, and that even if some Picts had survived the Viking colonization and continued to live on Orkney and Shetland, their numbers and status must have been so reduced as to render all aspects of their culture invisible to the archaeologist. Of course, one may hope that future discoveries may still throw new light on this question.

Scotland and the Western Isles

Lack of written evidence means that we are again almost totally dependent on place-names for assessing the nature and impact of Scandinavian settlement in Scotland and the Hebrides. In Scotland, the map of Scandinavian place-names seems very much to be an overspill from Viking colonies on the islands along its coast: in Caithness in the north-east, the overwhelmingly dominant Scandinavian names reflect the area's close connections with Orkney, especially after it became part of the earldom; along the west coast, the Scandinavian names can be linked to the Norse settlements in the Hebrides. On the basis of the place-name evidence, the Outer Hebrides appear to have been more thoroughly Scandinavianized than the southern

Isles, with the Isle of Lewis retaining some 99 purely Scandinavian place-names and a further nine partly Scandinavian names out of a total 126 village names. The proportion of Scandinavian place-names drops as one moves south through the islands, so that about sixty per cent of place-names in Skye are Scandinavian, and some thirty per cent in Islay. The intonation of Lewis Gaelic also reflects the island's Scandinavian linguistic heritage, although there are only a few actual Scandinavian loans in Lewisian dialect. Norse loans are particularly frequent in the maritime vocabulary of the Outer Hebrides, especially Lewis, Uist and Tiree. However, the number of -*bólstaðr* ('farm, settlement') place-names on Coll, Tiree, western Mull and Islay also suggests a strong Norse presence. While there are fewer Scandinavian place-names in the southern islands, such as Arran, this linguistic impact is still generally greater than that found in the areas of England settled by Scandinavians. Apart from a few island names, very few of the Gaelic place-names in the Isles can be proved to pre-date the Viking period, and it has been suggested that the Norse language did not totally drop out of use in the Hebrides until the early sixteenth century. Yet, Gaelic seems to have re-emerged and spread throughout the former Norse-speaking areas from the twelfth century. A total absence of documentary evidence makes it impossible to be sure whether Gaelic survived in the islands or else was wiped out and reintroduced at a later date. However, literary and historical sources hint at intermarriage between Norse and native in the Hebrides. The survival of Gaelic seems likely given this factor, and the lack of Gaelic place-names does not necessarily mean there were no Gaelic speakers. The names of larger nucleated settlements — villages and towns — seem to have been more resilient to change than the names of individual farms and smaller settlements. The relatively low number of large settlements in the Hebrides may therefore mean that the place-names of the islands have been changed more frequently, reflecting their turbulent linguistic history. Even on Lewis, the names of natural features have a much higher Gaelic proportion than village names.

Manx Gaelic

When the Vikings arrived on the Isle of Man at the end of the eighth century, the island's inhabitants probably spoke a form of Gaelic very close to that spoken in Ireland. This language seems to have been first established on Man in the fourth century, replacing native Brythonic, another Celtic language that was also spoken by the island's close neighbours in Wales, Cumbria, and Galloway. Gaelic was certainly used on the island in the sixteenth century, when it was used to compile tax records. However, the linguistic situation on the island between the arrival of the Vikings and the relinquishment of Norwegian sovereignty in 1266 is shrouded in uncertainty. The linguistic evidence for Scandinavian influence is considerable but its significance is much debated. Manx Gaelic contains Scandinavian loans that are not found in other forms of Gaelic, including *spret* ('start'), *grinney* ('gate'), *oalsun* (rope from head to foreleg of cow); the island's place-names have a very strong Norse flavour, with two-thirds of treens (local administrative units) having Norse names in sixteenth-century tax records, while only three Gaelic place-names (Douglas, Rushen, and Man itself) can be shown to pre-date Norse settlement. Yet, in the sixteenth century, some ninety per cent of quarterland (a smaller administrative unit, reflecting local farming divisions) names were Gaelic in origin. How old were these Gaelic names — had they existed throughout the Viking Age, reflecting the continued use of Gaelic by peasant farmers on the island? Or are they more recent than that, given in the period after the Scandinavian language ceased to be spoken on the island?

The place-name scholar Margaret Gelling argues that Norse was the dominant language on the Isle of Man between about 900 and 1300, and that Gaelic had probably died out during the period of Norse hegemony. She suggests that the re-emergence of Gaelic on Man was probably the result of later immigration by Gaelic speakers from Scotland or Ireland and that Norse only finally died out in the fifteenth century. But her argument is fiercely contested by other scholars, particularly Basil Megaw, who highlights Celtic influence on the personal and place-names of the island. For example, many of the people mentioned in the island's Scandinavian runic inscriptions have Celtic names or patronymics: the cross-slab Braddan I commemorates a man with the Norse name of Ófeigr who is described as *sun:krinais* 'the son of Crínán'. Crínán is a Celtic man's name and the word-order in the inscription follows Celtic practice, rather than Norse (where we would expect *krinais:sun*). Another rune-inscribed cross-slab from Bride was raised by a man called 'Druián Dubgaill's son', whose name, and that of his father, are Gaelic, and the word-order again follows Celtic rather than Norse practice. Similarly, several members of the Scandinavian dynasty of kings established by Godred Crovan at the end of the eleventh century have Celtic rather than Norse nicknames — the name Crovan is itself probably derived from Gaelic *crobh-bhán* 'White-Hand'. Megaw also points out the fact that there seem to have been a number of Gaelic alternatives to Norse place-names on the island. He concludes that the written evidence is biased in favour of the aristocratic Norse names for places, which were then later anglicized and consequently preserved for posterity. He also revises the date of a key document in Gelling's argument for thirteenth-century Gaelic immigration, showing that there were already a substantial number of Gaelic names in use on Man by the end of the thirteenth century. His conclusion is that Gaelic remained the language of the native peasants throughout the Norse period, and that Norse settlement was, in fact, a small-scale aristocratic take-over. Dolley sums up this view succinctly: 'Norse...[was]...the language of the thing and of tribunals and taxation, while proto-Manx was the language of pillow, kitchen and farm.'[20] However, Gelling maintains that in order to change the language of so many place-names, the number of newcomers must be relatively high and the social status of the majority of them relatively low. As in England, the reality that underlies the linguistic evidence is highly controversial.

Unanswered Questions

Although written sources tell us, in some cases at least, that Scandinavians settled throughout the British Isles in the ninth and tenth centuries, they do not answer many of the most important and interesting questions that this colonization raises: exactly where did they settle, how many settlers there were, and perhaps most crucially, what happened once these people had settled in an area. As this chapter has demonstrated, linguistic evidence — principally from place-names and loan-words — is one of the main ways of trying to reconstruct the process of settlement and exploring the relationship between the Vikings and their new neighbours. Yet, as should be clear by now, the process whereby one language influences another is not a simple or straightforward one: it is affected by the nature of the two languages that meet, as well as by the political, social, and economic circumstances of their meeting. When this meeting happened about a thousand years in the past, our understanding is furthermore fundamentally limited by the nature of the evidence that has survived. So much of the evidence we have was not recorded until hundreds of years after the Vikings are known to have settled in particular regions, and this can raise doubts about how 'Viking' some place-names or loan-words were. Nevertheless, a comparison of the linguistic evidence for Scandinavian influence across the British Isles reveals the sheer variety of linguistic change experienced in these different regions: from the very few Scandinavian loan-words and place-names in Ireland to the near total dominance of the Scandinavian language in the Northern Isles. These differences show us, perhaps more than anything else, that we are dealing with real people, not some kind of mathematical formula where you add *a* to *b* and end up with *c*.

The question of numbers, which has dominated scholarship on the Danelaw for so long, is quite simply impossible to resolve when added to this already complex equation — there are simply too many variables. But the evidence of language can tell us something about the status of the settlers, their culture, and the part that they played in local society and landscape. The picture of Scandinavian linguistic influence in the British Isles is as diverse as the different areas and peoples that encountered the Vikings. Nowhere is this illustrated more clearly than in the Hebrides, stretched along Scotland's west coast. As Barbara Crawford has written: 'As always the exact location is all-important; it is impossible to describe the relationship between Norse and Gaelic speakers in the Hebrides as a whole when it probably differed from one island to another, so much are the islands' cultural entities.'[21] The differences in the level of linguistic influence from the Scandinavian languages reflect the very different historical experiences of all the inhabitants of Britain and Ireland, both native and newcomer.

4
VIKING KINGS

Although the Vikings are well known as raiders and pillagers, it is easy to forget that they were also rulers of large parts of the British Isles during the Viking Age, wielding power over areas as far apart as southern England and the Northern Isles of Orkney and Shetland. In some places, this rule was fleeting, a short interlude before native kings reasserted their control, but in other parts of the British Isles, Scandinavians and their descendants managed to hold on to power long after Viking raids stopped and well into the medieval period. How did these men come to power? How did they hold on to their thrones? And what was being ruled by Vikings like for the people of the British Isles?

The Danish Kings of England

The most famous of these Scandinavian kings is Cnut or, as most of us know him, Canute. Even today, the story of his vain attempt to turn back the tides over a thousand years ago is still told (although this story is based on a misunderstanding), but what else do we know about him and his eighteen-year rule of England? Cnut's father was the Danish king Svein Forkbeard and his mother was probably the widow of Erik the Victorious of Sweden. He had one older brother, Harald, who became king of Denmark upon his father's death in

England in 1014. Cnut was with his father, Svein, when he died at Gainsborough in Lincolnshire, but although Svein had just driven the English king, Æthelred II, into exile and had received the surrender of 'the whole nation', Cnut was forced to fight on in the confusion that followed his father's death. Early in 1017, this young Danish prince was crowned king in London's Westminster Abbey. There was certainly a degree of luck involved in Cnut's capture of the throne: the English king Æthelred II died during the battle for his throne, and the machinations and eventual defection of Eadric Streona, a powerful Mercian noble, seriously weakened the rule of Æthelred's son and successor, Edmund Ironside. Following Eadric Streona's flight and a Danish victory at the unknown place called *Assandun*, Edmund came to terms with Cnut at Olney near Deerhurst in Gloucestershire, agreeing to give a substantial slice of his kingdom to the Dane. In the same way that Alfred the Great had given land to the Viking leader Guthrum, Edmund offered and Cnut accepted control of Mercia. But just over a month after this meeting, Edmund died and Cnut lost no time in claiming the entire kingdom for himself. That he was able to make good this claim shows very clearly, however, that Cnut owed his victory to more than luck. He saw off the threat of several rival claimants to the throne: Edmund's sons and wife were exiled; Edmund's brother, Eadwig, was exiled and then murdered; and Cnut married Emma, Æthelred's widow and the mother of Edmund's young half-brothers, Edward and Alfred, who had fled to the safety of their uncle's court in Normandy. Cnut managed to neutralize politically the most powerful of his remaining opponents through a skilful blend of diplomacy, bribes, threats, and outright violence: the Viking leader, Thorkell the Tall, who had fought for Æthelred II against Cnut's father was given the earldom of East Anglia and, ultimately, the position of regent in Denmark; while the treacherous Eadric Streona was first given Mercia and then

90

conveniently murdered at the Christmas gathering at Cnut's court in 1017, along with three other prominent nobles.

Although we might expect this victorious Viking to set about plundering further wealth from his newly conquered kingdom and to run it as some kind of military protectorate, Cnut appears to have done everything possible to avoid alienating his new subjects and disrupting political life any more. To this end, the new law-codes he drafted with the help of the Anglo-Saxon archbishop of York, Wulfstan II, were to all intents and purposes identical to those of Æthelred, and contained the promise to observe zealously the laws of Edgar established in the mid-tenth century. At the same time, most of Cnut's army was disbanded, eliminating the need for heavy taxation of his new kingdom and providing an important psychological step in helping to restore a sense of normality to English political life. The men that Cnut gathered around him at court included English nobles, although many of these were new men who owed their rise to power and therefore their loyalty to Cnut. The most famous of these was Godwine (d. 1053), who was given the prestigious earldom of Wessex by Cnut in the early 1020s and who, before his death, was said to have 'been exalted so high, even to the point of ruling the king [by then Edward the Confessor] and all England.'[1] Godwine married Cnut's Danish sister-in-law, Gytha; his daughter Edith married king Edward the Confessor in 1045; and his son Harold became, however briefly, king of England in 1066. The family provides an outstanding example of the mixed Anglo-Scandinavian aristocracy that emerged during Cnut's reign, with three of Godwine's and Gytha's children bearing Scandinavian names (Swein, Harold, and Tostig), and four of them bearing Old English names (Edith, Leofwine, Gyrth, and Wulfnoth).

Such was Cnut's concern to set his throne on a firm footing that he wrote two open letters to his people explaining his absences from

England in 1019 and 1027 — an unprecedented move by an English monarch, which underlines the importance Cnut attached to popular support for his reign.

> *Then I was informed that greater danger was approaching us than we liked at all; and then I went myself with the men who accompanied me to Denmark, from where the greatest injury had come to you, and with God's help I have taken measures so that never henceforth shall hostility reach you from there as long as you support me rightly and my life lasts.*[2]

In the letter that he sent following a visit to Rome in 1027, Cnut seems even more anxious to justify his absence from England and to inform his subjects of his achievements on their behalf, his concern suggesting that all was not well at home:

> *I make it known to you that I have recently been to Rome to pray for the remission of my sins and for the safety of the kingdoms and of the people which are subjected to my rule [...] I therefore spoke with the emperor [Conrad] and the lord pope and the princes who were present, concerning the needs of all the peoples of my whole kingdom, whether English or Danes, that they might be granted more equitable law and greater security on their way to Rome, and that they should not be hindered by so many barriers on the way and so oppressed by unjust tolls; and the emperor and King Rodulf [of Burgundy] consented to my demands [...] Now, therefore, be it known to you all, that I have humbly vowed to Almighty God to amend my life from now on in all things, and to rule justly and faithfully the kingdoms and peoples subject to me and to maintain equal justice in all things; and if hitherto anything contrary to what is right has been done through the intemperance of my youth or through negligence, I intend to repair it all henceforth with the help of God [...] And therefore I wish to make known to you, that, returning by the same way that I went, I am going to Denmark, to conclude with the counsel of all the Danes peace and a firm treaty with those nations and people who wished, if possible for them, to deprive us of both kingdom and life.*[3]

Looking at the documents that have survived from Cnut's reign, it is very easy to forget that Cnut was a Scandinavian conqueror who had no hereditary claim on the English throne. Interestingly, many of the Norse skaldic poems composed at his court, which must have been intended for a Scandinavian audience, emphasize both his right to the English throne and his godliness (see, for example, Hallvarðr Háreksblesi's *Knútsdrápa*). Cnut clearly saw skaldic poetry as an important form of propaganda, legitimizing his rule of the kingdom he had conquered by force. The poets who composed these stanzas recognized the importance of these issues to their king.

His reign was a time of stability for many of his English subjects, who were now spared the threat of Viking attacks and the punitive taxes needed to fund defences against the raids. This is clearly seen in the fact that there is no indication of any serious rebellion or popular opposition to his rule, such as that which followed the Norman Conquest of 1066. Rather ironically, Cnut's control of England instead coincided with a period of political turmoil in Scandinavia, as Cnut sought to extend his control over his Scandinavian neighbours. In a remarkable turnaround, the king of England was no longer preoccupied with defending his kingdom from Viking attacks; he was attacking them in their homelands of Norway and Sweden. And he appears to have enjoyed some, admittedly short-lived, success, for in the 1027 letter to his English subjects, Cnut describes himself as 'King of England, Denmark, Norway, and part of Sweden'.

However, the North Sea Empire that Cnut carved out for himself rapidly disintegrated following his death at Shaftesbury in Dorset on 12 November 1035, during the short and turbulent rules of his two sons and successors, Harold I Harefoot and Harthacnut. Harold and Harthacnut had different mothers — Harold's mother was the Mercian noble lady, Ælfgifu of Northampton, whom Cnut had married before he became king of England, while Harthacnut's mother was Cnut's Queen, Emma of Normandy.[4] The two half-brothers were bitter enemies and, immediately after their father's death, there was

93

a battle for power. Harold won the first round in this contest, and was crowned king of England in 1036, while Harthacnut was securing his throne in Denmark, where he had been brought up. Here, Harthacnut was preoccupied with an invasion by the Norwegian king Magnus the Good and, in 1036, was forced to sign a peace treaty in which Harthacnut renounced all Danish claims to Norway, recognized Magnus as king of Norway and, most humiliating of all, made Magnus Harthacnut's heir (incidentally, it was this treaty that Harald Hard-Ruler later claimed gave him the right to the English throne, and which triggered the (unsuccessful) Norwegian invasion of 1066).

Although he had the support of Earl Godwine of Wessex in England, Harthacnut's absence in Denmark meant that he was unable to press his claim to the throne over that of his half-brother, and he only succeeded to the English throne following Harold's death from a mysterious illness in 1040. One of the first acts of his reign was to have Harold's body dug up and unceremoniously thrown into a bog. In contrast to his father's reign, Harthacnut's rule in England was short and unpopular: he levied a tax of 21,000 pounds of silver to pay for the expansion of his fleet from 16 to 62 warships, and he was accused of murdering Earl Eadulf of Northumbria. Danish rule over England came to a rather inglorious end just two years after Harthacnut's succession: he died at a wedding feast on 8 June at Lambeth in present-day London where, according to the *Anglo-Saxon Chronicle*, he was seized by convulsions as he drank. Who poisoned him is not known, but there was certainly no shortage of discontented candidates. Harthacnut was succeeded by his half-brother, Edward the Confessor (d. 1065), the son of Æthelred II and Emma. Edward, who had been bought up at the Norman court, was keen to cut off all links with the Scandinavian past, and even forced his Norman mother, Cnut's widow Emma, into political obscurity amid rumours that she had promised to support an invasion by Magnus of Norway. Yet the Anglo-Scandinavian Godwine family, who had enjoyed an extraordinarily rapid rise to fame under Cnut, remained powerful despite Edward's attempts to reduce their influence. He had them exiled following a dispute in October 1051 but was reluctantly forced to welcome them back in 1052. Only Edward's cousin (once-removed, through Emma of Normandy), William, was able to finally remove the Godwines from power and to reorient English politics away from the North to Normandy in the South in the bloody conquest of 1066.

While a good deal is known about Cnut's reign and those of his two sons, the history of Viking rule in the Danelaw over 100 years earlier is much more shadowy and elusive. As early as 876, one of the leaders of the 'Great Heathen Army', Halfdan, is said to have taken some of his warriors and settled in Northumbria (north-east England), where they set about the very un-Viking-like activities of 'ploughing and providing for themselves.' This is the first recorded Viking settlement in England, but little more than these bare facts are known, as the *Anglo-Saxon Chronicle* was more concerned with the continuing atrocities performed by Viking armies further south than with the peaceful ploughing by Viking farmers in the far north of the country. Clearly, however, Halfdan must have wielded some political power in the area where he settled. The most likely candidate for Halfdan's seat of government is York, the capital of the kingdom of Northumbria, which had been captured by the Great Army in 866-67 and whose warring kings, Ælla and Osberht, had both been killed by the Vikings. York certainly became the most important seat of Scandinavian power in northern England in the following years, and the first definite reference to a Scandinavian king of York was made by *The Chronicle of Æthelweard*, which noted the death of a king called Guthfrith (also known as Guthred) on 24 August 895.

Guthfrith seems to have become king of York at some point between 880 and 885, and was converted to Christianity around 883. Like Cnut, he enjoyed the support of the Church — in this case, the important monastic community of St Cuthbert, which had relocated from the vulnerable monastery of Lindisfarne to Chester-le-Street in County Durham. It may seem startling to us that these monks had such short memories and were willing to support a Viking usurper, whose countrymen had wreaked such bloody havoc upon their holy monastery of Lindisfarne less than a hundred years previously. But, in the complex web of political rivalries in the north, it seems that ethnicity never mattered as much as we might suspect. What was important was that political and economic privileges were secured for the monks, and a Viking king, dependent on the monastic community for his power, was much less likely to interfere than the Saxon kings of Wessex, who were currently adding the non-Scandinavian areas of Mercia to their own kingdom and were threatening to swallow up the rest of England.

Coins minted in York provide the names of two kings with Scandinavian names, who probably ruled York shortly after Guthfrith: Cnut and Siefrid. These coins, with Latin legends and modelled on the coinage of the kings of Frankia, provide an important illustration of how, already, these conquerors were absorbing and adapting west European customs to their own advantage. No Scandinavian king minted his own coinage in Scandinavia until around 995, and these early coins in Denmark, Norway and Sweden were essentially copies of Anglo-Saxon ones, but the new Viking kings of York recognized the enormous propaganda value of circulating their own proclamation of victory and power. Every time someone used one of these coins, they were reminded who was king of York. The names of the people who produced these coins, which were normally given on the reverse of the coin, were predominantly Anglo-Saxon or Frankish during the early years of Viking power in York, which demonstrates the conquerors' dependence on the expertise of native or 'imported' craftsmen at this point — as well as these craftsmen's co-operation with their new rulers. This was to change dramatically over the following century and, by around 1000, some three-quarters of moneyers had Scandinavian names. At the time of the Norman Conquest, all moneyers operating in York had Scandinavian names — a clear testimony to the popularity these names had enjoyed in the town following its capture by the Great Army in 866.

Although York was remote from the West-Saxon court, the Viking rulers of the north were inevitably drawn into the political struggles of the south. Indeed, it is likely that they encouraged them and tried to use them to their own advantage. Perhaps one of the most significant threats to the rule of the kings of Wessex in the period after the Scandinavian settlements was reported in the *Anglo-Saxon Chronicle* entry for 899. Æthelwold, the nephew of King Alfred the Great, revolted against his newly crowned cousin, Edward the Elder, and was accepted as king of Northumbria by the Danish army. The young prince was later also acknowledged as leader by the Vikings in Essex and incited East Anglia to rebellion before being killed by Edward the Elder's army. His threat to Edward's throne, rather than his alliance with Vikings, was probably the greater of his crimes and in its description of Æthelwold's death one version of the *Chronicle*, compiled at Winchester in the heartland of Wessex, stresses that it was Æthelwold who had incited the Scandinavian king of East Anglia, Eohric, to hostility. Interestingly, the so-called northern version of the *Chronicle* has slightly different wording at this point, and simply states that the Scandinavians had chosen Æthelwold as their king. To the southerners, emphasizing Æthelwold's treachery was the most important fact because he was so close to the throne that he could pose a real threat. A number of other significant facts un-

97

derlie the *Chronicle*'s account of Æthelwold's defection: clearly there was serious political unrest in Wessex and the Scandinavians in the north of England were quick to take advantage of it. Interestingly the *Chronicle* still describes the Scandinavians of Northumbria as a Danish army, an alien force to be reckoned with, despite its earlier talk of ploughing and settling down. Were the descendants of Halfdan's army still really organized into an army over twenty years after they settled in Northumbria, or did the court-based chronicler want to play up the treachery of Æthelwold and the threat that Northumbria posed to Wessex in order to justify and glorify Edward's actions and achievements? The Anglo-Saxon word for army is *here*, and as late as 1013, when describing Svein Forkbeard's campaign of conquest in England, the Chronicle refers to the Scandinavian settlers of the Danelaw in this way:

> And then Earl Uhtred and all Northumbria immediately submitted to him [Svein Forkbeard], and all the people in Lindsey, and afterwards the people of the Five Boroughs, and quickly after, all the raiding army [here] to the north of Watling Street.

Dorothy Whitelock notes that the word *here* seems to be 'used in the sense of the organised inhabitants of an area of Danish settlement.'[5] Clearly, almost 150 years after the first Scandinavians settled in northern and eastern England, the colonists were no longer the soldiers of a Viking army, but memories of their ancestors lived on in English minds.

The episode of Æthelwold's rebellion neatly demonstrates that the Viking Age in England was more than the straightforward clash of Scandinavians and English: there was north-south rivalry and, more particularly, conflict between Wessex and the rest of England as Alfred the Great's descendants sought to unite the country under their own rule. In the north of England, this brought them into conflict with the Scots as well as the Vikings. Edward's 'reconquest' of the

Danelaw was a campaign to strengthen his own position rather than an idealistic or ethnically driven crusade to put England under English kings again — the fact was that the kings of Wessex had never before held power in northern England. The presence of the Vikings in the north provided a convenient excuse and a once-in-a-lifetime opportunity to extend southern power into the north, where long-established English dynasties had been driven out by the Scandinavians and where the new rulers were not yet properly or securely established.

As the Æthelwold episode and the 'reconquest' show, however, the Viking kings of York were not the only force to be reckoned with in the Danelaw — East Anglia, the Five Boroughs of Leicester, Nottingham, Derby, Stamford, and Lincoln, and areas of the present-day counties of Cambridgeshire, Bedfordshire, Hertfordshire and Northamptonshire had each been occupied by different 'armies' which recognized different leaders and rulers, some of whom are named in the *Anglo-Saxon Chronicle's* account of the reconquest of the Danelaw. Many of these men bore the title of *jarl*, the Scandinavian word for earl, or *hold*, a lesser noble, but some are called king: for example, Eohric of East Anglia who was killed in 904 with Æthelwold; Eowils and Halfdan of Northumbria who were killed in the Battle of Tettenhall in 910; and an unnamed king killed at Tempsford in 920. The geopolitical fragmentation of the Danelaw is also reflected in the way that Edward and his sister, Æthelflæd, Lady of the Mercians, won territory from the Vikings bit by bit: the southern part of Danelaw (Cambridgeshire, Bedfordshire, Hertfordshire) had fallen to Edward and Æthelflæd by 914; East Anglia was brought under English control in 917; the reconquest of the Five Boroughs was accomplished in the period 917-920; while, despite the capture of York by Æthelflæd in 918, the southern part of Northumbria, the old kingdom of Deira, remained intermittently independent until the death of its last Scandinavian king in 954.

York and Dublin

Indeed, the forty years after Ætheflæd's victory in York saw a remarkable tug-of-war between the Scandinavians and the English in northern England. Viking power in York was immeasurably strengthened by the arrival of a new pretender to its throne, a warrior called Ragnald who had been fighting in Ireland until the defeat and expulsion of the so-called 'Dublin Norse' in 902. The Norse kings of Dublin were among the most significant political figures in the Scandinavian settlements of the British Isles during the ninth century. The first known king of Dublin was Olaf the White (*Amlaíb, mac righ Laithlinde* 'son of the king of Laithlinde'), who defeated Viking rivals and won control of the town in 853, ruling for around twenty years with his brothers Ivar (*Ímar*, who has been identified with Ivar the Boneless) and Auðgisl (*Auisle*). But the real zenith of Dublin's power came shortly after the recapture of the town by Sigtrygg Cáech (Old Norse *Sigtryggr*, Irish *cáech* 'squinty') in 917, at around the same time that his brother Ragnald also established Norse control of York. Sigtrygg of Dublin and Ragnald of York were the grandsons of Ivar (*Ímar*) of Dublin and therefore part of the dynasty established by Olaf the White in the mid-ninth century. It has been said that the Viking monarchy of York was only really established with the arrival of the Norse in the early tenth century, and that the Danish rule in York before this was more like an oligarchy.[6] Coins suggest that Ragnald may possibly have established himself in York as early as 914 and he certainly (re)captured the town just one year after Æthelflæd's victory there in 918. Under Ragnald, York, already an important regional centre, became the joint capital of a wealthy and powerful Norse kingdom stretching from the North Sea to Dublin, and the town was able to take full advantage of trading connections with the Irish Sea that this new political axis offered. But it may come as a surprise to us to realize that these Vikings were not welcomed with open arms by the Scandinavians who had settled in York around fifty years before. The coins that Ragnald and his successors minted give some clues as to why this was so — these suggest a much clearer break with the past than the coins of the first Scandinavian kings of York. Ragnald's coins were decorated with swords, ravens (birds of the battlefield that were closely associated with Odin), and Thor's hammers. In short, the new rulers of York were pagan conquerors who imposed themselves upon a Christian, Anglo-Scandinavian population. The new political leaders seem to have made no attempt to establish any permanent roots, but were content to simply milk York and its hinterland for wealth and power, and to use it as a power base for further expansion of their control into the surrounding areas. The Danes who had colonized north-eastern England in the ninth century had long since been converted, had settled down to farming and trading, and were now an integral part of the political and social structures of the region. They were as keen to rid York of its new Norse kings as the kings of Wessex were.

In 919, the *Annals of Ulster* recorded a Norse victory (under Sigtrygg) at Dublin, which led to the death of the Irish high king, Níall Glúndub, five other Irish kings and many nobles. This event is also recorded in the *Anglo-Saxon Chronicle* for 921, where it clearly had repercussions for Norse power in York, although it mistakenly describes Níall as Sigtrygg's brother. The *Annals of Ulster* record that Sigfrith, Sigtrygg's brother, was killed by a 'kinsman' in 888, so it seems that the English version of events is a misunderstanding, confusing the events of 888 and 919. In 920, Sigtrygg is said to have abandoned Dublin, but the following year saw the arrival of his brother, Guthfrith, another grandson of Ivar (*Ímar*) in that town,

101

and the death of another of Sigtrygg's brothers, Ragnald. Sigtrygg appears to have succeeded Ragnald as king of York sometime around 921, and in the *Chronicle* for 925 he is described as king of Northumbria. A number of coins, minted at York and inscribed with the legend SITRIC REX, survive. In the same year, he came to terms with the English king, Athelstan, at Tamworth, was baptized, and married Athelstan's sister, Eadgyth. However, the Anglo-Norman historian, Roger of Wendover, writes that shortly afterwards he renounced both his new faith and his bride. Sigtrygg died the following year ('at an immature age', according to the Irish annals), and Athelstan is said to have succeeded to Sihtric's kingdom of Northumbria. But the reality of making good this claim must have been more difficult than it sounds, as Athelstan is said to have captured York from the Norse just one year later in 927, driving out another king, Guthfrith. Guthfrith's son, Olaf of Dublin, reappeared on the scene some eleven years later when Athelstan died, reasserting Norse control over the town with the support of Wulfstan (d. 955), the archbishop of York. Clearly the Norse leaders had quickly discovered the political advantages that acceptance of Christianity could bring. This remarkable archbishop even accompanied Olaf on his campaigns to extend Norse power into the once-Danish Five Boroughs in 940. However, in 944, the English under King Edmund recaptured York once again, and another two Scandinavian kings of York, Olaf Cúarán and Ragnald Guthfrithsson, were expelled on this occasion.

The most famous Scandinavian king of York, however, was Erik Blood-Axe, who defeated Irish and English rivals for the town in 948, with the support of Archbishop Wulfstan.[7] Erik had been king of Norway but was driven out of his homeland by his brother, Hákon, who had been raised at the court of the English king, Athelstan. Erik's reputation was that of a pagan warrior, as his nickname

102

suggests, and Snorri Sturluson, writing in the thirteenth century, described him as 'a large and handsome man, strong and of great prowess, a great and victorious warrior, violent of disposition, cruel, gruff, and taciturn'.[8] But while mugs and t-shirts decorated with a fierce-looking Erik are popular with tourists visiting the Jorvik centre in York today, it has to be said that virtually nothing is known about his very brief rule over the Viking kingdom of York, although he did have his own coins minted. His present-day fame probably owes more to his appropriately violent Viking nickname than to any real achievement. Erik's position in York certainly seems to have been precarious: Olaf Cúarán of Dublin returned to York in 949 and ruled there until 952, when Erik regained the town. He struggled to control York for a further two years, before being driven out of the town by the Northumbrians in 954. With Erik's murder at Stainmoor on the road from Carlisle to York, apparently at the hands of an Earl Maccus (who was possibly a son of Erik's old rival, Olaf Cúarán), independent Viking rule of York had finally come to an end.

English rulers in the south rarely visited this northern outpost and either appointed Anglo-Scandinavian earls to control the region and protect their interests, or entrusted the native earls of Bernicia (the northern part of Northumbria, centred on their residence at Bamburgh) with the same task. When Cnut became king of England he continued this policy and, having murdered the hostile Earl Uhtred of Bamburgh, gave Northumbria to his trusted Norwegian brother-in-law and brother-in-arms, Earl Erik Hákonarson of Lade. Erik last appears — as a witness to a charter — in 1023, but we do not know what happened to him, nor do we hear of his successor to Northumbria until 1033, when an Earl Siward (Old Norse *Sigvarðr*) is mentioned in a charter that Cnut granted to Archbishop Ælfric of York. Siward dealt a blow to the native house of Bamburgh in 1041, killing Ealdorman Eadulf of Bamburgh and marrying his

103

niece Ælfflaed, actions which strengthened his position in the north and enabled him to rule Northumbria until his death in 1055. His nickname, the Scandinavian word *digri*, could mean 'great, strong', but also 'stout' — it would be interesting to know which meaning his contemporaries favoured! When Siward died, his son, Waltheof, was too young to succeed and so the earldom was given to Tostig, son of Earl Godwine of Wessex. This was a disastrous appointment by Edward the Confessor — although Tostig had a Danish mother and a Danish name, he was a southerner by upbringing, and never before had a southerner been appointed to the earldom of Northumbria. By 1065 Tostig had succeeded in alienating his Northumbrian subjects through a combination of higher taxes, harsh justice and unfair laws. He had failed to defend Northumbria against the Scots who won control of Cumbria, only recently incorporated into Northumbria by Siward; he made powerful enemies and murdered the nobles Gamel son of Orm, Ulf son of Dolfin, and Gospatric; he also succeeded in antagonizing the important religious community of St Cuthbert. Rebellion was declared in October 1065 while Tostig was in the south; York was rapidly taken by the rebels, Tostig was declared an outlaw, and the Northumbrians chose Morcar, a member of the ruling dynasty of Mercia, as their earl. Marching south, the rebels advanced to Oxford and finally, on 28 October, their demands were met by Harold, Tostig's brother: Tostig and his family fled to Flanders, where his wife Judith's brother ruled. The next time Tostig stepped on Northumbrian soil was almost a year later, as part of the army Harald Hard-Ruler had assembled for the invasion of England. But then Tostig died with his Norwegian ally at Stamford Bridge.

Ireland

Some of those who survived defeat at Stamford Bridge fled to Orkney, others to Dublin, which in the mid-eleventh century was still an important part of the Scandinavian world. Scandinavian colonies in the Isle of Man and even as far away as Orkney had recognized the overlordship of Dublin for a considerable part of the tenth century. Yet, during the reign of Sigtrygg Cáech's son, Olaf Cúarán (an Irish nickname meaning rather obscurely 'sandal'), Dublin's political independence was to be severely compromised. After failing to establish himself as king in York in the middle of the tenth century, Olaf was baptized as part of a deal with King Edmund of England and left to rule Dublin. Despite further attempts in 949 and 952 to oust rivals in York, he was unsuccessful, and even on his home ground in Dublin his rule is associated with the end of Viking independence and the re-emergence of Irish overlordship. The crushing defeat that Olaf suffered at the Battle of Tara in 980 was a crucial turning point in the fortunes of the Norse in Ireland. Broken by the battle, Olaf himself subsequently retired to the monastery on the Scottish island of Iona where he died in 981. Nevertheless, Olaf is the only Norse king for whom Irish praise poetry survives. In England there was no tradition of employing court poets, but the situation was different in Ireland and the Celtic world, where professional poets were employed at royal courts. Cináed ua hArtacáin composed a stanza in honour of Olaf Cúarán, and another Irish verse, praising Olaf the 'good king of Dublin', has survived, although it has been argued that this commemorates the first king of Dublin, Olaf the White (d. 871). Although the poetry itself is not particularly informative, the very fact that an Irish poet composed it provides invaluable evidence of acceptance and integration.

The changing political landscape in Dublin and Ireland as a whole is clearly demonstrated in the rule of Olaf's son, Sigtrygg Silk-Beard (Old Norse *Sigtryggr silkiskegg*). Sigtrygg was king of Dublin for a substantial length of time, between 989 and 1036. Sigtrygg's autonomy as king of Dublin was limited by two successive Irish high kings, firstly Máel Sechnaill II of Meath and then, after 997, Brian Boru of Munster. Sigtrygg allied himself with the king of Leinster and rebelled against Brian's overlordship of Dublin in 999, but was soon forced to submit to the Irish king (who also became his step-father through his marriage to Sigtrygg's mother, Gormlaith), and he married Brian's daughter, Sláine, in the settlement that followed. However, some years later, in 1012, Sigtrygg once again used Leinster support to challenge Brian's overlordship, and he helped to forge the anti-Brian coalition that faced the Irish high king at Clontarf in 1014. Sigtrygg himself did not fight at Clontarf; in fact *Orkneyinga Saga* claims that he actually ran away from the battle! The Dublin Vikings were instead led by Sigtrygg's brother, who interestingly has the Irish name Dubhgall, reflecting his mixed parentage. Sigtrygg's and Dubghall's mother was Gormlaith (d. 1030), the Irish daughter of Murchad mac Finn, king of Leinster, whose own complicated life also offers a fascinating insight into the nature of Irish-Norse relations at the end of the tenth and beginning of the eleventh century. Gormlaith was married three times: her first husband was Olaf Cúarán; she then married and later divorced Máel Sechnaill (d. 1022), the Irish Uí Néill rival to Brian Boru; finally, Gormlaith married Brian Boru, Irish high king, and bore him a son called Donnchad, before apparently leaving Brian. At the Battle of Clontarf, her son Sigtrygg's Dublin Vikings and her brother, Máel Mórda of Leinster, fought against Brian Boru (although Sigtrygg himself was by then married to one of Brian's daughters, Sláine). In addition to these marriages, Gormlaith was apparently promised to Sigurd the Stout of Orkney and Brodir of the Isle of Man in the negotiations that surrounded Clontarf, with Dublin as her dowry.

The famous battle at Clontarf was fought to the north-east of Dublin on Good Friday (23 April) 1014. Vivid descriptions of the circumstances leading up to the conflict and the battle itself can be found in both Norse and Irish sources, such as *Njal's Saga* and the twelfth-century *War of the Irish with the Foreigners*. The Dublin Norse allied themselves with Sigurd the Stout, the earl of Orkney, and Máel Morda, king of Leinster (and Sigtrygg's uncle), in opposition to Brian and his supporters, who included Máel Sechnaill, king of the Southern Uí Néill. The battle lasted all day and although the Dublin alliance was defeated, Brian was killed — and was soon hailed a holy saint in Norse and Irish sources. Although later acclaimed as a major conflict, in order to enhance the prestige of Brian's dynasty in the twelfth century, the Battle of Clontarf in fact failed to alter the political landscape of Ireland. With his rival, Brian, out of the way, Máel Sechnaill simply reclaimed his control of Dublin, so that Sigtrygg's position as a vassal of the Irish high-king was essentially unaltered. During his reign, however, the first Hiberno-Norse coinage was struck at Dublin (c. 995-1020). Sigtrygg's coins were closely related to the contemporary coinage of King Æthelred II of England, and some of them were more or less straightforward copies. Others, however, bear the legend SIHTRC REX or occasionally SIHTRC CVNVNC (from Old Norse *konungr* 'king'), alongside the Dublin mint-signature. Sigtrygg was a Christian king and undertook two pilgrimages to Rome, in 1028 and 1042;[9] he also founded Dublin's Christ Church cathedral c. 1030. He abdicated in 1036, and Sigtrygg's nephew Echmarcach mac Ragnaill became king of a Dublin that was much reduced in its political, if not its economic, power. Dublin ultimately remained subject to increasingly powerful Irish kings, and was never to again have the independence it had enjoyed in the tenth century. The last king of Dublin, Ansculf Torquilsson, lost control of the town in 1169 to an Anglo-Norman invasion force, which effectively signalled the death knell of Dublin's special status in Ireland.

Man and the Isles

The Isle of Man lies in the middle of the Irish Sea and at the cross-roads of two key maritime routes in the Viking world — the east-west crossing between Ireland and northern England, which became particularly important during the Norse rule in Dublin and York in the first half of the tenth century; and the north-south seaway that ran from the islands in and around Irish Sea up to the Northern Isles and, ultimately, the west coast of Norway. The strategic and economic importance of these routes made the Isle of Man an important place for the Vikings, and its collection of rune-inscribed cross-slabs is unique in the British Isles. It is therefore perhaps rather surprising that the island does not seem to have produced any strong Norse rulers until the very end of the Viking Age. Instead, occasional references to Man in both contemporary chronicles and later sagas suggest that the island was overshadowed by its more powerful neighbours in Ireland, England and Orkney. The *Chronicle of Melrose* records that Maccus, 'king of very many islands', was one of six petty kings who swore allegiance to King Edgar of England. According to the later Icelandic *Njal's Saga* and *Egil's Saga*, Earl Sigurd the Stout of Orkney is said to have defeated Godred Haraldsson, king of Man, in the latter part of the tenth century, and to have incorporated the island into his own earldom. The island may have remained under Orkney's control until the death of Earl Thorfinn the Mighty in 1065, but Dolley suggests that the Dublin Norse regained control of Man after Orkney's disastrous involvement in the Battle of Clontarf.[10] The Isle of Man was certainly in the hands of a king with Dublin connections in 1066 — Godred Sihtricsson.

In that year, in the aftermath of the Norwegian defeat at Stamford Bridge, Godred Haraldsson, nicknamed Crovan, took refuge on the Isle of Man and was welcomed at the king's court. Godred Crovan was the son of an Icelander called Harald the Black, and the grandson of Olaf Cuárán, one time king of Dublin and York. He does not appear to have had any links with Man before his visit in 1066, nor any other credentials to establish a claim to the Manx throne. Yet, following his victory at the Battle of Sky Hill in 1079, he founded a new dynasty of Norse kings on Man and, in a dramatic turnabout of fortunes, shortly afterwards added Dublin and part of Leinster to his domain. Godred passed into popular Manx legend as 'King Orry', and his ancestors ruled the island for almost 200 years, until Scotland purchased it from the king of Norway.

How did Godred and his descendants establish themselves on Man? The main source for Manx history between 1066 and 1377 is the mid-thirteenth-century *Chronicles of the Kings of Man and the Isles*, produced by the monks of Rushen Abbey in the south of the island. Unfortunately, this does not give us many clues with which to attempt an answer to this question, nor does the other main source — Icelandic sagas — which concentrates on the activities and accomplishments of Norwegian kings in the Scottish Isles and Man. But we can piece together a rough picture. The beginning of Godred's rule certainly coincides with the much-reduced power of the Dublin Norse and the earls of Orkney, as well as with the establishment of Norman rule in England. This allowed Godred sufficient breathing space to attempt a further expansion of territory, and the kings of Man became the kings of the Hebrides, ruling a scattered Norse community as far north as Lewis. Such a disparate kingdom needed a central focus and this was provided by the Manx parliament at Tynwald in the German parish, where the forty-eight representatives of the *Suðreyar*[11] met around Midsummer (see Chapter 6 for more details). But by the time of Godred's death in 1096, there were new threats — Magnus Bare-Foot, king of Norway, launched two expeditions (in 1098 and 1102) to establish his direct control over the Northern and Western Isles, ending their political freedom and the largely nominal homage that rulers in these areas had paid to his predecessors. Magnus established his own puppet king, Ingimund, on Man. However, Magnus's death in Ireland in 1103 saw the return of Olaf, Godred Crovan's youngest son, from the Anglo-Norman court of Henry I, and he ruled Man for another forty years. Olaf's longevity seems to have been a key factor in establishing the new dynasty firmly in place, and the entry for 1102 in the *Chronicles of the Kings of Man and the Isles* suggest that Olaf's skilful diplomacy was also crucial in maintaining peace on the island: 'He was a peaceable man and had all the kings of Ireland and Scotland as confederates in such a way that no-one dared disturb the kingdom of the Isles during his lifetime.'[12] Yet Olaf's cousins, the three sons of his older brother Harald, who had grown up in Dublin were 'engineering a villainous plot among themselves to assassinate the king' (they succeeded) and Olaf's own private life also sowed the seeds of future conflict, or, as the *Chronicles of the Kings of Man and the Isles* puts it, 'was the cause of the collapse of the entire kingdom of the Isles.'

Although the independence of these island kingdoms was threatened by monarchs in Norway and Scotland throughout the early medieval period, their distance from the Norwegian and Scottish courts allowed their rulers to hang on to power against all the odds. The main threat to the kingdom of Man and the Isles in this period was not the Norwegian or Scottish king, but instead a rival Hiberno-Norse dynasty that established itself on the west coast of Scotland. In 1102, the *Chronicles of the Kings of Man and the Isles* tells how Olaf, Godred Crovan's son 'had many concubines from whom he begat three sons, namely Reginald, Lagman and Harald, and many daughters, one of whom married Somerled, ruler of Argyll [...] He had by her four sons, Dougal, Reginald, Angus and Olaf.' The Crovan dynasty on Man spent much of its 200 years in power in conflict with Somerled and his sons and relatives (who became known as the *mic Somhairle*) and, in 1156, the Manx king, Godred II, was forced to hand over the southern islands in the western archipelago. Godred II kept the Outer Hebrides, those islands most remote from Man, while Somerled took the islands south of the Ardnamurchan Point, which were closest to his power-base on the south-west coast of Scotland. The number of Tynwald representatives was reduced to thirty-six to reflect the new political order.

Earls on Orkney

Finally, although they never bore the title of king, the earls of Orkney enjoyed considerable political power in the north of Scotland and, during some of the Viking Age, even further afield — in the Western Isles, the Isle of Man and even Dublin — rivalling the control of native and Scandinavian rulers in these areas. The heartland of their power was of course the group of islands that lies just six miles north of the Scottish coast. Despite their northern latitude, the Orkney Islands were fertile, with good low-lying agricultural land, and the excellent supplies of easily worked sandstone compensated for the lack of timber on the windblown islands. Although we, with our land-based, car-centred culture, might think that these islands are remote and inaccessible, communications were not a problem for the sea-going Vikings. Indeed, the islands became one of the northerly staging points on a coastal 'motorway' that stretched from Norway in the north to Ireland and Wales in the south. The islands also enjoyed a strong defensive position, surrounded by the sea and relatively distant from the power centres of both Scotland and Scandinavia, for although Orkney was close to the north-east Scottish coast, the 'political centre of gravity for a viable Scoto-Pictish kingdom lay in the region between Perth and Edinburgh',[13] while the 300-mile journey between Orkney and Norway gave the earls of Orkney a good degree

111

of political independence — even when Norwegian kings periodi-
cally tried to clamp down on this freedom.

The early history of the Earldom is, like so much of the Viking
Age, shrouded in mystery, even though the islands have the distinc-
tion of being the only area in the British Isles that is the subject of an
Icelandic saga. This *Orkneyinga Saga* was written in Iceland around
the year 1200 and covers a period stretching from the rule of the first
earl, Sigurd the Powerful (d. c. 870), in the late ninth century to the
death of 'the ultimate Viking', Svein Asleifson c. 1171. But Icelandic
sagas were not written as straightforward histories in our sense of the
word, they were works of entertainment. The people in these sagas
therefore had narrative roles to play and, like every good story, the
sagas had a moral, a point or a judgment to make about these people,
about the past and, not least, about the present. Saga-writers seldom
worked with contemporary records and documents because, as far
as we know, these did not exist — one of the most serious Icelandic
writers of history, Snorri Sturluson (1179-1241), described skaldic or
praise poetry as his most important and reliable source because, as he
saw it, to recite false praise in front of an audience would be 'mockery,
not praise'. Although this poetry was probably composed during the
Viking Age, it was not written down for posterity — instead, it was
remembered, repeated and passed down from generation to generation until medieval writers decided to include it in their works. Skaldic poetry provides a vivid insight into the values and achievements
that were admired at the courts of Viking kings and princes, but the
information it provides is not the stuff of conventional history.

> *Against England the Earl*
> *urged his banner;*
> *oft his war-band*
> *blooded the hawk-beak;*
> *fire shrank the halls*
> *as the folk ran, flame*

ravaged, smoke reared
reeking skyward.

This verse, composed by the poet Arnorr Jarlaskald ('Earl's poet'), describes a campaign of one of Orkney's most powerful earls, Thorfinn the Mighty, who ruled the islands between about 1014 and 1065. Thorfinn was, in fact, the grandson of the Scottish king, Malcolm III Canmore (1005-34), and grew up in his court (his mother was Malcolm's daughter and his father was Earl Sigurd the Stout of Orkney). Almost twenty of *Orkneyinga Saga*'s 112 chapters are devoted to Thorfinn's career, which was a significant period in the history of the earldom. As well as considerable territorial conquests in Scotland and the Hebrides, Thorfinn's rule marked a new stage in the relationship between Orkney and Norway. From the time of Sigurd the Powerful, the earls of Orkney had tended to seek marriage, and therefore political, alliances in the British Isles rather than Scandinavia, as well as concentrating their energies on conquest in the west. However, Thorfinn married a Norwegian woman, Ingibjorg, and maintained closer connections with the Norwegian court than previous earls of Orkney: he visited the court of King Olaf Haraldsson of Norway twice and, later on, established friendly relations with Olaf's uncle, Harald Hard-Ruler. Why did he do this? Perhaps because he was one of the first earls whose family connections were all in the British Isles and because he needed Norwegian support if he was to see off rival claims to his title. To judge from *Orkneyinga Saga*, this political balancing act was essential for an ambitious earl of Orkney — the islands were frequently divided between brothers into two or more 'kingdoms', but these brothers seldom seem to have been content with their lot, and sought the backing of Scottish and Norwegian factions in an effort to oust their brother(s) from power. Thorfinn himself was the youngest of four brothers and it is notable that the saga's description of Thorfinn's visits to the Norwegian court are nearly all followed by an expansion of his power in Orkney. Thorfinn's career is also interesting in its combination of traditional Viking activities with the role of a Christian ruler: he raided in the British Isles and served as a mercenary in Cnut the Great's army, but in his latter years he also visited the Imperial court, made a pilgrimage to Rome and is credited with establishing the first fixed bishop's see in Orkney about 1050 at Birsay.

The writer of *Orkneyinga Saga* concludes that people believed that there were three great earls: Thorfinn was one of them; the other two were Sigurd the Powerful, the very first earl of the islands, and Harald Maddadarson, the son of Earl Maddad of Atholl (who was brother of King David of Scotland) and Margaret, the great-granddaughter of Thorfinn the Mighty. Harald, who died in 1206, seems a strange choice in many ways, because the end of his career was marked with failure: he was forced by the king of the Scots to pay a quarter of the revenue from his lands in Caithness and, after losing a battle against the Norwegian king, Sverrir, Harald had to surrender the Shetland Islands and all their revenue to Norway. Perhaps Harald's greatness lay instead in his capacity for survival — he was said to have first been made earl at the age of five, to have ruled jointly with his uncle, Rognvald, for twenty years and to have been earl for a further forty-eight years after Rognvald's death, seeing off rival claimants and retaining lands in Scotland despite Scottish attempts to oust the earl. Even Harald's failed attempt to unseat Sverrir of Norway demonstrates the military and political power that the earl of Orkney must have wielded in order to launch such an expedition. The end of Harald's rule is, however, the last chapter of the saga and it marks the beginning of a shift in the political realities of the Norse earldom. The earls were no match for increasingly powerful rivals in the south and the east and the alliances they were forced to seek for their survival ironically contributed to their downfall — they

114

soon became an extension of the Scottish royal house and it was not long before the earldom was swallowed up into the patrimony of the Scottish kings.

Another surprise in the saga's conclusion is that neither Earl Magnus (d. 1117) nor Earl Rognvald (d. 1158) is listed among the great rulers of the islands. Magnus's father, Erlend, had ruled Orkney peacefully with his brother Paul, but there was considerable hostility between their sons. During Erlend's and Paul's lifetimes, the islands were divided into two separate earldoms in order to minimize conflict between Magnus and Hákon, Paul's son. As Paul was the oldest brother, he received the West Mainland, including the prestigious centre at Birsay and the southern Isles of Orkney; while Erlend received the East Mainland and the northern Isles of Orkney. Hákon, the great-grandson of the Norwegian king Magnus I the Good, looked to Norway to support him, while on the other hand Magnus commanded considerable support in Scotland and Shetland. Hákon hoped that Magnus Bare-Foot of Norway would back his claim to be sole ruler of Orkney during his western expedition of 1098 (see Chapter 7), but instead King Magnus deposed Hákon's father, Paul, and Erlend, and sent them back to Norway (where they both died that winter), and set up his own son, Sigurd, to rule Orkney with the help of a council. Both Hákon and Magnus accompanied Magnus Bare-Foot on his journey south to the Hebrides, the Irish Sea, and the Menai Straits, where Magnus Bare-Foot fought against the Normans for control of Anglesey, possibly with the aim of restoring the native Welsh ruler, Gruffydd ap Cynan, as a Norse puppet king. Here, Magnus of Orkney refused to fight, a decision which Magnus Bare-Foot attributed to cowardice, but which *Orkneyinga Saga* ascribed to his piety. After the battle, Magnus of Orkney managed to escape and took refuge with King Edgar of Scotland, who helped

115

him to become earl of Caithness, as a preliminary to reclaiming his half of Orkney.

The death of Magnus Bare-Foot led to his son, Sigurd, being recalled from Orkney in 1102, and in 1104 Hákon was named earl of Orkney once more. Magnus returned to Orkney to contest Hákon's position, and it was agreed that he should visit Norway to obtain the royal verdict on his claim. As a result, Hákon and Magnus shared the earldom from about 1105 to 1114, during which time Magnus married a woman from 'the noblest family there in Scotland'. However, after Magnus left Orkney to take part in a campaign against the Welsh with Henry I of England and Alexander I of Scotland, Hákon took over the rule of the whole earldom. On Magnus's return, the two earls and their armed followers met at an assembly-place and a temporary peace was negotiated before they agreed to meet on the small island of Egilsay during Easter week to finalize the terms of their treaty. It was here that Magnus met his death, killed by Hákon's cook. Magnus's skull, discovered in a pillar in the cathedral at Kirkwall in 1919, shows that he was probably killed by a blow to his skull.

Hákon went on a pilgrimage to Rome and Jerusalem following the murder of Magnus, receiving absolution from the pope, and he arranged for Magnus to be buried in Christchurch in Birsay. However, miracles began to be reported at Magnus's grave. This cult was strongly encouraged by Magnus's nephew, Earl Rognvald Kali Kolsson, in his bid for the earldom of Orkney, and he was responsible for the building of St Magnus Cathedral in Kirkwall (1136-7), where Magnus's body was moved. Rognvald was himself known as 'the Holy'. He ruled as earl between 1136 and 1158 and was canonized after his death. The impact of his rule is neatly summed up by the title of a recent book: *St Magnus Cathedral and Orkney's Twelfth Century Renaissance*. Rognvald epitomized the contemporary Norse 'gentleman', and was renowned, among other things, for his skills as a poet:

> *At nine skills I challenge –*
> *a champion at chess:*
> *runes I rarely spoil,*
> *I read books and write:*
> *I'm skilled at skiing*
> *and shooting and sculling*
> *and more! – I've mastered*
> *music and verse.*

Yet, paradoxically, during Rognvald's rule the earldom was open to increasing influence from the wider Christian world. The Cathedral of St Magnus, the very symbol of the Norse earldom, was based on models from England (Durham) and Scotland (Dunfermline). Some of the verses attributed to Rognvald are more reminiscent of troubadour love poetry than the heroic skaldic tradition. His pilgrimage to Rome and Jerusalem brought him into close contact with continental Christianity, and the long-serving Bishop William was trained at Paris. Wainwright saw the death of Earl Rognvald in 1158 as the end of the 'Golden Age' of the Norse earldom, with art and architecture already dominated by the Romanesque tradition.[14]

Indeed, 'Scottification' of the islands was weakening Scandinavian cultural and political influence. Scottish earls held the earldom from 1231 and, following the loss of the Hebrides in 1266, Orkney became potentially vulnerable to Scottish take-over. There were Scottish bishops and clergy from the fourteenth century and by the fifteenth century the clergy appear to have been entirely Scottish. The arrival of a considerable number of settlers from Scotland, particularly in the fourteenth and fifteenth centuries, and the growing trade with Scotland accelerated 'Scottification'. The language of government, religion and trade increasingly became Scots, and the last extant document in Scandinavian is dated to about 1426. Scandinavian ownership of

117

the islands was formally surrendered to Scotland in 1468, and the transfer of the bishopric to the jurisdiction of St Andrews followed shortly afterwards.

The Norwegian Withdrawal

Hákon Hákonarson, king of Norway, launched a last desperate attempt to maintain his control of the Northern and Western Isles in 1263. The battle that he fought against the Scots at Largs was inconclusive, but the Norwegians were forced to withdraw and retreat northwards to safer territory in Orkney. This spelled clearly the end of Norwegian ambitions in the west. Hákon fell ill at Kirkwall and died on 16 December, having had the sagas of all the Norwegian kings since Halfdan the Black read to him. The sale of Man and the Hebrides to Scotland followed shortly afterwards. It is surprising, with the advantage of hindsight, that Norway was able to keep possession of the Northern Isles for another two hundred years, particularly given that the earls of Orkney were Scottish from 1231. This survival testifies to the political strength and independence of the earldom rather than Norway's effective control or resistance to Scottish encroachment. Efforts were made to tie Orkney and Shetland closer to Norway, and trade and family connections bound the islands to their Scandinavian motherland. Similarly in the west, the Hiberno-Norse institution of the Lords of Argyll and the Isles vigorously asserted its independence well into the fourteenth and fifteenth centuries. Nevertheless, although the territories and titles remained in the remoter Scottish Isles, there were no Scandinavian rulers in the British Isles from about the mid-thirteenth century onwards.

5
PAGAN MEETS CHRISTIAN

When we think of the Vikings we tend to think of pagan barbarians, of the brutal murder of defenceless monks and priests, and of the wanton pillage of sacred treasures from holy places across western Europe. As we have already seen in Chapter 2, the raid on the Northumbrian monastery of Lindisfarne in 793 provides a neat illustration of this kind of Viking atrocity, which is probably why it is described in virtually every book and television programme about the Vikings. We are lucky enough to have the letters of the Anglo-Saxon monk, Alcuin, which record the Church's response to the attack in vivid and shocking language:

> *...heathens desecrated God's sanctuaries, and poured the blood of saints within the compass of the altar, destroyed the house of our hope, trampled the bodies of saints in God's temples like animal dung in the streets.*[1]

This letter was written immediately after the raid and addressed to the religious community on Lindisfarne — who were still there — but Alcuin was not himself a victim of these attacks. Nor in fact was he living anywhere near the monastery, as he was based at the court of the Emperor Charlemagne in Aachen, in present-day Germany. Nevertheless, the shockwaves of the attack reverberated throughout the Christian community of western Europe. Indeed, the Vikings were seen by many churchmen as a tool of divine justice, sent to punish sinful Christians: Alcuin believed that Northumbria was being punished by God for its moral degeneracy, and he also wrote a letter to its king, Æthelred, calling for a return to Christian piety. His only consolation for the monks of Lindisfarne was that they had been punished more severely than others in Northumbria because of God's greater love for them. But if monks were not safe from this kind of retribution, who was? Alcuin clearly expresses the fears raised by such an unexpected, lightning attack on the monastery: '...It was not thought possible that such an incursion could be made from the sea...' And even a century later, the psychological shock caused by this raid can be seen in the *Anglo-Saxon Chronicle*, compiled at the court of King Alfred in southern England: the attack was preceded by 'terrible portents', and the Vikings are described as 'heathen' who 'miserably devastated God's church in Lindisfarne island by looting and slaughter.'

This connection between the religion and the raids of the Vikings implies that it was their paganism that drove them to attack their Christian neighbours. But despite the best efforts of monastic chroniclers, the Viking Age was more than a battle between pagans and Christians. Certainly, during the early years of the Viking Age, the raiders from Scandinavia were pagan and the monasteries of the British Isles suffered from frequent attacks. But the Vikings targeted monasteries not out of any anti-Christian crusading zeal but for reasons of straightforward opportunism — monasteries were generally isolated and undefended, were located on the coasts and islands of the British Isles, and, most important, housed considerable wealth. In other words, monasteries were the perfect targets for hit-and-run raids, performed by small groups of men, who sailed across the North Sea in their state-of-the-art longships. Moreover, the Vikings also raided other desirable and easily accessible targets — the market places of western Europe were a particular favourite as they too were located along the coast and major rivers and there were also rich pickings that could be grabbed, at least in the early years of the Viking Age before defences were organized.

From Pagan Pillagers to Christian Kings

By the mid-ninth century, the Vikings seem to have become a permanent fixture on the Anglo-Saxon scene, but the most important record of their activities in England, the *Anglo-Saxon Chronicle*, no longer describes them as heathen looters of religious treasures. Instead, the Vikings are more often described simply as 'Northmen' or 'the army', and their targets included towns, royal manors and the countryside in general — apparently nowhere was safe. This might reflect a change in the sources used by the *Chronicle* — monastic records seem to have been used by its authors for writing about the years before about 870, but during the reign of King Alfred the Great (878-99) the *Chronicle* was probably composed at the royal court. Nevertheless, at around the same time there is a similar shift in the vocabulary used to describe the raiders in the *Annals of Ulster*, which documents events in Ireland. And, shortly afterwards, we start to find that some Viking leaders in the British Isles were converted to Christianity.

> *Guthrum, the king of the Vikings, with thirty of the best men from his army, came to King Alfred at a place called Aller, near Athelney. King Alfred raised him from the holy font of baptism, receiving him as his adoptive son ... Guthrum remained with the king for twelve nights after he had been baptised, and the king freely bestowed many excellent treasures on him and all of his men.*[2]

It may seem strange to us that the peace treaty agreed between Alfred and Guthrum at Wedmore in 878 insisted upon the baptism of the defeated Viking leader. Today, the adoption of a new religion is

121

generally regarded as a matter of personal choice, reflecting the private beliefs of an individual, but in Viking-Age Europe religion and politics were closely bound together. Throughout western Europe, kings were crowned by churchmen, and the evangelical Christian Church legitimized 'crusades' against those leaders and countries who were not yet believers. Guthrum's baptism was therefore as much a political as a religious gesture, a huge propaganda coup for Alfred that won him the support of his people, the nobles, and of course the Church, which helped to secure Alfred's hold on the crown. And the lavish gifts given by Alfred to Guthrum as part of the peace — hardly the way we would expect a victorious king to treat his defeated rival — demonstrated Alfred's generosity, a quality that was regarded as necessary to being both a good king and a good Christian. It was another gesture designed to win favour with his own people and with religious leaders, as well as being a pay-off to the Vikings, a Danegeld in disguise. Certainly Alfred and his contemporaries must have hoped that the conversion of the heathen Vikings would bring an end to their raiding, by 'civilizing' them and bringing them into a Christian brotherhood, but the baptism of the Viking leader and his chief men was primarily about securing Alfred's own hold on the throne and building up a reputation that had suffered during his 'exile' in the marshlands of Somerset the previous year.

As well as Guthrum, there were other converts to Christianity, such as Guthfrith, the first known Viking king of York, who was converted around 883. One of Alfred's successors, King Æthelred II, had the defeated Norwegian Olaf Tryggvason baptized at Andover in 994, and Olaf promised to 'never come back to the English race in hostility', a promise that he kept. However, conversion to Christianity did not necessarily stop the raids. Guthrum broke the terms of Wedmore in 885, although the time that the deal had bought Alfred allowed him to build fortifications and establish a naval defence, and in 886 Guthrum was forced to reconfirm the peace of 878. In the 890s, Alfred captured the wife and two sons of the notorious Viking, Hastein, who was harrying Essex at the time: one of the sons was Alfred's own godson, and the other was the godson of Alfred's son-in-law. The largest Viking military campaign of all, which resulted in the conquest of England at the beginning of the eleventh century, was led by the Christian Danish prince, Cnut the Great. As we saw in Chapter 4, Cnut ruled England for almost twenty years (1017-35) and his reign was certainly not that of a pagan barbarian: he adopted, with remarkably few adaptations, English law, promoted new English men at his court, married Æthelred's widow, Emma, and was an enthusiastic patron of the Church.

The Gods and Myths of the Vikings

What do we know about the religion that Guthrum gave up, in name if not necessarily in deed, at Wedmore? Most of us have heard of the Viking gods — the one-eyed god of battle, Odin; Thor, the hammer-wielding god of thunder — and a few of us may even be familiar with some of their beliefs about the afterlife, where brave warriors feasted in Valhalla awaiting their final battle. But unfortunately we know very little about the religion of the Vikings. The Vikings do not seem to have written down their beliefs and myths, and the oldest surviving Scandinavian descriptions of the pagan religion were not recorded until well after the Norse conversion to Christianity. This means that there is a gap of around four hundred years between the earliest Viking raids and the earliest Scandinavian accounts of Norse mythology, a gap that is about the same as that which separates us from the late Elizabethan period (Queen Elizabeth I died in 1603). But while we have written records to help us reconstruct what people believed during the past, it seems that medieval Scandinavians had little to work with apart from some oral poetry and traditional tales that had been passed down the generations. How accurate this oral tradition was is something of which we can never be sure. Another serious point to consider too is that these descriptions of Viking beliefs were written by Christians — how much did they really know about how the religion of their ancestors worked?

The most important of the medieval works on Norse mythology were both written down in Iceland in the thirteenth century: the *Prose Edda* of Snorri Sturluson, around 1220, and the anonymous collection of poems known as the *Poetic Edda*, around 1270. Both *Eddas* describe the beginning of the universe, the main pagan deities and some of the stories told about them, and the collapse of this world — Ragnarok or 'The Twilight of the Gods' — and its ultimate rebirth. From these two works we learn that there were two distinct 'races' of gods — the Æsir and the Vanir — that had once been at war with one another. The former included Odin and his wife Frigg; their son Balder; Thor; Heimdall, who guarded the rainbow bridge that led to the gods' world; and a series of more obscure gods about whom very little is known, including an ageing god of battle called Tyr. The main gods of the Vanir were Niord and his twin children, Frey and Freya. These gods and goddesses each had their own distinct attributes and controlled different aspects of everyday life, and each had their own hall in Asgard, the 'land' of the gods. In this way, paganism was much more complex than the monotheistic Christianity which replaced it. Instead of one god, one heaven, one devil, and one hell, there were several gods, several final resting places, and no single or simplistic force of evil. But both *Eddas* offer frustratingly little information about the multiple worlds of Norse mythology. Valhalla was not a Nordic heaven, it was Odin's hall and it was only brave warriors who won a place there in the afterlife; we know that some women might end up in Freya's hall, Vanadis, but what happened to everyone else? The Scandinavian Hel was the home of a goddess of the same name, but exactly who was thought to go there after death and for what reasons is not clear: Snorri writes that 'wicked' people went there, but also people who died from old-age or sickness. And Odin's son, Balder, described as the most pure and beloved god, was rescued from Hel — why was he there in the first place? Hel was not a pleasant world, but its description as a cold, damp and gloomy place — as an underworld for the damned — may well owe a good deal to its equation by medieval writers with Christian hell, the Eastern concept of hell fires replaced with Northern ice and numbing cold.

Norse paganism, as we know it, is full of contradictions and complexities — are these the result of medieval misunderstandings, or incomplete information, or was this always the case? Certainly the two *Eddas* do not always agree in detail. This may reflect different myths that were told by the Vikings, but we cannot be sure. The gods themselves are not described as infallible, all-powerful and all-conquering beings in the *Eddas*, but appear rather like humans, with their own faults and weaknesses. For example, Odin seems to have been the most powerful god of battle in the Viking Age, the 'chief' of Asgard, and is sometimes called 'The High One', but those who followed Odin were warned that he was also capricious and unreliable. This is at least partly the result of medieval writers' attempts to discredit pagan gods — Snorri himself argued that the Æsir were 'men of Asia' who had tricked the Vikings into thinking they were divine beings. The main enemies of the gods were said to be the giants, who lived in Jotunheim, but the gods were nevertheless not averse to marrying giants from time to time — Niord, for example, took the giantess Skadi as his wife. This absence of clear-cut 'goodies' and 'baddies' in Norse religion is nowhere more confusing than when considering the role of the god Loki. Loki is said to be one of the Æsir, but while he sometimes helped them in their ongoing conflict with the giants, at other times he deliberately hindered them and caused trouble. He was able to change shape, into an otter, a mare, and a salmon, and his offspring include the most fearsome beasts in Nordic mythology — Fenrir the wolf and the Midgard serpent — as well as Odin's incredible eight-legged horse, Sleipnir. Loki, Fenrir and the Midgard serpent were all key players in the destruction of the world, Ragnarok.

Both *Eddas* are concerned primarily with myths about the gods; they do not offer any real information about the day-to-day practice of religion in the Viking Age. For that we have to turn to archaeology and some contemporary accounts written by observers of Viking rituals. The archaeological evidence comes mainly from pagan graves, as it seems that feasting and worship usually took place out of doors, in sacred groves, on burial mounds, and by holy springs and wells, or in the halls of chieftains. No definite example of a temple exclusively dedicated to the practice of religion has been found, even though Adam of Bremen, a German monk writing in the 1070s, claimed that the people of eastern Sweden had built an enormous golden temple at Old Uppsala, just north of present-day Stockholm. Nevertheless, the sacrificial ritual that Adam described with disgust centred on a nearby grove:

> *The sacrifice is of this nature: of every living thing that is male, they offer nine heads, with the blood of which it is customary to placate gods of this sort. The bodies they hang in the sacred grove that adjoins the temple. Now this grove is so sacred in the eyes of the heathen that each and every tree in it is believed divine because of the death or putrefaction of the victims. Even dogs and horses hang there with men. A Christian, seventy-two years old, told me that he had seen their bodies suspended promiscuously.*[3]

Place-names back up this link between pagan worship and natural features in the landscape, for nearly all places that contain the names of pagan gods also contain words such as 'grove', 'spring', 'headland' and 'harbour'. Place-names also help us to assess just how popular different gods were in the Viking Age. For example, there are many more place-names that contain the name Thor than there are containing the name Odin, even though medieval Icelanders describe Odin as the most important god. Many Scandinavian personal names also include the name Thor — Thorkell, Thorbjorn, Thorbjorg — but there are none based on the name Odin. Interestingly, Adam of Bremen claimed that of the three gods worshipped at Uppsala, Odin, Thor and Frey, Thor was 'the mightiest of them'. Perhaps the medieval Icelandic accounts had got it wrong; perhaps they assumed the god of battle should be the most important of gods, just as Mars and Zeus were the most important gods in the Roman and Greek pantheons. Did the skaldic poetry on which they relied, composed in praise of warrior kings, exaggerate the importance of Odin to most people?

The evidence of graves shows clearly that Vikings believed in some kind of afterlife — people were buried with those items that they had used in their everyday life and which they might also need after their death. Men were buried with their weapons and/or farming tools, and women with domestic equipment, such as needle cases and looms for weaving. The most prestigious burials also contained boats, carriages or horses, by which the dead person might be able to travel to their final resting place; food for their journey; and, it seems, in some cases servants to help them. Ibn Fadlan's description of a Viking funeral that took place on the River Volga in Russia around 922 is a well-known illustration of how Scandinavians buried their dead in the days before they were converted, and is worth quoting at some length as it is the only detailed written evidence for this kind of ritual.

> *I heard one day that one of their chief men was dead. They laid him in his grave and roofed it over for ten days, while they cut out and made ready his clothes. What they do is this: for a poor man, they make a small boat, place him in it and then burn it; but if he is rich, they gather together his wealth*

127

and divide it into three – one part for his family, one part to provide clothes for him, and a third part for nabidh (a fermented drink), which they drink on the day that the slave woman is killed and burned together with her master. When a chief has died, his family asks his slave women and slaves, 'Who will die with him?' Then one of them says, 'I will.'

…When the day came that the dead man should be burned together with his slave, I went to the river where the ship lay. It had been hauled up on land and supported by four posts of birch and other wood. Around it was arranged what looked like a large pile of wood. The ship was then drawn up and placed on the wood. People began to go to and fro and spoke words which I did not understand, but the corpse still lay in the grave from which they had not yet taken it … They had put with him in the grave nabidh, fruit and a lute, all of which they now took out. The corpse did not smell at all and nothing but the colour of his flesh had changed. They then clothed him in drawers and trousers, boots and tunic, and a brocade mantle with gold buttons on it. They placed a cap made of brocade and sable on his head. They carried him into a tent which stood on the ship … Then they brought nabidh, fruit and sweet-smelling herbs and laid these beside him. Next they brought bread, meat and onions and threw these beside him. Next they took two horses which they caused to run until they were sweating, after which they cut them in pieces with a sword and threw their flesh into the ship. Then they brought two cows, which they also cut into pieces and threw them in. The slave woman who wished to be killed went to and fro from one tent to another, and the man of each tent had intercourse with her and said, 'Tell your master that I have done this out of love for him.'[4]

Although the ship and its contents were set alight and reduced to ashes in Ibn Fadlan's account, excavations have shown that some burials were instead covered with mounds of earth. The contents of these graves support Ibn Fadlan's description: for example, the Oseberg ship burial (see Fig. 1) in southern Norway contained a huge array of goods — a sleigh, a carriage, beds, buckets of food, horses, dogs — placed on a ship with the bodies of two women, one of whom is assumed to be a servant. When more than one person is found in a grave, however, it can be difficult to say if they were ritually sacrificed or if there had been some kind of family accident or illness. There are nevertheless some clear-cut cases: the burial from Ballateare on the Isle of Man, containing the remains of a man and woman, is usually said to be an example of ritual sacrifice as the woman's skull has a huge hole in the back of it, consistent with a blow by a heavy implement.

Mission Accomplished

In the Viking homelands, German and Anglo-Saxon preachers were starting to spread the Christian word from the 820s onwards. The German missionary Ansgar built churches in the Danish towns of Ribe and Hedeby, and although these seem to have had a fairly short life, Ansgar returned in the 850s to re-establish Christianity in these towns. At least one Danish king at this time, Harald Klak, was Christian. Admittedly, his conversion, like that of Guthrum's, seems to have been prompted by political rather than religious considerations — he was baptized at the court of the Frankish emperor, who in turn offered Harald support against a political and pagan rival in Denmark. In spite of this help, Harald was still driven out of his kingdom, and there is virtually no record of internal events in Denmark from the mid-ninth until the mid-tenth century, when another Harald is said to have come to the Danish throne. This Harald, nicknamed Blue-Tooth, was the first Christian king of Denmark with sufficient power to impose his religion on his subjects, an achievement which is proudly recorded on a rune-stone that Harald had made to commemorate his parents:

King Harald had this monument made in memory of his father, Gorm, and his mother, Thyre. Harald won all Denmark for himself, and Norway, and made the Danes Christian [the final part of this inscription is carved underneath a picture of Christ crucified].

By this time, Denmark had three bishops with cathedrals in the towns of Ribe, Hedeby and Århus, and the basic administration of

129

the Church was being established in the country. Yet, according to Adam of Bremen, Harald was driven into exile by his son, Svein Forkbeard, in what is described as a pagan revolt against the Christian Harald. However, closer examination of the political situation in Denmark suggests that it was more likely that Svein's rebellion was motivated by widespread resentment at his father's attempts to extend his power, which were funded by new and heavier taxes on his people. Adam of Bremen's portrayal of Svein as the arch-enemy of the Church owes more to his resentment at Svein's refusal to acknowledge the primacy of Adam's church, the archbishopric of Hamburg-Bremen in present-day Germany. The Scandinavian countries of Denmark, Iceland, Norway and Sweden were potentially big catches for the church that could win control over them — in economic, political and religious terms — and there seems to have been fierce competition between English and German archbishops over who was in charge of establishing church life in Scandinavia. The long reign of Cnut the Great led to close ties between the English and Danish churches, but Cnut also appeased Hamburg-Bremen. By 1103, the Danish Church was considered mature enough to have its own archbishop, based in Lund (in present-day Sweden).

Attempts to convert Norway and the Norwegians were slower in meeting success — the country was much bigger than Denmark, the population more dispersed, and the mountainous landscape made inland travel more difficult. These problems also made it more difficult for any one king to assert his control of the country — it was not until the eleventh century that an effective central kingship was established — and so there was no Norwegian Harald Blue-Tooth to impose the new religion on his subjects during the tenth century. Geography meant that the missionaries of Hamburg-Bremen made no sustained effort to convince Norwegians of the merits of Christianity — the predominantly coastal population of Norway had always looked westwards to the British Isles. So instead the Anglo-Saxon Church led the way, and its efforts were supported and encouraged by a number of Norwegian kings who had been baptized abroad. The first of these, Hákon, was brought up at the court of the English king Athelstan. Athelstan was the grandson of Alfred the Great and had been entrusted with Hákon's upbringing as part of a political deal, an arrangement that was very common in medieval politics. Hákon, nicknamed *Aðalsteinsfóstri* 'Athelstan's foster-son' in Norway, returned to his homeland in 960. He defeated his pagan rivals, was declared king of Norway shortly afterwards, and set about converting his countrymen. Hákon brought English monks and missionaries to Norway and had a number of churches built, but his efforts were given short shrift by other Norwegian chieftains and petty kings. His churches were burnt down and, as a final irony, a poem composed to commemorate Hákon after his death recounted his arrival in Valhalla, Odin's hall for fallen pagan warriors. Nevertheless, the connection with the English church persisted, and two of Hákon's successors, Olaf Tryggvason and Olaf Haraldsson, employed English churchmen in their own attempts to Christianize Norway. According to the later evidence of sagas, their methods were fairly primitive — if their subjects would not accept Christianity, the king burnt their lands and killed them. Olaf Haraldsson's unpopularity was such that he was killed in battle by a peasant army, which was led by his political rival, the earl of Lade. Yet in death Olaf attained a popularity of which he could only have dreamed, and which accomplished the two main objectives of his reign: to unite Norway under one king and to convert the country to Christianity. Against the backdrop of harsh rule by Olaf's successor, Svein, the English-born son of Cnut the Great, miracles began to be reported around the place where Olaf had been buried and when his coffin was opened a year later, by Olaf's Anglo-Saxon bishop, Grimkell:

...there was a delightful and fresh smell. Thereupon the bishop uncovered the king's face, and his appearance was in no respect altered, and his cheeks were red as if he had but just fallen asleep. The men who had seen King Olaf when he fell remarked, also, that his hair and nails had grown as much as if he had lived on the earth all the time that had passed since his fall.[5]

Olaf's death and subsequent elevation to sainthood marked the effective breakthrough of Christianity in Norway, and Olaf became arguably the most important Christian figure in early medieval Scandinavia — at least until Denmark and Sweden acquired their own saints, Knut II (another martyr king) and Birgitta (a visionary nun). Nidaros (present-day Trondheim) in Norway became the centre of Olaf's cult and Olaf's shrine was visited by pilgrims from all over Scandinavia and Europe. The archbishopric of Nidaros, established in 1153, had a huge archdiocese that included the Norwegian colonies of Orkney, Shetland, the Hebrides, and as far south as the Isle of Man. It is hardly surprising therefore that church dedications to Olaf can be found in the British Isles, in places such as Norwich, York, and London.

Vikings and the English Church

Guthrum's baptism was accompanied by that of his 'best men' who went with him to Wedmore, presumably because Alfred wanted to do his best to ensure that they would also uphold the terms of the peace. However, other leaders of the Viking armies in the British Isles may well have encouraged and insisted on the conversion of their followers, just as Harald Blue-Tooth and Olaf Haraldsson in Scandinavia undertook the Christianization of their countrymen. But many Vikings who settled in the British Isles probably converted to Christianity voluntarily. To the Viking kings of York and Dublin, to the earls of Orkney, and to other local leaders like the kings and princes of Scandinavia Christianity offered prestige and status, bringing them into the larger community of Christian Europe and conferring the recognition and potential support of other leaders in Christendom. On a more local level, Viking leaders could count on Church support — economic, political, and social — if they were Christian. For example, in Yorkshire, several Viking kings won the backing of the archbishop of York and, on a number of occasions, this was used to stave off interference in the affairs of northern England from the royal house of Wessex, based in southern England. Although the Vikings are often credited with the wanton destruction of churches and churchmen, the reality was that once they were a permanent fixture on the political scene, they saw that the Church could be a valuable ally. The Vikings were opportunists — and Christianity offered far more opportunities through working with it than through its destruction. In Ireland, where for a long time conflict between a series of different local chieftains persisted, there were plentiful opportunities to divide and rule, but once England was united under one king, only the Church provided a powerful enough counterpoint to the king's rule. In northern England this could be used to particularly good effect by the Vikings because of the tension between northern and southern England and a strong feeling of regional identity. Cnut, as king of England, worked particularly closely with Archbishop Wulfstan II of York in a shrewd attempt to bridge the political gap between north and south, and he was a generous patron of the Church. Indeed, he had to be, because an alienated Church would provide a perfect rallying point for other disaffected elements in his kingdom. The Church hierarchy was dominated by members of noble families and therefore sensitive to their political feelings, particularly as the Church's economic strength rested partly upon the gifts and bequests of these families. In addition to this, a disaffected Church could call upon the Pope and other Christian leaders in Europe for assistance if they felt unhappy with its ruler.

Crosses and Christ ... and Odin

It was not only the Scandinavian kings and chieftains who embraced Christianity. In the decades after Vikings colonized northern and eastern England, settling down to farm their new land, stone crosses were produced there in vast numbers: the churches and churchyards of Yorkshire and Cumbria are liberally peppered with the remains of these tenth-century monuments; and, similarly, on the Isle of Man and in the Hebrides there are more than 150 Celtic-style cross-slabs decorated with Viking art styles, some of which have inscriptions in Scandinavian runes. Interestingly, many of these Christian crosses are also decorated with motifs from Norse mythology and with traditional Norse heroes. Perhaps the most famous of these is the Gosforth cross from Cumbria, a ring-headed cross that depicts the crucifixion of Christ alongside Ragnarok — the story of the overthrow and destruction of the gods of Norse mythology. The exact significance of this combination of scenes has been debated for many years, but it is worth noting that the subjects are not so incongruous as they may at first seem. For example, above the crucifixion on the east side of the cross is a man with a spear battling with a monster. His foot is thrust between the monster's forked tongue and his one hand is holding the monster's upper jaw. This man has been identified with the Norse god Viðarr, who takes revenge against the wolf Fenrir, who had killed his father Odin. Viðarr is one of the few Norse gods who survives Ragnarok, and so, like the crucifixion, we here have another triumphant victory of good over evil.

In northern England and on the Isle of Man, several cross-slabs represent scenes from the legend of Sigurd the Dragon-Slayer, paralleling representations that can be found on Swedish rune-stones and even on the doors of a twelfth-century Norwegian church. According to Old Norse literature, Sigurd was the son of a dead hero, Sigmund, and was brought up by the smith, Regin. Regin had a brother who had been turned into a dragon and who guarded an immense but cursed treasure of gold. Sigurd was encouraged by Regin to steal this treasure, and the smith gave him a specially forged sword that incorporated part of Sigmund's sword to help him. Following Regin's advice, Sigurd dug a pit, hid in it, and when the dragon passed over the pit on its way to drink at a nearby pool, Sigurd stabbed and killed it, and could thus take the unguarded treasure. Sigurd cut out the dragon's heart and roasted it as Regin had requested, but he burnt his thumb while doing so. As he sucked his thumb to cool it, he tasted the dragon's blood, which gave him the ability to understand the speech of birds. These promptly informed Sigurd that his foster-father, Regin, was going to betray and kill him and take the treasure for himself. Sigurd preempted this by beheading Regin and then proceeded to load up his horse Grani with the treasure. At Jurby (Isle of Man), Sigurd is shown in the pit, stabbing the dragon from below; stones from Ramsey, Andreas, Malew, all from Man, illustrate the dragon's heart roasting on the fire; and Malew and Ramsey also show Sigurd sucking his thumb, while Sigurd's horse, Grani, is depicted on the Ramsey cross-slab. At Halton, in Lancashire, a smith is shown next to a decapitated body, and there is also a thumb-sucking figure shown underneath a tree with birds sitting in it.

Why were these Sigurd scenes portrayed on Christian monuments in areas settled by Vikings? To us, this seems a strange and perhaps blasphemous blend of ideologies. How could the Christian Church sanction carvings of Odin on a cross that stood in the parish churchyard? Why did the people who commissioned these monuments feel the need to portray the Germanic hero Sigurd the Dragon-Slayer on a cross that declared their commitment to the Christian Church? Were they linking Sigurd's heroic deeds and reputation with the person being commemorated? Or perhaps his struggle against evil was being recast in a Christian mould, in the same way that St Michael's triumph over a dragon was a popular theme in medieval art? There are a number of possibilities: placing pagan and Christian images next to each other on a cross could be a way of emphasizing the superiority of Christianity over paganism; and it also highlighted similarities between the old and new religions that might help persuade doubtful converts. Indeed, it is well known that the missionary Church happily adopted old pagan burial grounds and sacred festivals and restyled them as Christian churches, graveyards and feast days. Perhaps the stone crosses expressed a coming-to-terms with the new religion, which was accompanied by a nod to the old beliefs. Icelandic sagas mention a man, Helgi the Lean, who prayed to Christ for most things but in matters of seafaring continued to put his trust in the pagan god Thor, and the crosses may well represent a similar hedging of the Vikings' bets. As for the heroic accomplishments of traditional figures such as Sigurd, they could equally well impart a Christian as a pagan message. In this sense, the missionary Church in Scandinavia was careful to portray the crucified Christ as a hero, a victor, with an almost defiant air as he was hung on the cross. Indeed, the word 'hung' is hardly appropriate for the Christ shown on the Jelling rune-stone — there is no hint of suffering or weakness like that to be found on later medieval depictions of Christ. Christ was a victor not a victim.

Pagan Graves

Before Scandinavians were converted to Christianity, burials usually contained what are known as grave-goods. The number and the quality of these indicate clearly the wealth and status of the person who was buried, as well as that of the family that buried him or her. There are also differences between the grave-goods of men and the grave-goods of women: while men were generally buried with tools and/or weapons, women's graves usually contain household utensils, such as the equipment used in weaving and sewing. Perhaps one of the most famous and fabulous archaeological treasures from Viking-Age Scandinavia is the Oseberg ship burial from Vestfold in Norway. On the deck of this 75-foot-long ship was a burial chamber, richly hung with tapestries, and containing the fully-dressed bodies of two women who had been laid on beds. One woman was about 50-60, while the other is estimated to have been 20-30 years old. Accompanying their bodies was a wagon, four sledges, 12 or more horses, a tent, food including an ox and bucket of apples, five beds, storage chests, oil lamps, a chair, wall hangings, farming and kitchen tools, personal items and stuff for weaving. The sumptuous nature of the grave goods show that the family was rich, and that they could afford to dispose of all these possessions. They also show the importance of the women buried, and the simple fact that women could be accorded such an elevated social status. The nature of the burial and grave goods may also suggest that these people believed in some kind of journey to another world after death.

There is nothing quite so lavish as the Oseberg ship burial in the British Isles, but several boat burials have been found. One of the most recently excavated of these is one at Scar on the Orkney island of Sanday, found in 1991. This wealthy, 'yet distinctly odd', burial contained, very unusually, three bodies: a man in his late twenties or thirties, a child of around ten and a woman, perhaps in her seventies. The relationship between these three and why they were buried together is puzzling — were they three generations of a family that were killed in a terrible tragedy? Although the woman and child occupied pride of place in the grave, the man's grave goods — including a magnificent sword — clearly demonstrate that he was a rich warrior. Perhaps he died a little later than the woman and child, and his body was hastily placed in the grave after it had been prepared? The boat and grave goods, with the exception of a spindle whorl made out of Orkney sandstone, all hail from Scandinavia. How long had these three been in Orkney? We would not really expect a woman of sixty or seventy years to sail across the North Atlantic to start a new life, but if they had been living near Scar for a while, why did their grave goods betray so little evidence of their new home? One of the excavators of Scar, Olwyn Owen, has suggested that perhaps this burial represents 'a self-conscious flourishing of pagan belief and ritual in the face of encroaching acceptance of Christianity in the tenth century'.[6] In other words, the grave and the goods placed in it were an assertion of the social and cultural identity — pagan and Scandinavian — of the dead and the people who buried them. Careful excavation and close examination of graves can, in this way, offer significant insights into the new societies established by Scandinavians in these islands.

In northern and eastern England, the area known as the Danelaw, archaeologists have long been puzzled by the scarcity of pagan Viking-Age graves, particularly when tenth-century stone crosses decorated in Viking art styles can be found in abundance throughout Yorkshire and Cumbria. Scandinavian place-names in these regions suggest a large-scale settlement by former Viking warriors, so what happened to these pagans who died in England? A survey of pagan Viking graves, published in 1967, listed just sixteen certain burials. Since then, excavations have revealed two crucial new sites, at Repton and Ingleby Heath on the River Trent in Derbyshire, which have altered this picture, even though the precise significance of these extraordinary sites is still a matter of speculation. Repton is mentioned in the *Anglo-Saxon Chronicle* entries for 874 and 875, where it is stated that the Viking 'Great Army' took winter quarters there before splitting up into two factions. The remains of a Viking camp and a burial mound have been found on the site of Repton's Anglo-Saxon church. The burial mound contained the disarticulated remains of approximately 250 people, placed around a separate high-status male burial that has been dated to the mid-870s. About eighty per cent of the bodies found in the grave were male, between the ages of 15 and 45. In addition to this mass grave, a number of burials were found close to the church, and one of these contained a man, aged 35-40, who had been buried with a Thor's hammer amulet, his sword and scabbard, and two knives. He had been killed by a large blow to his groin and was apparently castrated: the tusk of a wild boar had been placed in between his legs when he was buried. The excavators, Martin Biddle and Birthe Kjølbye-Biddle, interpreted the mass grave at Repton as the remains of some of the Great Army, although other scholars have suggested that these may in fact rather be the remains of the victims of the Great Army.

Ingleby Heath lies just two and a half miles away from Repton and the site appears to have been in use for no longer than twenty or thirty years in the second half of the ninth century. There, a group of some sixty burial mounds contains the only definite examples of Viking cremation burials in England, with traces of burnt animal bones and the remains of grave-goods, including two swords, nails and iron buckles. There were also some apparently empty mounds, interpreted as cenotaphs. The archaeologist Julian D. Richards has suggested that the two sites may physically represent the division of the Great Army into two, led by Halfdan and Guthrum respectively, that is recorded by the *Anglo-Saxon Chronicle*, and that at Ingleby the Vikings were making a clear statement of their religious and political affiliations in a hostile and unfamiliar landscape.[7] Yet the extraordinary nature of these sites simply emphasizes the lack of other evidence for Viking paganism in England. Those Vikings who stayed and made the Danelaw their home seem to have been

139

rapidly converted to Christianity, and to archaeologists their graves are therefore indistinguishable from those of the Vikings' Anglo-Saxon neighbours.

There is rather more archaeological evidence of pagan Viking burials elsewhere in the British Isles, although this may simply reflect the fact that the landscapes of Scotland, including the Northern and Western Isles, and Ireland are today rather less built-up than those of northern and eastern England, and so less archaeology has been destroyed. Until relatively recently, most of the known Viking graves in the British Isles were those of male warriors, and some scholars argued that this suggested that most of the Scandinavians who settled here were young men, who then married local women, had families and were consequently fairly rapidly assimilated into the local population and the local way of life. The Isle of Man provides a good case in point. The earliest evidence for Viking society on Man is provided by a number of pagan burials from the late ninth and the early tenth century which have been excavated around the island's coast. These include ship burials at Knock-y-Doonee, Andreas and Balladoole, Arbory and burial mounds at Ballateare, Jurby and Cronk Moar, Jurby. At Peel Castle on St Patrick's Isle, a tenth-century pagan cemetery, closely associated with a pre-existing Christian cemetery, was excavated in the 1980s. All but one of these pagan burials contain the bodies and grave-goods of men. Just one pagan female burial has been found on the Isle of Man (in the cemetery at Peel), although this is admittedly the richest female grave from this period in the whole of the British Isles, containing an iron cooking spit, a spectacular necklace of amber and glass beads, two knives, shears for cutting cloth, a bone comb, a work box containing needles and beads, a feather pillow, a pendant with a fossil ammonite and a tiny mortar and pestle. But there is still some doubt as to whether this lady was a Scandinavian or a Celt married to a Scandinavian

— her clothing lacked the characteristic 'tortoise' brooches that Viking women used to hold their dresses in place. The finds from the male pagan burials on Man — swords, shield bosses, knives, tools — indicate a rich, land-owning warrior aristocracy that had connections with Norway and the Irish Sea region. As at Peel, many of the loose finds of weapons and some of the burials are found in Christian cemeteries that were still in use by Christian Celts. This suggests that there was some contact, and more importantly some kind of compromise, between incoming Norse and native Celt on the Isle of Man — a situation that would presumably have been helped by the absence of Scandinavian women on the island.

It is important to remember that in the early days of archaeology, before rigorous modern excavation techniques were developed, many finds were made by accident or by amateurs interested only in more lavish finds, such as swords and weapons, and more frequently than not the excavations were not properly recorded. The graves of warriors are generally more easily identified as they contain distinctive Viking swords and weaponry, and they may also be marked out from the landscape in other ways, such as a raised mound over the top of the grave. It may well be that in some cases and places the graves of women were simply not noticed or recorded by early excavators because their grave-goods lacked the more sensational objects. Some of the earliest and most spectacular finds of Viking graves in the British Isles were made at Kilmainham and Islandbridge, approximately one and a half and two miles respectively from the centre of Dublin, in the mid-nineteenth century. The first finds at Kilmainham were made during the excavation of a rail cutting, and were recognized as Scandinavian grave-goods in 1846. The burials were not excavated properly, and the finds are recorded in a series of catalogues and a watercolour painting, made in 1847. More burials were uncovered at Islandbridge in 1866 and 1869, but these were not fully recorded at the time. It was not until 1933-34 that the first and only controlled excavation at Islandbridge took place, revealing two further accompanied burials. Despite the imperfect record of the nineteenth-century finds, it seems that there are at least 43 individual accompanied burials at these two sites, thirty at Kilmainham (27 male and three female) and 13 at Islandbridge (ten male and three female). The finds include at least forty swords, spears, axes, oval brooches, weighing scales, and lead weights. The cemeteries appear to be associated with the Viking *longphort* established in 841 and were probably in use until the expulsion of the Dublin Norse in 902. Although women's graves are clearly outnumbered by men's, there were, it seems, Scandinavian women there in Dublin during the very earliest period of the town's history, when it was still a military encampment rather than the cosmopolitan trading centre that it became.

Certainly, the picture of Viking society in the British Isles is changing as more graves are excavated. For example, around thirty or forty pagan Norse grave-finds have been recorded in the Hebrides, some of which date from as early as the second half of the ninth century. A large number of these finds are from the southern islands of Colonsay (including the rich boat burial from Kiloran Bay), Oronsay, and Islay, and early references to a number of pagan burials indicate that there were probably pagan cemeteries at Cornaigbeg on Tiree and Ballinbay on Islay. In recent years, a series of burials, including inhumations of a female and a child, have been discovered at Valtos on the north Hebridean island of Lewis. Of the 32 graves where it is possible to identify the sex of the interred, there are 14 female graves. Approximately forty pagan burials, including cemeteries at Westness on Rousay and Pierowall on Westray, have been uncovered on Orkney, with a roughly equal number of male and female burials. While only two pagan graves are known from Shetland, both are apparently female as they contained the distinctive bronze 'tortoise' brooches used by Scandinavian women to hold their dresses in place. Barbara Crawford highlights the difference in numbers of pagan burials found on Orkney and Shetland, suggesting that the rich arable lands of Orkney were able to support a larger and wealthier population than Shetland. It also seems possible that Scandinavian settlers on Shetland may have been Christianized more quickly, perhaps because fewer Vikings settled there and more Christian natives survived. The Orkney grave finds also contrast with those from the Western Isles and Man: on Orkney, farming equipment is often found in male graves, suggesting a rather more settled Scandinavian society than in the Western Isles, where weapons predominate in male graves.[8]

The Death of Paganism

Yet even though pagan burials can be found in the British Isles, the numbers of graves are not huge. Once again it seems that the Vikings rapidly abandoned their own religious practices in favour of new ones — even in Orkney where place-names and archaeology suggest that the native Picts were all killed or driven out of the islands. Why was this so? As well as the impact of marriage between Vikings and the natives of the British Isles, a respected nineteenth-century historian suggested as an explanation that the pagan religion of the Viking warriors was too disorganized a system of belief to withstand the well-oiled machinery of the Christian Church, and there is probably some truth in this. Christianity was backed up by the written word, and centuries of tradition and teachings; it was supported by a powerful and wealthy infrastructure; and the concept of one, all-powerful God was a simple philosophy both to teach and to grasp. In contrast, Norse paganism apparently did not consist of a standard set of beliefs and practices, it did not have a priesthood dedicated to teaching and practising the religion, and it did not exclude other gods and religions. In short, it was too flexible a religion — people could pray

143

to whichever god they thought might help them, including Christ; beliefs and practices appear to have varied in different places and at different times during the Viking Age; and there were no spiritual authorities to enforce and protect the religion. Much of paganism's strength was derived from tradition — traditional locations, such as burial mounds and springs, where rites might be carried out; a local chieftain's traditional position as leader of festivities; and the role of the family in perpetuating traditions associated with birth, marriage and burial. Settling in a new country took Vikings away from their religious landscape, their families and, often, their ruling chieftains — they could start a new life and, although expatriates are frequently notoriously conservative, it seems that Norse paganism withered and died; its roots were simply cut off and there was nothing to sustain it.

Fig 1: Restored prow of Oseberg ship, now at Viking Ship Museum in Oslo
(Author's own photograph)

Fig 2: The Gokstad ship, Viking Ship Museum, Oslo
(Author's own photograph)

Fig 3: Ruins of the later Benedictine monastery on Lindisfarne
(Author's own photograph)

Fig 4: Remains of a
Norse farmhouse at
Jarlshof, Shetland
(Author's own
photograph)

Fig 5: View of Norse buildings on the Brough of Birsay, looking towards mainland Orkney (Author's own photograph)

Fig 6: Tynwald, Isle of Man. Site of the island's Viking-Age parliament
(Author's own photograph)

Fig 7: Site of the Althing, Iceland's Viking-Age parliament, at Thingvellir
(Author's own photograph)

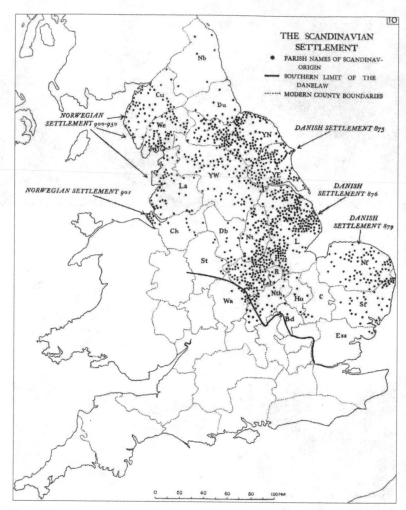

Fig 8: Map showing the distribution of Scandinavian place-names in England. Reproduced from A. H. Smith, *English Place-Name Elements*, 2 vols, Cambridge 1956. Copyright English Place-Name Society, used with permission.

Fig 9: Cross from Middleton church, North Yorkshire, showing Viking warrior (Author's own photograph)

Fig 10: Sundial with Anglo-Scandinavian text at St Gregory's minster, Kirkdale, North Yorkshire (Author's own photograph)

Fig 11: Pub sign from Stamford Bridge, East Yorkshire showing legendary Viking who, according to later tradition, heroically held the bridge single-handedly against the English in September 1066 (Author's own photograph)

Fig 12: The Martyrdom of St Edmund. Fifteenth-century wall-painting from the church of St Peter and St Paul, Pickering, North Yorkshire. Reproduced with permission from Heritage House Group.

6
SCANOINAVIAN SOCIETY

'The reformed and placated pirate-mariners brought with them many customs. They had a different notation, which they would have been alarmed to hear described as the 'duodecimal system.' They thought in twelves not tens [...] They had a different view of social justice [...] Their customary laws as they gradually took shape were an undoubted improvement upon the Saxon [...] Scandinavian England reared a free peasant population which the burdens of taxation and defence had made difficult in Wessex and English Mercia.'[1]

We have already seen how the Scandinavian settlement of England has been linked to the existence of a large number of freemen in northern and eastern England. To medieval Icelanders too, the Vikings were the embodiment of freedom, heroism and bravery, establishing a new republican society in the North Atlantic. Of course, it is no accident that the Icelanders wrote their sagas recounting the adventures of their brave and free ancestors after the Icelandic republic had fallen into the hands of the king of Norway (in 1262; Iceland was not to be independent again until 1944). Similarly the idea of the 'noble savage' enjoyed widespread popularity during the romantic movement of the Victorian era, and has done much to shape our views of the Vikings. British and Irish readers, all too aware of the atrocities that the Vikings committed in their raids, will probably be surprised to learn that these same people are credited with establishing the oldest parliament in the world — the Althing in Iceland

— and that many of the Scandinavian words which have passed into English, Scottish Gaelic and Irish are linked with law and legal procedures. It seems quite extraordinary that English speakers adopted the word 'law' from the language spoken by the armies that attacked their country! This alternative view of the Vikings — as freedom-loving, law-abiding citizens who established democratic institutions in their new colonies — is very definitely at odds with most people's perceptions and expectations, but how accurate is it?

Reading the Runes

Unfortunately for us, Scandinavian society during the Viking Age does not appear to have had a literary culture, and so there are no written histories, poems or tales that have survived to tell us about the Viking homelands in any detail. But the Vikings did have their own alphabet — the runic alphabet — that they used to carve short texts into objects made from wood, bone, stone and metal. Around 2,500 runic inscriptions have survived from the Viking Age. These are the only written texts that the Vikings have left us, and they are therefore the starting point for anyone wishing to find out more about Scandinavian society in the Viking Age.

The overwhelming majority of the inscriptions from Viking-Age Scandinavia are fairly short, memorial texts, following the same basic pattern: 'X [one or more names] raised this stone in memory of Y [one or more names]', with the relationship between the people usually given. This is hardly the sort of detail that we would wish for in our task of trying to understand Scandinavian society. In addition to their limitations in content, the majority of inscriptions that have survived come from the end of the Viking Age — the eleventh century — and from eastern Sweden: how useful are they then for tenth-century Norwegian society, for example? Despite these problems, taken together, runic inscriptions do provide quite a large body of evidence for customs of commemorating the dead (and in some cases the living), for the Scandinavian languages, and for the names of Scandinavians who never made it into the history books. In addition to this, some runic inscriptions contain extra snippets of information that not only tell us about the person who had died, but also help to give us an idea of the society that produced them. At the very simplest level, runic inscriptions indicate that it was important for some people to commemorate relatives and friends — to record the names of the deceased people and perhaps some details about their status, their life, or their manner of death. Runic inscriptions, cut into stone monuments, were one way in which your name and achievements could live on after your death. This idea of leaving a positive memory behind you is also powerfully expressed in the poem, *Hávamál* (verses 76-77), preserved in a medieval Icelandic manuscript:[2]

Cattle die, kin die,	*Cattle die, kin die,*
The man dies too.	*The man dies too.*
But good fame never dies	*One thing I know that never dies*
For the man who earns it.	*The good name of the dead.*

The raising of a rune-stone was probably a fairly costly business — stone would need to be cut and worked, a rune-carver employed, and the completed monument placed in a suitable and visible place — and this suggests that the custom was practised by the wealthier sections of Viking society. Indeed, the tenth-century Danish king, Harald Blue-Tooth, raised an imposing rune-stone to commemorate his mother and father, and, perhaps more important, to record for posterity his own achievements: winning all Denmark and part of Norway for himself, and making the Danes Christian. Many other inscriptions also demonstrate clearly that Viking-Age Scandinavia was a hierarchical society rather than a society of freedom-loving equals. There are references to different social ranks and occupations, many of them associated with a warrior-type society — *dreng* ('young warrior'), *thegn*, *jarl* ('earl'), lord, retainer, marshal, steersman — but there are also references to business activities, landownership and farming. Runic inscriptions also occasionally give us a glimpse of the qualities which were admired in individuals: the heroic valour of a fallen warrior, for example, is praised on the Sjörup stone in south-west Sweden: 'He fled not at Uppsala, but struck while he had a weapon.' From Spånga in eastern Sweden, we hear that Gudmar 'stood like a man in the stem of the ship.' Other inscriptions praise more peaceful qualities: 'he was gentle in word and generous with food' (Hagstugan, Sweden); 'there shall not come to Hassmyra a better housewife who controls the farm' (Hassmyra, Sweden); and 'she was the most skilful girl in Hadeland' (Dynna, Norway).

Apart from preserving the memory of the dead, the names of the people who had these monuments raised are also recorded on most rune-stones. Well over ninety per cent of runic memorial stones record some kind of relationship between the people who were commemorated and the people who had the rune-stone made. Some scholars, most notably Birgit Sawyer, have argued that rune-stones are more than mere memorial stones to the dead — that they were important for the living too because they are in some way tied to making a claim to inheritance rights. Very few inscriptions specifically mention inheritance, although one famous exception to this, the Hillersjö inscription from eastern Sweden, provides a thought-provoking insight into family life in the Viking Age:

> Read! Germund took Gerlög, a maiden, as wife. Then they had a son before [Germund] was drowned and then the son died. Thereafter she had Gudrik as her husband...[damaged part of inscription which probably refers to Gudrik as the owner of Hillersjö]...Then they had children but only one girl survived, her name was Inga. Ragnfast of Snottsta had her as his wife. Thereafter he died and then the son. And the mother [Inga] inherited from her son. Then she had Erik as her husband. Then she died.

Then Gerlög inherited from Inga her daughter. Torbjörn skald carved the runes.

As well as inheritance customs, this inscription also says something about mortality in Viking-Age Sweden, confirming the ever-present danger of death that we can read in the advice of *Hávamál*. Gerlög outlived two husbands, all her children, one son-in-law and her grandson. Unlike the Hillersjö inscription, the majority of Scandinavian rune-stones were commissioned by men to commemorate male relatives: just four per cent of rune-stones are raised in memory of women only, a figure which clearly cannot reflect a demographic reality. Women are found more frequently as sponsors of rune-stones — raising about twelve per cent of the total number of rune-stones — which shows that some women, such as Gerlög, had sufficient resources and independence to commission their own monuments. Yet this is still well below what we would expect on the basis of demography, and it seems that in the majority of cases, male relatives took responsibility for raising rune-stones, and women only appear when there was no male relative to undertake the task. Interestingly, on the Isle of Man, this situation is a reversed: a large proportion of the Manx runic crosses are raised in memory of women, although no inscription records a woman raising a cross. Judith Jesch comments that '...although the proportion of stones commemorating women is high enough to suggest a society which accorded a certain respect to women, there is no evidence that it accorded them any power to go with that respect.'[3] But perhaps, given the lack of female pagan burials on Man, there were simply very few Scandinavian women, who might have commissioned such monuments, living on the island.

Viking Women in the British Isles

Odd references, such as the *Anglo-Saxon Chronicle's*, to the families of Vikings certainly suggest that some Scandinavian women did travel to the British Isles as part of fleets that contained warriors: in 895, for example, the Chronicler records that 'the Danish had secured their women in East Anglia before they went out from that fortification.' If there were a secondary migration of Scandinavians into the English Danelaw, as some linguists argue, then we would expect more Scandinavian families, including women and children, to have settled in the wake of Viking warriors. The colonization of Iceland was certainly not limited to men only (the new settlement would not have lasted long if it had been!), and it seems quite natural that once some Scandinavians had made homes for themselves in the British Isles, they might be joined by their friends and families. Certainly, as we have seen in the previous chapter, a fair number of pagan female burials have been uncovered in recent years, suggesting that some Viking women at least were living in the British Isles during the early years of the Viking Age. As always, the picture is likely to have varied across the country — in the settled farming community that developed on Orkney after the native population had disappeared, there are likely to have been many more Scandinavian women than, for example, in the Hebrides, where the native population survived and intermarried with the Viking warriors who used the islands as raiding bases.

Icelanders' Views of Viking Society

A poem recounting the mythical beginnings of Viking society was copied out and preserved in an Icelandic manuscript at some point in the mid-fourteenth century. *Rígspula* or 'The Lay of Rígr' tells how the god Heimdall, who disguised himself as a solitary traveller and took the name Rígr, created human society and its social hierarchies. On his journey, Heimdall/Rígr was welcomed in three different households. The first house he came to belonged to Ái and Edda ('Great-Grandfather' and 'Great-Grandmother'). Heimdall shared their meal and later their bed, staying for three days. After nine months, the woman, Edda, gave birth to a son called Thræll ('thrall', 'slave') and we are told that 'his face was ugly, his back was crooked.' Thrall married a woman of equally low status, who is described as being bandy-legged and having a bent nose. She was called Thír (which means 'slave', 'slave-girl'), and together they had a succession of children, all given extremely unflattering names such as Foul, Lump, Thickard, Sluggard and Thicklegs. In this way, Thrall and Thír founded the race of slaves. The poem describes slaves as doing the hardest and nastiest work — feeding pigs, muck-spreading and carrying heavy loads. Rígr, meanwhile, continued his travels and arrived at another house, that of Afi and Amma ('Grandfather' and 'Grandmother'), where the same thing happened: he stayed and Amma later gave birth to a son, called Karl — a word that means a freeman or farmer. Karl's marriage to Snør ('string') resulted in the birth of more children, this time endowed with more positive characteristics, including Pretty-face, Lady, Wife, Strongbeard, Dreng ('young warrior'), Smith ('smith') and Bóndi ('farmer'). The race of freemen (*karlar*) is said to have been descended from Karl and Snør. Finally, Rígr visited the rather splendid house of Mother and Father. Nine months later, a third son was born: Jarl ('earl') hunted and was an accomplished archer, swordsman and horseman. He married Erna ('the capable one'), daughter of Lord, and the children that they had are described in noble terms (indeed one is called Aðal, which means 'noble'). Their youngest son was called Konr Ungr ('young Kon'), clearly a pun on the Old Norse word for king, *konungr*, and he was the wisest and most accomplished of all. Konr Ungr knew how

151

to read and write runes, he was able to understand birdsong, he was strong but also capable of pacifying men, and as a adult he assumed the name Rígr, another word for king, derived from Irish *rí*.

The account of the foundation of human society as presented in *Rígspula* is clearly mythological, and the society presented in the poem appears contrived and artificial. But the poem does provide some clues to the nature of Scandinavian society, or at least to how the poem's author saw it. Scandinavian society is presented as a collection of individuals, each of whom had their own place in a rigid hierarchy, rather than a society of equals (of the type envisaged by Victorian romantics). The king was at the very top of this social pyramid and the slaves were at the bottom. The basis for social status was the ownership of land — this is what separates the freemen from the slaves. Wealth and social status seem to be relatively fixed, for there is no mention of the slaves being freed or earls marrying into a lower social class: according to *Rígspula*, you were born into your social class and you stayed there for the rest of your life.

What do we know about the author of *Rígspula* — and therefore about the usefulness of this poem as a source for Viking-Age society? Unfortunately, very little — in its current form, it was written down by an unknown Icelander, who was undoubtedly a Christian (Icelanders converted in the year 1000), centuries after the Vikings had harried western Europe. Although some scholars have argued that the poem is much older than this, and may even have been written as early as the tenth century, others have suggested dates in the twelfth and thirteenth centuries. The mention of the god Heimdall and the acceptance of slavery hint at a time before the official conversion to Christianity, and the presence of the king at the top of the social hierarchy probably rules out a date very early in the Viking Age, when there were many regional rulers rather than one high king. But even these indicators are not without problems — what if the poem was written by someone who was interested in his pagan past and created this poem for his own amusement or the amusement of others? Perhaps the poem might even have been a late justification for the Norwegian king's seizing of power from the formerly free republic of Iceland — and the pagan details were added to give the claim a touch of authenticity? Perhaps it was an attempt to eradicate slavery, by linking it with a pagan past that was no longer acceptable in polite Christian society?

Another poem presents a less 'storybook' version of Scandinavian society, although unfortunately it too is only preserved in a late Icelandic manuscript. *Hávamál* or 'The Sayings of the High One [Odin]' is a compilation of some 160 verses, which includes almost eighty verses offering advice to the reader/listener on how to live their life. Surprisingly, given the Vikings' reputation for excess, moderation in all things is seen as the best way to survive the dangers of the Viking Age. For example, travellers are advised to be cautious and keep their weapons to hand, not to talk or drink or eat too much, and not to outstay their welcome at any house. There are tips, sometimes openly cynical, on how to make and retain friends ('open your heart to him, exchange gifts, go to see him often'), how to woo women (with 'sweet talk and gifts'), how to treat guests and travellers (provide 'food and clothes' and a 'warm welcome'), how to stay alive ('A flying spear, a tumbling wave, overnight ice, a coiled snake … let no man trust'), and how to be successful ('He should get up early, the man who plans to kill or steal'). The importance of avoiding death underlies much of this advice, suggesting that life for the unwary or unprepared was dangerous, and injury is said to be preferable to death because 'What good is a corpse to anyone?'

Law and Disorder

Another important source of information about the structure and the functioning of Viking society in Scandinavia and the British Isles is the legal codes these societies produced. We know from a number of sources — principally Icelandic — that Viking-Age Scandinavia was an organized society with local assemblies (called *thing*s) that kept order and proclaimed a set of laws. In the eleventh century, Norway was divided into four legal provinces, each known by the name of its local assembly: the Gulathing for western Norway, the Frostathing for Trøndelag (around present-day Trondheim), the Eithsifathing for inland, eastern Norway, and the Borgarthing for the area around Oslofjord. Each legal province had its own law, and complete examples of the medieval versions of the Gulathing and Frostathing law-codes have survived to this day. Life in the towns of Viking-Age and medieval Scandinavia was clearly different enough to merit separate laws, which are often known as Bjarkøy laws, perhaps named after the great trading centre of Birka in eastern Sweden. The danger of fire in the closely packed streets of wooden houses seems to have been a particular concern in the towns, as well as the noise and disruption associated with taverns frequented by locals and visiting merchants alike.

The surviving Scandinavian law-codes, all of which date unfortunately from the medieval period, tend to back up the impression that it was one's birthright that was important in determining social status and that society was hierarchical — the primary social group in the laws is the kin, members of one's family (sometimes including fourth or fifth cousins). When fines had to be paid in compensation for a crime, it was the family that was responsible rather than an individual, and the fine (*mansbot*) was calculated according to the social status of the victim. Icelandic sagas are full of details that emphasize the family's responsibility to protect and avenge members. The ultimate sanction in Scandinavian law was to be declared an outlaw, for once someone stood outside the law then he or she could be legally killed by anyone. Indeed, the killer

154

was in fact doing society a favour by getting rid of the unwelcome troublemaker.

These medieval law-codes suggest that, despite the Church's wish to improve conditions for slaves and ultimately eradicate slavery, the legal status of a slave was more or less identical to that of livestock and other property belonging to an individual. For example, the owner of a slave could buy, sell and otherwise exchange him or her as they saw fit; owners were not liable before the law for hurting or killing a slave; and if the slave was harmed or killed by another person, that person paid compensation to the slave's owner, not to the victim's own family as was normally the case. Some Christian influence is nevertheless evident; for example, Icelandic laws included an injunction against killing slaves during Lent. And we also know that some slaves were freed: one Viking-Age rune-stone, from Hørning in Jutland in Denmark was raised by an ex-slave, Toki, to commemorate his former master: 'Toki the smith set up the stone in memory of Thorgisl Gudmund's son, who gave him gold and freedom.'

Thanks to the literary endeavours of medieval Icelanders, much more is known about the way law and order functioned in Iceland than in mainland Scandinavia, at least during the Viking Age. The national assembly of Iceland, the Althing, was probably established in the year 930 (although most of what is known about it post-dates reforms made in the mid-960s), with a legal system modelled on that of Norway's Gulathing. The Althing was held in the open air, on the plain known as Thingvellir, about thirty miles east of present-day Reykjavik in south-west Iceland. Every free man (there is no evidence that women had the right to attend the *thing*), except those excluded by outlawry, met at Thingvellir for two weeks at Midsummer. Here complaints were made, compromises negotiated, solutions reached, and the most important legal decisions were made by the head of the Althing, the Law-Speaker. Most famously, the decision to make Iceland Christian was taken by the Law-Speaker, Thorgeir, in the year 1000:

> *Thorgeir set himself down and spread his cloak over him, and lay there all that day and the following night, and not a word did he say. And the next morning he sat up and sent round for everyone to go to the Law-Rock [...] He said that, as he judged it, men's affairs would get into an impossible state if they should not all have the same law in this land [...] 'So it seems advisable to me', he said '[...] we all have the same law and the same religion.'*[4]

The Law-Speaker was elected for a three-year period by the island's goðar 'chieftains', and had to recite a third of the island's law every year at the Law-Rock (Old Norse *lögberg*), so that all of Iceland's laws were declared in the course of the Law-Speaker's three-year office. Not until 1117 was a law was passed in Iceland which required that all the laws of Iceland be written in a book. The first Law-Speaker was a man called Ulfljót, who was also responsible for drawing up Iceland's first law-code, *Úlfljótslög*. In the 960s, four new 'quarter courts' were established, where cases from the newly established four quarters of Iceland (North, South, East, and West) were heard, if they could not be settled in their respective district *thing*s. Later, in 1005, a fifth court was set up in order to deal with cases that the quarter courts were unable to solve. In this court, a majority verdict was acceptable, in contrast to the quarter courts, where decisions had to be unanimous. After the Icelanders' conversion to Christianity, a further court, 'the priests' court', was founded to administer Christian law. The official end of each Althing was marked by the beating of weapons, *vápnatak*, a word that also appears to have given its name to the local administrative divisions of the Danelaw — wapentakes.

Scandinavian Law in England

Some time after the Viking settlement of northern and eastern England, the 'Danelaw' — a district run according to Danish law — emerged. Exactly where and what this was is extremely hard to define. To Anglo-Norman writers, such as Simeon of Durham, the Danelaw was an enormous region, consisting of fifteen shires (as opposed to the nine shires of West-Saxon law and the eight of Mercian law): Yorkshire, Nottinghamshire, Derbyshire, Leicestershire, Lincolnshire, Northamptonshire, Huntingdonshire, Cambridgeshire, Bedfordshire, Norfolk, Suffolk, Essex, Hertfordshire, Middlesex and Buckinghamshire. As Henry Loyn has pointed out, this huge territory constituted approximately one-third of the total area of the English kingdom at that time,[5] and many scholars are sceptical about the accuracy of these boundaries, especially given that evidence for Scandinavian influence in this region varies dramatically. Sometimes the Danelaw is simply identified with those areas that were settled by Scandinavians in the ninth century.[6] As we saw in Chapter 3, defining the scale and extent of this settlement is in itself problematic: the Scandinavian settlement of Mercia, Northumbria and East Anglia is described in just three terse sentences in the *Anglo-Saxon Chronicle*, and while it tells us that the western part of Mercia was left under the control of a puppet king, Ceolwulf, it does not mention that the northern part of Northumbria, Bernicia, remained in the hands of the native Anglian earls. Although there are considerable methodological problems concerning the age and the significance of place-names, they are frequently the only source for the geographical extent of this settlement. The distribution of these names is, however, extremely uneven, with major concentrations in Lincolnshire and Yorkshire; other areas, such as East Anglia, have significantly fewer Scandinavian place-names, and the southern parts of Danelaw — Buckinghamshire, Middlesex, and Hertfordshire — have virtually no Scandinavian place-names. Therefore, to equate the Danelaw with the areas settled by Scandinavians in the ninth century, or with the distribution map of Scandinavian place-names, is too simplistic and misleading.

A further point of confusion is found in the treaty between Alfred and Guthrum, often called the Treaty of Wedmore. This is sometimes regarded as formally establishing the Danelaw by defining Danish and English spheres of control, along the line of the old Roman road, Watling Street. This road is generally used by historians as a convenient border for delimiting the extent of ninth-century Danish settlement in England, and also as the border between Danelaw and the rest of England, but the treaty itself does not actually specify that the boundary ran along the whole length of Watling Street to Chester. Indeed, it seems to suggest that the border zone actually ended at the beginning of Watling Street:

> First as to the boundaries between us: up the Thames, and then up the Lea, and along the Lea to its source, then in a straight line to Bedford, then up the Ouse to Watling Street.

In addition to this, the Treaty of Wedmore itself was not, as is often implied, a treaty between the Danes and the English, it was:

> ...[the] peace which King Alfred and King Guthrum, and the councillors of all the English nation and all the people who dwell in East Anglia, have all agreed upon and confirmed with oaths, on their own behalf and for their subjects.

By the time this treaty was signed, the Scandinavian settlement of Mercia and Northumbria had already taken place, and the treaty terms agreed with Alfred were only applicable to the Scandinavians of East Anglia. That this treaty was perhaps less significant than modern scholars generally regard it, and that other agreements were made, is clear from the *Anglo-Saxon Chronicle* which, for example, talks of peace being broken by Viking armies in 893. Similarly, in

905, terms are said to have been agreed by Edward the Elder and the East Anglians and Northumbrians at Tiddingford in Buckinghamshire. Several scholars have argued convincingly that the treaty between Alfred and Guthrum was in fact of fairly short duration, perhaps lasting less than a few years.

It is not until later on, in the *Anglo-Saxon Chronicle* for 1013, that we have some contemporary evidence that Watling Street had come to be generally recognized as the dividing line between Anglo-Scandinavian and English England:

> *And then Earl Uhtred and all Northumbria immediately submitted to him [Svein Forkbeard], and all the people in Lindsey, and afterwards the people of the Five Boroughs, and quickly after, all the raiding army [*here*] to the north of Watling Street.*

But how Danish was the law of the Danelaw? The apparently straightforward equation of the Danelaw with Danish law runs into serious problems when considered in detail, particularly given the current consensus that the Viking armies that settled England numbered in their hundreds rather than their thousands. How far can the 'strong individuality' of the customary law of the Danelaw be attributed to specifically Danish or Scandinavian influences rather than other social, economic and political factors that followed the Scandinavian conquest and settlement? More fundamentally, was the law of the Danelaw really that different from the law of the rest of England?

The term 'Danelaw' first occurs in two legal compilations made by Archbishop Wulfstan II of York during the reign of Æthelred II (978-1016). The so-called Laws of Edward and Guthrum, dated to between 1002 and 1008, refer to the compensation to be paid 'in the Danelaw' (*on Deone lage*) if a slave was compelled to work on a church festival,[7] while the following is found in the law-code known as VI Ethelred:

And if anyone plots against the king's life, he shall forfeit his life and all that he possesses, if it is proved against him; and if he seeks and is able to clear himself, he shall do so by means of the most solemn oath or by the triple ordeal in districts under English law, and in those under Danish law in accordance with their constitution.[8]

This law-code was issued in 1008, that is 130 years after the *Anglo-Saxon Chronicle* described the settlement of the Viking armies in Northumbria, Mercia and East Anglia, and some ninety years after Edward of Wessex and Æthelflæd of Mercia had re-established English control of these territories. Nevertheless, English kings had legislated for the Scandinavians within their kingdom well before the reign of Æthelred II. The law-code known as IV Edgar, issued in the form of a letter from King Edgar (959-75) to the rulers of Northumbria, Mercia and East Anglia, does not refer to the Danelaw, but it does stipulate that:

*...it is my will that there should be in force among the Danes (*mid Denum*) such good laws as they best decide on, and I have ever allowed this and will allow it as long as my life lasts, because of your loyalty, which you have always shown me.*[9]

While this suggests that Edgar allowed the Danes a considerable degree of independence in their law-making, he also makes it clear that:

...this measure is to be common to all the nation, whether Englishmen, Danes or Britons, in every province of my dominion, to the end that the poor man and rich may possess what they rightly acquire.[10]

Therefore, while both Edgar's and Æthelred's laws testify to the legal distinctiveness of the areas settled by Scandinavians, they also provide clear evidence of their integration into the kingdom of England. This is also demonstrated by comparing Edgar's legal policy towards the Scandinavian settlers in England with that of his grandfather, Edward the Elder:

*If anyone subsequently harbours him, he shall pay such compensation as the written laws declare of him who harbours a fugitive, if the offence is committed in our own kingdom. If the offence is committed in the eastern or northern kingdoms, compensation shall be paid in accordance with the provisions of the treaties (*friðgewritu*).*[11]

Here, northern and eastern England clearly stand outside the legislative authority of the king of Wessex, and legal relations with those areas are governed by special treaties.

The earliest evidence for the use of the term 'Danelaw' therefore clearly indicates that it was a legal province of the kingdom of England, in spite of the emphasis on 'Danishness' in the term itself. Indeed, there appears to have been some movement towards legal integration in the fifty years which separated Edgar's and Æthelred's law-codes, for while Edgar permitted the Danes their legal autonomy, in return for their support against his brother Eadwig, Æthelred apparently extended English customs to the *Dena lage* in his law-codes. The single most important legal source for the Danelaw is Æthelred's Wantage Code, which was intended for circulation in the Scandinavian dominated Five Boroughs of Lincoln, Stamford, Derby, Leicester and Nottingham, but large parts of this code simply concern the extension of English practice to the Five Boroughs. Indeed, Charlotte Neff's assessment of the Wantage Code is that: '...the law of the Danes had to accord in principle with that of the English. Differences of procedure were acceptable. Different standards of justice, law and order were not.'[12]

When the term 'Danelaw' was next used by the king of England, in the law-codes issued by Cnut, England was ruled by a Danish king. However, Cnut's laws were by no means inspired by Danish law: according to the *Anglo-Saxon Chronicle* (D version only) entry for 1018 and Cnut's proclamation of 1020, they were modelled on those of King Edgar. Yet Cnut's laws also have much detail in common with the laws of Æthelred and were almost certainly drafted by the same man, Archbishop Wulfstan of York. The term *Dena lage* occurs five times in these codes; there are also four references to *mid Denum*, as found in Edgar's laws, and one further reference to Danish men (*denisc*). Niels Lund has argued that Cnut's policy towards the Danelaw, as seen in the law-code known as II Cnut, was in fact '...much more like that of Æthelred than Edgar', and that while he was willing to permit regional variation in the fines which were paid in the Danelaw, he differed from Edgar, in that he did not '...leave the maintenance of peace and justice to the Danes themselves.'[13]

Significant Scandinavian influence on English legal terminology is generally recognized by scholars: terms such as *lándcóp* 'purchase of land' or 'a fine paid when buying land', *lahslit* 'penalty for breaking the law', and *witword* 'agreement' or 'the right to prove one's case' testify to the distinctive legal vocabulary of the Danelaw. But differences in legal terminology may mask similarities: for example, the administrative districts known as wapentakes in Yorkshire and the Five Boroughs apparently served the same function as the hundreds found elsewhere in England. This suggests that Scandinavian settlers may often have simply taken over and renamed existing legal institutions and practices, rather than establishing their own customs. While the laws of the English kings demonstrate that there were much larger penalties in the Danelaw than in the rest of England, these probably reflect different conditions in the Danelaw rather than a distinctively Scandinavian approach to law, and simply may reflect the English king's attempt to enforce his laws in this remote part of his kingdom. Interestingly, many of the Scandinavian legal terms found in the Danelaw do not appear to have ever been used in Denmark. There are Scandinavian parallels for the Danelaw institution of a 'jury' of twelve leading thegns, mentioned in the Wantage Code, although the claim that this established the institution of a jury in English law is controversial. While acknowledging the Scandinavian character of its legal terminology, the Danish historian Ole Fenger emphasizes the organic nature of the Danelaw, and how the rules and institutions associated with it must have been altered and applied in different ways in different places at different times, resulting in the gradual emergence of an Anglo-Scandinavian, rather than Danish, legal province. He suggests that the Danelaw should be redefined as: '...that part of England in which neither Danish nor English law and custom prevailed.'[14]

In summary, it seems highly likely that the boundaries of the Danelaw were neither fixed nor clear-cut when referred to in Æthelred's law of 1008. Moreover, there is no straightforward relationship between the area described as the Danelaw by Anglo-Norman writers and the fluctuating area under Scandinavian control in the Viking Age. While the terms *Engla lage* and *Dena lage* are used in contrast to each other in the laws of Æthelred, Cnut and Edward the Confessor, there is no real evidence that the area under Danish law ever formed a single political counterpart to the English of Wessex and West Mercia, as is sometimes implied. Certainly, the Viking armies that settled in northern and eastern England co-operated with each other from time to time, but the reference to 'treaties' by Edward the Elder's laws testifies to the lack of political cohesion in the areas so often referred to under the convenient umbrella of the Danelaw. Edward's and Æthelflæd's campaigns in northern and eastern England demonstrate this political fragmentation very clearly: the southern part of Danelaw had fallen to the English by 914; East Anglia was brought under English control in 917; the reconquest of the Five Boroughs of Leicester, Nottingham, Derby, Stamford, and almost certainly Lincoln, was accomplished in the period 917-920; and the southern part of Northumbria, the old kingdom of Deira, remained intermittently independent until the death of the last Scandinavian king of York, Erik Blood-Axe (controlling all of England north of

Watling Street for a brief period), in 954. A final reminder is also needed about the status of north-west England, which is sometimes included in the Danelaw, as it lies north of Watling Street: Cheshire, Lancashire and Cumbria, settled by Norwegians from Ireland and Scotland in the tenth century, were never included either in the Danelaw or in Domesday Book, and formed a contested border zone between the English and Scottish well into the post-Conquest period. It was Domesday scholar F.W. Maitland who first cautioned, 'We must be careful how we use our Dane.'[15] It is equally important that we use the term Danelaw as carefully as possible, and recognize that there probably never was one single Danish law-code in operation throughout northern and eastern England.

Things *in the British Isles*

There are no surviving copies of laws from other Viking colonies in the British Isles — indeed, there may never have been any written documents for these areas, for as we have seen, laws were often made and publicized orally, by word-of-mouth at the *thing* place. Nevertheless, Scandinavians certainly established their own local assemblies in their new settlements. The most famous of these Norse parliaments is the Manx assembly at Tynwald, a place-name derived from Old Norse *þing* 'thing' and *vollr* 'plain', and a direct parallel to the name Thingvellir on Iceland. Most remarkably, this parliament still meets every summer to formally ratify new laws. Here the forty-eight representatives (reduced to thirty-six when the Inner Hebrides were conceded to Somerled in 1156) of the Isle of Man met. Place-names show us that there must once have been similar assemblies at Tingwall (also Old Norse *þing* 'thing' and *vollr* 'plain') in both Orkney and Shetland (on Law-Ting Holm), Thingwall in Wirral, Thingwall Hall (in the Knotty Ash district of Liverpool) in south-west Lancashire, Tiongal on the Isle of Lewis, Tinwhil on the Isle of Skye, Dingwall in Rosshire, north-east Scotland, Tinwald in Dumfriesshire, Dingbell Hill in Northumberland, Thingwalla in Whitby in north-east England, Thinghou (Old Norse *þing* 'thing' and *haugr* 'mound') in Lincolnshire and Norfolk, Thingoe in Suffolk, and Fingay Hill in North Yorkshire. The names of many of these places show us that they were chosen for providing a relatively flat piece of land, where crowds could gather, and that natural or man-made hills were used by the law-speakers to address the listening people.

Administration and Tax

As well as the remnants of the local assemblies established by Vikings, there are other possible traces of Scandinavian influence on local administration throughout the colonies they established in the British Isles. The best known of these are recorded in Domesday Book, compiled in 1086, and their significance has been debated by scholars for well over a hundred years. The principal differences that Domesday records in counties that were settled by Vikings are: land is measured, for taxation purposes, in carucates, also known as ploughlands, rather than hides; the principal units of local administration and justice were called wapentakes rather than hundreds; fiscal assessments seem to be calculated on the basis of the duodecimal (with 12 as the basic unit and 'long hundreds' of 120) rather than the decimal system (with 10 as the basic unit); large numbers of freemen or, as they are usually called, 'sokemen' are listed among the inhabitants of the areas settled by Scandinavians; and the land and settlements in northern and eastern England often appear to have been divided into what are known as 'sokes' rather than distinct manors, which were the main units of land ownership (and thus taxation and administration) in post-Conquest England. These sokes generally consist of a central settlement, with several smaller dependent sub-settlements scattered

165

around it, and Stenton, amongst others, argued that this reflected the nature of Viking colonization in the ninth century — with the leader taking the main settlement and allocating smaller parcels of land to his loyal soldiers.

However, research in the last half century or so has destroyed much of Stenton's thesis about the supposedly Scandinavian character of local administration and society in northern and eastern England. For example, the sokes mentioned in Domesday Book appear to have once been found in other parts of the British Isles, including Wales and the northern part of Northumbria that was not settled by Vikings, and most likely are a relic of the time when all land was divided into estates that were administered from a centre, providing their lord with food and other kinds of produce, such as timber or salt, as their rent. Social, economic and political conditions were clearly different enough in the former Viking colonies to preserve this form of land organization, but the sokes were only taken over by Scandinavian settlers, not established by them. Similarly, given the small size of the Viking armies, the vast numbers of sokemen recorded in Domesday Book can hardly be the descendants of Scandinavian warriors — they may in some cases reflect differences in terminology and procedure for recording the status of the population, although the large numbers of freemen may also represent different social and economic conditions in districts settled by Scandinavians, which allowed them to retain their freedom. The wapentake and carucate are probably just Scandinavian names for units that are known and used elsewhere in England (hundred and hide), and the carucate seems to have been introduced at the beginning of the eleventh century. And, finally, the duodecimal valuations are also found in non-Scandinavian areas of England and in Normandy, where they are seen as Frankish, while the decimal system is seen as Scandinavian! Another important point is that all of these 'Scandinavian' characteristics are not found across

166

the entire area that was settled by Vikings in the ninth century. For example, in East Anglia there are relatively few Scandinavian place-names, but masses of sokemen; and in East Yorkshire there are very few sokemen, hundreds rather than wapentakes, even though there are large numbers of Scandinavian place-names and the area itself was known as the East Riding. Undoubtedly 'the eastern counties are the home of liberty', in the words of F.W. Maitland, but as he and many others have noted, there are considerable differences in the number of sokemen across the vast area that became known as the Danelaw.

The lack of a Domesday Book for other parts of the British Isles makes it harder to trace Viking influence on administration — and increases debate about the real age of some features that are claimed to be Scandinavian, for many details are not recorded until the sixteenth century and even later. However, several basic units of justice, taxation and military obligation in the former Viking colonies have Scandinavian names. In some cases, these can be paralleled across the North Sea. For example, in Orkney there is evidence for a centralized administrative structure based on the Earls' farmsteads (*húsabýr* 'house farm') being imposed from above (four such Husebys have been identified across Orkney, with a further two possible examples, making a total of six). Such Huseby farms can be found in Denmark, Norway and Sweden, where many former centres retain the name 'Huseby' or 'Husaby', and they seem to have been the places where tax and food rents paid to rulers were collected. The Scandinavian administrative unit known as a *herað* (a local court similar to the English hundred) can be recognized in several place-names across the Scottish Isles: for example, Harris in the Outer Hebrides; Harray on mainland Orkney; Harris on the islands of Rhum and Islay in the Inner Hebrides, and 'de Herra' in three places on Shetland. The Norwegian naval levy, known as *leiðangr*, was a system for the provision and manning of a longship, and there is a hint that this may have been transferred to Norse colonies in the British Isles: there is a payment called 'leanger' in some late tax records from Shetland.

Yet other features of tax and administration, despite there being a clear link with a Scandinavian presence in the British Isles, have no obvious Scandinavian parallels. The Isle of Man was divided into six administrative sheadings (from Old Norse *séttungr* 'a sixth part'), each of which consisted of three parishes. In the parish, land was divided into 'treens' (possibly from Gaelic *tirunga* 'land-ounce'), the basic area of land-holding, generally between about 200 and about 500 acres. These treens were further sub-divided into quarterlands or 'kerroos', the basic farm holding of between 50 and 180 acres. The antiquity of these administrative units has long been discussed, but the debate is still unresolved. The treen divisions are first recorded in detail in the sixteenth century, and it has been suggested that these divisions were introduced by Scandinavian settlers for they are directly paralleled by the ouncelands (sometimes called *eyrislands*) that are known from across Scandinavian Scotland — in the Hebrides, Caithness in north-east Scotland and the west coast of Scotland. Yet these territorial divisions, and the smaller pennylands into which they are sometimes subdivided, have no parallel in Norway. These units are obviously connected with tax, but while ouncelands suggest that the tax was, at least originally, paid in silver bullion (the ounce was the basic unit of weight used for silver payments), the name 'pennyland' indicates payment in coin. The distribution of these two units is not identical across the Scottish colonies — in some places, particularly south-west Scotland, there are pennylands but not ouncelands, and in others, such as the Isle of Man, it is the opposite. This rather confusing situation is also made worse by the fact that in Orkney an ounceland consisted of 18 pennylands, while in the Hebrides there are more usually 20 pennylands in an ounceland. Furthermore, in

Orkney, the ounceland was also divided into four 'skattlands' ('tax lands'). All this suggests that the remants of Norse administration that we can still see must date from several different periods, and to have performed several different functions.

Orkney and Shetland are frequently treated as a single unit of Scandinavian settlement, the northern outpost of Vikings in the British Isles that were ruled by earls based in Orkney. For taxation purposes, both groups of islands were divided into ouncelands and pennylands, but this is where the similarities end — which suggests that Scandinavian society on Orkney and Shetland was quite different in character. As we have seen in the previous chapter, the evidence of pagan graves suggests a contrast in the wealth and number of early settlers, with Shetland appearing to be the poorer cousin. The fertile and rich soils of Orkney produced one of the most significant political institutions in the Viking west — the earldom of Orkney — and local administration there seems to reflect this, with the centralized Huseby system. However, in contrast, several parishes or parts of parishes in Shetland have names in -*ting* 'local assembly' (Delting, Nesting, Lunnasting, Sandsting, Aithsting), suggesting local self-governing communities. These divisions also formed the basis of the twelve to fifteen priest districts (*prestegjeld*) into which Shetland was divided, with the parish having rather less importance in the islands. This arrangement is again in clear contrast to Orkney and similarly suggests a more organic, grass-roots growth of such units rather than their imposition from above. There even seems to have been a difference in the relative importance of the ouncelands in the administration of Orkney and Shetland, with the so-called 'scattald', rather than the ounceland, forming the most important unit of social organization on Shetland. These 'scattalds' were often closely associated with local chapels, and it has been suggested that they originated in pre-Norse divisions. There is indeed some slight

169

evidence of religious continuity on Shetland, particularly in the continued production of Christian sculpture well into the tenth century, suggesting that picture of wholesale destruction of the natives by the Vikings there is too simplistic. Despite the near total Scandinavianization of place-names, it certainly seems that Viking society on Shetland was not so destructive as is sometimes believed.

Viking Art

Archaeological finds have helped to create another image of the Vikings to place beside their reputation as fearless and fearsome warriors. A favourite illustration for books and articles on the Vikings is one of the earliest and most spectacular archaeological finds — the Oseberg ship burial, discovered in 1904. But while the ships of the Vikings certainly made their raids possible,[16] the Oseberg ship and the grave-goods that were buried with it reveal much more about Viking craftsmanship than Viking warfare, decorated as they are with intricate and accomplished wood-carving. As well as the longship, with its beautifully decorated prows, excavators found a cart, sledges, a bedstead and a mass of other everyday objects at Oseberg, many of which were decorated with intricate interlacing patterns. Perhaps most stunning, however, are the animal-head posts that clearly demonstrate the main feature of the so-called Oseberg style: myriads of small creatures, twisted and distorted into fluid patterns that make them virtually unidentifiable as animals. The craftsmen responsible for this work transformed functional objects into things of great beauty, and the Oseberg ship burial has given its name to the first of the great Viking-Age art styles.[17]

Art historians have identified six distinct art styles that were in use between the second-half of the eighth century and the mid-twelfth century in Scandinavia, demonstrating how artists and craftsmen developed their skill and repertoire of motifs as the Viking Age progressed. As with the Oseberg style, the names of these art styles are taken from classic examples of the motifs and characteristics that they include. In roughly chronological order, they are: Oseberg (750-840); Borre (835-970); Jellinge (880-1000); Mammen (950-1060); Ringerike (980-1080); and Urnes (1035-1150). As can be seen, there was often quite a long overlap between the different styles — and one style may have had a longer life in some parts of the Viking world than in others, an important point when discussing Viking art in the British Isles. By the same token, new trends and motifs may have reached British and Irish shores some time after taking root in Scandinavia. It should also be remembered that these dates are approximate, based as they are on the archaeological dating of the artefacts on which they have been found.

What does Viking art in the British Isles tell us about the societies that were created following the Scandinavian colonization? At the very simplest level, a piece of Viking art shows us that the people who decorated the object were either Scandinavian or influenced by Scandinavian art. Some pieces of Scandinavian art are more useful than others. A brooch might be an import from Scandinavia, brought over by a settler, a warrior, a tradesman, or a Viking tourist! Such highly portable objects generally do not provide particularly helpful clues to the nature of the Scandinavian presence in the British Isles. There are some exceptions to this rule nevertheless. In Lincolnshire and Norfolk, for example, a combination of field-walking and metal-detecting has uncovered large numbers of Viking-style brooches and women's dress fittings in recent years, the sheer number of which suggests that they were being produced in the region. Even more interestingly, most of this metalwork is of distinctly low quality, 'made using cheap materials and often of poor workmanship',[18] which suggests that they were worn by the families of peasant farmers rather than rich landholders. The quantity and quality of these finds lend considerable support to the idea that the Scandinavian settlement of eastern England was large-scale, and the coincidence between the distribution of metalwork and Scandinavian place-names is striking. Motifs found on this metalwork also demonstrate continued contact with Scandinavia, with eleventh-century Ringerike and Urnes styles represented, as well as the ninth- and tenth-century Borre and Jellinge styles. Indeed, examples of Anglo-Scandinavian art also seem to have been exported to southern Scandinavia, showing clearly the close connections that persisted across the North Sea.

Monuments in Stone

Although Viking art-styles can be found decorating numerous small objects recovered by archaeologists — jewellery, combs, knives, spoons, gaming pieces — the impact that the Vikings had on the art of the British Isles can perhaps best be traced today in the stone sculpture that was carved by craftsmen some thousand years ago, particularly in northern and eastern England. Much of this sculpture was funerary, designed to commemorate the dead, and perhaps surprisingly most are Christian monuments placed in churchyards. These monuments were made to last and can still be found scattered in the churchyards and churches across the land, as well as in the less exposed conditions of museums such as the National Museum of Scotland in Edinburgh. Throughout northern England, from the East Yorkshire coast to the Irish Sea in the west, Viking-Age stone crosses and grave-stones provide evidence of the popularity of Scandinavian motifs and styles, as well as of the local elites' wealth. These monuments are especially important because, as they are made from massive blocks of stone, it is very unlikely that they have been moved far from where they were produced and originally placed. Crucially, then, their current distribution almost certainly echoes their distribution at the end of the Viking Age, allowing art historians to trace regional trends. There are, of course, some exceptions: a cross-shaft from Crowle in Lincolnshire is made from millstone grit from West Yorkshire, and is decorated in a style usually found in the Vale of Pickering, North Yorkshire, in the first half of the tenth century. It has been argued that this cross is therefore an import, and represents a deliberate statement of political and cultural allegiance to York, then under the control of Hiberno-Norse kings from Dublin. Indeed, a recent study has traced the link between monuments and political history, arguing that the appearance of a new type of monument in Lincolnshire in the second half of the tenth century marks the ousting of the York affiliated elite and its replacement with one that looked towards Wessex.

It is important to realize that monuments decorated with Scandinavian motifs and style were not necessarily commissioned or even carved by Scandinavians. Art historians label this art as Viking-Age rather than Viking. Indeed, analysis of the sculpture has demonstrated that these are hybrid monuments. In the Danelaw, an Anglo-Scandinavian blend of two traditions and new innovations resulted from the Viking settlement. Perhaps one of the most striking aspects of this Viking-Age sculpture is the sheer quantity in which it was produced in the period that followed the Viking settlement. For example, one expert, Richard Bailey, contrasts the 25 Anglian monuments on 17 sites in Cumbria with the 115 Viking-Age monuments from at least 36 sites; and in Yorkshire and Cleveland a similar pattern can be found with 90 Anglian pieces on 41 sites and 325 Viking-Age monuments on 65 sites.[19] In Lincolnshire, there are over 350 stones from the tenth and eleventh centuries, found at almost 150 different locations. This growth in numbers was apparently accompanied by (or indeed the result of) a change in patronage, seen in a move away from the monasteries to the parish churches of the north, a secularization of setting that suggests that the people who were having these monuments made were no longer monks and monastic communities but relatively wealthy private individuals. There was no tradition of making monuments like this in Scandinavia, and although stone monuments had been made in the British Isles before the Viking Age, their form, their setting, their design and the people commissioning them were all quite different in the period after the Viking settlements. How did this artistic revolution come about? Perhaps the simplest answer here is right — if surprising — because for all the disruption that the Vikings and their settlements caused, they did bring about a phenomenal redistribution of wealth. Monastic communities were robbed and traditional landholding patterns were disrupted. Viking settlers gained from both, and were consequently in a position to spend and make money that had previously been tied up in the larger religious establishments or aristocratic households of the north. The reasons why they chose to invest their money in stone monuments have been briefly examined in Chapter 5, on the religion of the Vikings.

As well as religious reasons, however, it is important to remember that these memorials were also 'the ultimate statement of cultural and political groupings with which the deceased, or his surviving family, wished to be identified.'[20] Unlike the low-quality jewellery from Lincolnshire, these expensive monuments demonstrate the tastes of the elite. Indeed, in some cases it seems likely that they commemorate the founders or owners of the local churches of the Danelaw. In one case, we may even have a picture of such a wealthy Anglo-Scandinavian patron. The Middleton cross, near Pickering in North Yorkshire, shows a warrior figure, wearing a helmet and a knife or sword at his belt, and surrounded with his weapons: a spear, sword, axe and shield. This was once interpreted as showing a Viking lying in his grave, a kind of Christian nod to pagan burial practices, but scholars could not explain the significance of the two round shapes above the warrior's shoulders. This problem is resolved if we view this warrior as a local lord sitting on his throne, with the circular shapes marking the knots on the back of this throne. The other symbols of his status — his weapons — show very clearly that the process of integration still had some way to go when the cross was carved in the tenth century: his power was still very much grounded in his military superiority.

The Isle of Man is also rich in Viking-Age stone sculpture, with around seventy examples of crosses or cross-slabs made from Manx slate. Almost all of these were found on or near the sites of modern parish churches, and it seems a reasonable assumption that they were generally raised in churchyards. The collection of several monuments on one site suggests that these locations functioned as centres for a Christian community. Particularly interesting is the fact that just over thirty of these monuments, from the island's northern and central parishes, are also inscribed with runes, making the Isle of Man the only Viking colony with a custom of making runic memorials. Many writers have expressed surprise at the fact that most of the Vikings who settled in the British Isles (and elsewhere, such as Iceland) apparently did not raise rune-stones to commemorate their dead. However, perhaps this is not so unexpected as it may seem — very few runic inscriptions have been found in Norway, and the custom does not appear to have been particularly widespread in Denmark during the ninth century, when Danish Vikings colonized eastern England.

As Ray Page observes, the Manx monuments represent an intriguing combination of tradition and innovation. The Scandinavian memorial formula, 'X raised this...in memory of Y', is the traditional element in the Manx corpus. Innovation is found in the word 'cross', which replaces the more usual 'stone'. The monuments on which the inscriptions are carved also represent a visual innovation, taking the form of cross-slabs decorated with Borre-style interlace, creatures and figures, and forming a distinctive group of monuments. These runic crosses combine the Scandinavian runic tradition with the Celtic tradition of raising crosses. This merging of cultures also appears to be found in the mixture of Norse and Celtic personal-names that is found in the inscriptions. The evidence seems to suggest that, following a period of conflict, Manx society, like that of the Danelaw, developed a true hybrid culture, combining elements of the old and the new, and producing something entirely different. The people who produced and commissioned memorials such as those found in the Danelaw and on the Isle of Man were clearly living in these places, part of the local community — it is highly unlikely that a visiting Viking would commission or carve a huge piece of stone sculpture. Indeed, the absence of the first Viking art style on sculpture produced in the British Isles is testimony to this, but during the time the Borre style became popular in Scandinavia, Vikings were already becoming a permanent fixture on the scene. This art style, distinguished by the plait-like pattern known as the ring-chain interlace, enjoyed considerable popularity in the British Isles, and can be found on stone sculpture across northern England and in the Western Isles and Man.

The Ringerike style, popular in Scandinavia during the first half of the eleventh century, is particularly well-represented in England and can be found on a considerable number of artefacts from London and the south-east where, following Cnut's conquest of England, Scandinavian art became the art of the royal court. The prestigious nature of the art style is clearly seen in the sort of artefacts decorated with Ringerike motifs: a bronze panel from Winchester; a couple of stone fragments from Rochester; two stone fragments from the City of London; a fragmentary slab from All-Hallows-by-the-Tower, in the City of London; a bone pin from the Thames; and bronze plates from Smithfield, London. Most famous, however, is a rune-stone that was discovered in 1851 in the graveyard of St Paul's Cathedral. The St Paul's rune-stone demonstrates clearly all the classic features of the style, with its 'great beast' and tendril ornament. Who this grave-slab was meant to commemorate is, frustratingly, unknown, although such a high-status burial place suggests that he or she belonged to the very highest ranks of society (King Æthelred II was buried in St Paul's graveyard). The runic inscription that runs along the edge of the stone simply states that 'Ginna and Toki had this stone laid.' The history books contain no mention of Ginna and Toki, but the runes and the language of the inscription clearly suggest that they were Scandinavians, and their names and the Ringerike decoration point north too. Yet there are other things about the stone that are puzzling from a Scandinavian point of view: its shape is radically different from the rune-stones that are found in Scandinavia, and the inscription itself is rather different from those found on Scandinavian rune-stones, which normally mention the name of the person commemorated by the stone. Indeed, a gravestone without the name of the person being commemorated by it is not much of a memorial, so it seems likely there might once have been another stone that had the name of the person Ginna and Toki wished to honour with their rune-stone. The wording of the inscription itself suggests this — Ginna and Toki recorded that they had the stone *laid*, but the St Paul's rune-stone was found standing upright in soil. Perhaps the St Paul's rune-stone was originally a headstone for a larger monument that may also have included a flat slab lying on the grave, a type of gravestone that is known from Winchester. If so, this means that the stonemason that Ginna and Toki used was one who was familiar with the latest Scandinavian art styles, Scandinavian runes and the Scandinavian language, but also with the latest Anglo-Saxon designs for gravestones — presumably a Viking who had spent some time in this country. In this way, the St Paul's rune-stone provides a tantalizing illustration of the blending of Scandinavian and English cultures, a fusion of native and Norse tastes that can be witnessed all over the British Isles.

Making Connections

The picture of Scandinavian society that we have is undoubtedly an incomplete and partial one, and biased towards the wealthier and more powerful sections of society. For example, in 1096 a census was taken in Iceland, and this recorded the population of the island as 4,560. But this included only the fully free, grown men, and it has been estimated that in actual fact the population would have been approximately 80,000 if women, children, landless poor, tenant farmers and servants were included. If we remember that only freemen had the right to participate in local and national assemblies, this means that less than six per cent of the population of Iceland were involved in the making of law — this was hardly a democracy in any sense of the word. Yet it is important to remember that, as we have seen, the Vikings who settled down in Iceland and in the British Isles worked not only to make a living for themselves and their families, but also to establish and maintain an organized society that was controlled by laws, that paid taxes to the Church and to local rulers, and that was far removed from the wild and destructive barbarians of popular mythology.

All too often Viking art and culture are neglected at the expense of other sources providing more tangible and straightforward evidence of the Scandinavian impact on the British Isles. But these aspects of Scandinavian culture are invaluable in trying to construct a rounded picture of the society that emerged in the newly-settled areas of Britain and Ireland. We can trace connections that may not be evident in any other sources, such as the sculptural link between Lincolnshire and Hiberno-Norse York, or the presence of an Icelandic poet in

178

Yorkshire. We can also see how the process of integration proceeded, although the evidence of sculpture suggests that this was not simply a matter of Scandinavians adopting local customs and abandoning their roots — instead we have a more complex picture, with much more give and take between locals and newcomers. Taken together with other sources, this can provide some exciting and surprising new insights into the Viking Age.

7
AFTER THE
NORMAN CONQUEST

'And Harald, king of Norway, and Earl Tostig and their army had gone from their ships beyond York to Stamford Bridge [...] Then Harold, king of the English, came upon them beyond the bridge by surprise; and there they joined battle and were fighting very hard long into the day; and there Harald, king of Norway, was killed and Earl Tostig and countless people with them, both of Northmen and of English. And the Northmen fled from the English.'[1]

With the death of the Norwegian king, Harald Hard-Ruler, on 25 September 1066 in the battle fought at Stamford Bridge, and William the Conqueror's assumption of the English throne at Christmas in the same year, historians have traditionally declared the Viking Age at an end. The Battle of Stamford Bridge is often described as 'the last proper Viking raid', launched by one of the last 'proper Viking' kings: 'Never again was a Scandinavian army able seriously to threaten the power of an English king or the unity of the realm.'[2] But it is important to remember that classic Viking raids, on the monasteries around the British and Irish coasts, had long since ceased, replaced by increasingly organized attempts at settlement and political conquest from as early as the arrival of the Great Army in the mid-ninth century. The events that took place at Stamford Bridge, East Yorkshire, on 25 September 1066 are much less important in

English historians' definitions of the end of the Viking Age than the battle near Hastings that followed 19 days later, on 14 October. The Norman Conquest is seen as brutally and effectively ending England's long and close ties with Scandinavia, as well as bringing Viking raids to an abrupt end: 'The country [England] was summarily dragged from a niche in the Scandinavian world and with a jolt its face was turned firmly towards France.'[3] The new Norman king and aristocracy, with their political, social, economic, cultural, and linguistic implications for England and English, become the main focus of historians studying the period after the Norman Conquest, whose gaze consequently shifts from the North to the South.

The Norman Conquest certainly had a dramatic and profound effect on all aspects of English life, but it is important to remember that the people who lived through the Conquest did not have the advantage of hindsight. Nobody could have foreseen the long-term consequences of William's invasion of England — the Danish conquest of England just fifty years before had only temporarily disrupted the English royal succession. While many of Cnut's Scandinavian followers had settled near to his court in south-west England, bringing northern culture to parts of England that had not been settled by Danes or Norwegians in the ninth and tenth centuries, a great deal of Anglo-Saxon life continued as before: the economy, the law, the Church. Why should William's conquest be any different? And what about the claims of English and Scandinavian princes to the English throne? The English royal line had been restored in 1042 after twenty-five years of Danish rule, and while Edward the Confessor had certainly died childless, Harald Hard-Ruler's invasion had shown that the Viking threat was still there. Indeed, in many ways, it must have seemed a far more potent threat than William's, given the long and fearsome history of Viking raids in England, and the Scandinavian colonies that embraced northern Britain and Ireland. Normandy was, by way of contrast, a relative newcomer on the political scene, and had traditionally been absorbed in more local power struggles — with the French kings, as well as their Breton and Flemish neighbours. Cnut's great northern empire had admittedly disintegrated upon his death in 1035, and with hindsight it might seem that the Viking heyday was long over in 1066. But the defeat of Harald of Norway in 1066 has unfairly distorted our view of his achievements — and the threat he and his countrymen posed. Not for nothing was Harald called 'the thunderbolt of the north' by Adam of Bremen who, while deploring his 'greed and cruelty', acknowledged his reputation as a 'mighty man [...] renowned for the victories he had previously won in many wars with barbarians in Greece and in the Scythian regions.'[4] And despite Harald Hard-Ruler's failure at Stamford Bridge, the ambitions of Scandinavian kings did not die with Harald in battle — they continued to be an important political factor for some years after the Norman Conquest.

Danish Invasions

The Danish kings Svein Estrithsson (d. 1074) and his son Knut Sveinsson (d. 1086) both planned invasions of England in the twenty years after 1066. Although overshadowed in English historiography by his uncle, Cnut, and his more successful contemporary, William the Conqueror, Svein Estrithsson was a formidable figure. He began a long campaign to become king of Denmark in 1047. His claim to the Danish (and English) throne came from his mother, Estrith, who was Cnut's sister. Svein was later described in the Danish *Roskilde Chronicle* (c. 1140) as Svein the Great, in recognition of his reorganization of the Danish Church, and for his work in bringing the kingdom of Denmark into the religious and political community of Western Europe. Svein worked tirelessly to strengthen links between the papacy and the Danish Church, to reduce the influence of the German Church in Denmark, and ultimately to establish an independent archbishopric in Denmark. He was also one of the main informants used by Adam of Bremen when writing his account of Scandinavia in the *History of the Archbishops of Hamburg-Bremen* around 1070 (hence Adam's open hostility to Svein's rival, Harald Hard-Ruler). Adam praised the king for his learning, piety, and respect for Church law; a letter from Pope Gregory VII to Svein also mentions his superior 'book-learning'. Despite Adam's praise of the Danish king, he did also recognize Svein's weaknesses, described as gluttony and women. Indeed, Svein is known to have had at least 14 sons by a number of different mothers.[5] This weakness for women was to have important long-term consequences for the stability of the Danish state, as well as for Danish political ambitions abroad.

Politically, much of Svein's reign was spent in conflict with the kings of Norway. Following a deal with Cnut's son, Harthacnut, Magnus the Good of Norway had been recognized as king of Denmark since Harthacnut's death in 1042, a situation that Svein sought to remedy. Interestingly, the *Anglo-Saxon Chronicle* records that, in 1047, Svein asked for English help against Magnus, requesting some fifty ships. Although the Chronicler records that 'it seemed unwise to everybody', there is nevertheless some hint at a difference of opinion when he adds that 'then it [an offer of assistance] was hindered because Magnus had a great power in ships' (*Anglo-Saxon Chronicle* D, 1047). Indeed, the twelfth-century chronicler, 'Florence' (probably a monk called John) of Worcester recorded that Earl Godwine of Wessex wanted to help Svein, who was his wife's nephew, but that Earl Leofric of Mercia and 'all the people' were against it. Without English assistance, Svein was defeated in battle by Magnus shortly before the Norwegian king died. After Harald Hard-Ruler's accession to Magnus's kingdom in 1047, conflict continued with Norwegian attacks on Denmark in 1048, 1050, 1060, and a con-

184

frontation off the Swedish coast in 1062. In 1048, the *Anglo-Saxon Chronicle* reports yet another appeal to the English king, Edward the Confessor (d. 1065), to send ships to support Svein; again this was apparently opposed by 'all the people'. Svein was driven out of his kingdom at some point in this conflict, and according to Adam of Bremen spent twelve years in exile at the Swedish court. However, Svein and Harald Hard-Ruler of Norway came to terms in 1064, and Svein was finally recognized as king of Denmark. Finally secure in Denmark, Svein was keen to re-establish his uncle's North-Sea empire (as indeed was Harald Hard-Ruler, who traced his right to the throne through Harthacnut's deal with Magnus of Norway), and he launched an invasion of England in 1069. The invasion fleet of 240 ships was headed by three of Svein's sons, Harald, Knut, and an otherwise unknown *Beorn Leriz*, as well as two earls. According to the *Anglo-Saxon Chronicle*, the Danes sailed up the Humber, with York as their goal; they were apparently met by a huge 'greatly rejoicing' crowd and, together, the Danes and Northumbrians launched an attack on the symbol of Norman authority, the newly-built castle, killing the soldiers and looting treasure. Before the Danes had arrived the Normans had burnt down the town and York Minster, apparently accidentally, after they tried to destroy the houses near to the castle so that the Danes would not be able to use them to fill the ditch around the Norman castle. With York in ruins, William the Conqueror headed north and completed the destruction, laying the whole shire of Yorkshire to waste. The Danish fleet wintered on the Humber, and in 1070 Svein himself joined them, prompting locals to come and make peace with him because they 'thought that he would conquer that land.' Further south, the bishop of Aarhus and Danish soldiers under Earl Osbeorn were welcomed in Ely by the English 'from all the Fenlands', who also believed that the Scandinavians would be successful. But the momentum of Svein's

185

invasion was fizzling out. The minster churches at Peterborough and Ely were looted before the Danish fleet headed to the Thames, and William and Svein came to terms, signalling the end of Svein's English ambitions — and apparently the hopes of many Englishmen and women.

It seems no accident that the main opposition that William encountered — and the main support for Svein — was in those parts of England most thoroughly Scandinavianized: Yorkshire and Lincolnshire. Interestingly, these were also the places from where Svein Forkbeard launched his campaign for the English throne in 1014. Were the rebels of 1068-69 motivated by pro-Scandinavian sympathies or anti-Norman anger? Surely the descendants of Vikings, who had settled in these areas some two hundred years before the Norman Conquest, did not still see themselves as Scandinavian rather than English? We have become so used to seeing the Norman Conquest as a battle between the English and the Normans that it is all too easy to forget the importance of other regional and ethnic identities, which must have been all the stronger because of the difficulties of communication between the various parts of the kingdom of England. There was certainly a long tradition of northern independence, predating the Viking settlements, although undoubtedly the Scandinavians helped to reinforce and perpetuate the north-south divide. But is there any real evidence for an ethnically Danish or Scandinavian population in northern and eastern England during the second half of the tenth and the eleventh century? As we have already seen, although the Danes of the Danelaw are rather hard to track down in the sources, there does seem a good deal of evidence for the emergence of a new Anglo-Scandinavian society and culture in northern and eastern England. Just as the law of the Danelaw was neither Scandinavian or English, so the stone sculpture produced there in the tenth and eleventh centuries, the artefacts found in archaeological excavations and the personal names used by the settlers all testify to something that was different from what had gone before but also, crucially, from what was found back in Scandinavia. So, yes, there was both a regional and an ethnic dimension to the Danelaw — but the ethnicity in question is not Scandinavian, it is Anglo-Scandinavian. Yet whether these differences actually had any political significance is much harder to say. A sense of political identity is something more than simply and passively belonging to a particular group: it implies a consciousness of this difference and also conscious attempts to define those differences and actively construct an identity. There seems to be little evidence for this in the period before 1066, but there are some hints that inhabitants of the Danelaw regarded their Anglo-Scandinavian past as an important element of their identity after the Norman Conquest.

Conquest and Rebellion

Conquest by a foreign power and the systematic subjugation of the native population are certainly likely to spawn popular stories about a more heroic past, frequently rooted in perceived ethnic differences. We have only to think about the long popularity of King Arthur, who stood against the wave of barbarian Anglo-Saxon invaders, or Robin Hood, an outlaw defending the poor Anglo-Saxons against the rapacious Normans, to realize this. Is there any evidence that the Scandinavian heritage of Danelaw gave rise to similar legends following the radical changes that the Norman Conquest brought about? In a book on the literary history of England as a nation, Thorlac Turville-Petre has highlighted the interest in Lincolnshire's Scandinavian past through an analysis of the *Lay of Havelock the Dane*, first recorded some seventy years after the Norman Conquest.[6] *Havelock* was written for a Lincolnshire audience, and presents one of the earliest revisionist views of the Vikings, as instruments of the law,

187

justice and peace in this part of England. The local audience was clearly conscious of its Scandinavian past — but wished to distance itself from more sensational views of the Vikings as heathen barbarians inflicting destruction and bringing chaos and misery. One of the most famous rebels against Norman rule, Hereward the Wake, can also trace his roots to the east of England, the fenlands around Peterborough. Unlike Havelock, Hereward's opposition to the Normans was very real, but even so perhaps we can see his rebellion in this part of Lincolnshire as another expression of this region's feeling of distinctiveness.

With the advantage of hindsight, Svein Estrithsson's invasion in 1069 seems little more than a footnote, an interesting diversion from the main thrust of the post-Conquest period. But it is very clear that William the Conqueror took the Danish threat extremely seriously. As the *Anglo-Saxon Chronicle* stresses, the king unusually overwintered in England in 1069-70, and the vicious Harrying of the North that took place in that winter devastated large tracts of land in a ruthless attempt to dull the Northumbrian appetite for rebellion. It was apparently successful, for when Knut Sveinsson returned to England in 1075 at the request of Earl Waltheof of Bernicia, he met little enthusiasm or support from the people. Indeed, Waltheof, who with Earls Ralph of Norfolk and Roger of Hereford had rebelled against the king, had already been forced to seek William's forgiveness after the Danish fleet, delayed by conflict in Denmark that followed Svein Estrithsson's death, failed to turn up in time to challenge William. Knut's army 'dared not to join battle with King William' by itself, and so, after sacking York and its Minster in search of booty, the Danes headed south to Flanders, seeking additional support against William the Conqueror. Earl Waltheof was beheaded as a traitor by William at Winchester in 1076, and was buried at Crowland Abbey in Lincolnshire where a local cult, rooted in anti-Norman sentiment, quickly grew up and he was soon venerated as a saint. Intriguingly, Waltheof was commemorated in a skaldic poem, *Valþjófsflokkr*, composed by the otherwise unknown Icelandic poet, Thorkell Skallason. He is described as a warrior ('Odin of battle') and lamented as a brave man, deceived by William in a state of truce, and finally lamented: 'No more glorious king will die than my bold lord was.'[7] This poem gives a tantalizing insight into the political opposition that William encountered after the Norman Conquest. Waltheof was the youngest son of Scandinavian Earl Siward of Northumbria (d. 1055), who had been given the earldom by Cnut in 1033, and after initially submitting to William in 1066, had briefly become involved in the uprising of 1069. After the failure of Svein Estrithsson's invasion and the Harrying of the North, he had been, uncharacteristically, pardoned by William and even married the Conqueror's niece, Judith, an honour that no other English magnate was given. However, the fact that he employed a poet who composed in Old Norse suggests that Waltheof actively and consciously promoted Scandinavian culture, presumably as an expression of opposition to the new Norman regime. The poet's last stanza remarks, forebodingly, 'It is true it will take some time for the killings in England to cease.'

Rune-Writing in Norman England

Post-Conquest evidence for the continued importance of England's Scandinavian past is not just confined to the Danelaw. Five Scandinavian runic inscriptions, found in north-west England, provide another small piece in the jigsaw of post-Conquest society in northern England. These inscriptions are rather peculiar for a number of reasons: they all post-date the Norman Conquest, yet there are no indications that Scandinavian runes were used by the people living in the north-west before this date; the syntax and grammar of three of these inscriptions demonstrate influence from English, yet the runes used by the carvers of these inscriptions show that they were also familiar with recent innovations in the Scandinavian runic alphabet. This suggests that the people who carved these inscriptions in north-west England were familiar with either English or an Anglo-Scandinavian dialect; that they also had some kind of access to up-to-date versions of the Scandinavian runic alphabet; and that, for some reason, they chose to use this script, rather than the Roman alphabet, for their inscriptions. Apart from a piece of runic graffiti found in the cathedral at Carlisle, the other inscriptions come from what are now quiet rural locations: in the parish churches at Bridekirk, Dearham and Pennington, and in the remains of the Augustinian priory at Conishead. The twelfth-century font at Bridekirk is perhaps the most spectacular of these rune-inscribed artefacts, decorated with mythical beasts and biblical scenes, and bearing the Middle English rhyming couplet (written in a mixture of Scandinavian runes and English bookhand characters): 'Ricarðr, he made me and [...] brought me to this splendour.' Why did Ricarðr write his English message in Scandinavian runes?

One possible answer is that the inscriptions from Bridekirk, Pennington and possibly Conishead were carved by professional craftsmen: the Scandinavian runes they used must presumably reflect the interest of these people in the runic script. The fact that the Bridekirk carver uses Scandinavian runes alongside English bookhand characters to write a Middle English rhyming couplet certainly suggests a literate and sophisticated artist, and the self-conscious tone is reinforced by the little carving that shows Ricarðr at work on the font. It is also notable that all of the five inscriptions from north-west England were found in church buildings. The twelfth century saw the foundation of several monasteries in this area, and in spite of political upheavals, there was a blossoming of intellectual life in the monasteries. This religious renaissance might also explain the late date of

190

the inscriptions, providing new channels for the dissemination of literacy and learning. Indeed, a collection of miscellaneous documents from between the years 1296 and 1346 for the Benedictine Abbey of Whalley in Lancashire, known as the *Liber Loci Benedicti de Whalley*, includes an example of a late Scandinavian runic alphabet.[8] In this, the runes are placed in alphabetical order, rather than the traditional Scandinavian order,[9] and there are several so-called dotted runes — later innovations to make good the deficiencies of the original 16-character alphabet — as well as some more obscure characters that are directly paralleled in the inscription at Conishead. While there appears to be no direct link between Benedictine Whalley and Augustinian Conishead, about fifty miles apart as the crow flies, the presence of the runic alphabet in a north-western manuscript, the identity of these rare runic forms, and the coincidence in date with the Conishead inscription together strongly suggest some kind of antiquarian acquaintance with Scandinavian runes in the region.

The north-west's Scandinavian heritage might have led to a desire to find out more about the ancestors' runic alphabet. The church network certainly would have provided opportunities for transmission. Trading connections may also have played a part, but the inscriptions themselves, in terms of both their text and their location, do not seem to point in this direction. While there is no evidence to my knowledge of direct connections between the places where the inscriptions are found and any Scandinavian religious establishments, it is obvious that such links were fairly widespread. For example, Evesham priory, which had a daughter house at Penwortham in Lancashire, established another foundation at Odense in Denmark just before 1100, and personnel seem to have moved between them quite frequently in the twelfth and thirteenth centuries. The cult of St Olaf thrived in England during the same period, and Nicholas Breakspear, the papal legate responsible for establishing the Norwegian archbishopric of Nidaros (Trondheim) in 1153, was English. Church architecture shows that masons and craftsmen must have moved between England and Scandinavia. For example, Lincoln and Trondheim cathedrals share architectural and sculptural details.

These inscriptions demonstrate at the simplest level that people were carving Scandinavian runes in north-west England in the twelfth and thirteenth centuries. This might seem a rather obvious statement, but it is worth emphasizing given the tendency to gloss over England's continued links with Scandinavia in the post-Conquest period. These inscriptions remind us that the reality on the ground — in parts of northern England at least — was never so simple as English v. Norman.

Death of the Viking Age

Following his detour to Flanders, the Danish prince Knut Sveinsson married Adela, the daughter of Count Robert I of Flanders, an alliance that must have worried William the Conqueror. He continued to harbour ambitions of a Danish reconquest of England, but after he succeeded his elder brother, Harald Hén (r. 1074-80), to the Danish throne in 1080, he became increasingly involved in the protection of Denmark's southern borders against the expansion of the German emperor, Henry IV. At home, Knut introduced a number of financial measures to aid the clergy, and began the construction of a Romanesque cathedral in Odense. However, Knut was murdered in Odense in 1086, slain by rebels in the church of St Alban, which contained relics of the saint that he had brought back with him from his raids in England during 1069-70. The rebels were those nobles and farmers who were involved in another expedition planned against England in 1085. They were annoyed at Knut's attempts to introduce higher taxation to finance the Danish Church and also at his failure to join the invasion fleet in Jutland.

The Danish magnates involved in the murder of Knut promised to support his brother Olaf 'Hunger' (who ruled 1086-95), who in turn promised not to implement any of the financial and social reforms that Knut was threatening. This tense domestic situation meant that when William the Conqueror died in 1087 there was apparently no thought of a fresh Danish attempt on the English throne. Indeed, this seems clearly to mark an end to Danish hopes of recreating Cnut's empire — as well as the beginning of more troubled times at home in Denmark. During Olaf's reign, there was famine and an epidemic, and the clergy claimed that God was expressing his anger with the Danes for killing their king. By 1095, the last year of Olaf's rule, Knut's remains were being credited with miracle cures. Another of Knut's brothers, Erik Ejegod (ruled 1095-1103), succeeded Olaf. Knut's saintly status was used as a tool by Erik, as well as his brother and successor, Niels (ruled 1104-34), to enhance the prestige of their dynasty and to establish their divine right to the throne of Denmark. In 1099, Knut II Sveinsson was canonized by the Pope, and the dead king officially became a Christian martyr.

The failed invasions by the Danish kings, Svein Estrithsson and Knut Sveinsson, effectively ended Danish hopes of regaining the English throne, and were followed by a concerted attempt to establish good relations with one of Denmark's most important trading partners. But trade was not the only link between Denmark and England. For example, King Erik Ejegod invited the Benedictine monastery of Evesham in Worcestershire to set up a daughter priory in Odense on the Danish island of Fyn. One of its members, the Anglo-Saxon monk Ælnoth, wrote an extremely favourable history of Svein Estrithsson and his sons around 1120, including an account of Knut's martyrdom that promoted the dead king's cult. Erik was also responsible for the translation of Knut's relics to a new shrine on the altar of Odense's cathedral in 1100. This example very neatly illustrates the changing nature of contact between England and Denmark in the twelfth century, developments that also characterize relations between Scandinavia and Europe as a whole. Scandinavia was no longer a heathen outpost on the periphery of the known world; it was an integral part of Western Christendom. It is arguable that the cultural impact of Europe on Scandinavia, spread principally through religious channels, had a more significant long-term impact than Viking raids had on Europe. The evidence for this contact is scattered and fragmented, but nevertheless, taken together, demonstrates the continuing importance of links between Britain and the Scandinavian countries, especially Norway, Denmark, and Iceland, in the period after the Norman Conquest.

1066: Continuity and Change in the Celtic World

In tracing the history of Scandinavians in the British Isles, it is vitally important to remember that outside the borders of England there was no dramatic political dislocation in 1066. From the end of the eleventh century, Scottish kings were certainly threatened by their new and powerful Norman neighbours to the south, who sought to bring Scotland under their control, but in the Northern Isles of Orkney and Shetland people's lives were affected as much by events in Norway as by those in central mainland Scotland, if not more. In Ireland and the Isle of Man, the Normans appear more as one faction in a number of factions struggling for political supremacy, at least initially, and the people there retained a strong sense of its Scandinavian identity, as well as close ties with Norway, Denmark and Iceland. Nevertheless, there were a number of significant developments in the Scandinavian colonies of northern and western Britain around the time of the Norman Conquest. In 1065, Earl Thorfinn the Mighty of Orkney died, and his two sons were among those defeated with Harald Hard-Ruler at Stamford Bridge; a reduction in Orkney's power followed as the brothers fought over their shares of the earldom back home. In 1079, the Isle of Man was conquered by Godred Crovan, who had also fought with Hard-Ruler in 1066, and this heralded a new golden age for the Norse kings of Man, which included rule over Dublin for a time in the 1090s. The Welsh king, Gruffydd ap Llewellyn, who was the first king to rule the whole of Wales, died in 1063, leaving a power vacuum in Wales. A series of Viking attacks on Wales followed, closely linked to events in Hiberno-Norse Ireland. By this time, distinctions between Celt and Norseman were becoming blurred, and it is possible to talk of an Irish Sea political circle. For example, Gruffydd ap Cynan (d. 1137), intermittent ruler of Welsh Gwynedd from 1075, was said to have been born in exile in Ireland in 1054 or 1055, of mixed Welsh-Hiberno-Norse ancestry, and to have been brought up in the Scandinavian settlement of Dublin. After the Norman Conquest, there was a prolonged struggle in North Wales between the Normans and native Welsh princes and kings. In 1098, the Welsh were forced to withdraw to Anglesey and to use Hiberno-Norse mercenaries to help control the seas. The mercenaries, however, betrayed their Welsh lords, and Gruffydd ap Cynan fled to Ireland. It was at this point that the last real Viking intervention in Welsh affairs came, with the appearance of King Magnus Bare-Foot and a Norwegian fleet near Anglesey. The Norwegians and Welsh united against the Normans and, following a successful engagement in the Menai Straits (between mainland Wales and Anglesey), both the Norwegians and the Normans withdrew from Wales. These developments demonstrate the continuation of Viking activity in the British Isles, and the increasing complexity of Scandinavian politics in the British Isles.

In Orkney, Shetland and the Isle of Man, where Scandinavians had settled in considerable numbers and where they held political power, the period after 1066 completed the transformation of these island raiding bases into mature political units, and that of their rulers from Viking leaders into earls and kings (see Chapter 4). This development was accompanied by the emergence of these places from the obscurity that had enveloped them during the tumultuous events of the Viking period, for the first time providing historians with the documents they need to be able to trace details of rulers, political alliances, and major social and economic developments. These documents are nevertheless still few and far between, but taken with archaeological finds, they allow us to flesh out a picture of Scandinavian rule in these remote regions. The main reason for this new light on these islands is the conversion of their rulers to Christianity and the subsequent integration of what were Viking raiding bases and colonies into the Christian community of western Europe. The realities of this integration meant that outsiders were sent to Orkney, Shetland and the Isle of Man to convert their people, to establish churches and parishes, to ensure that Christian law was observed and pagan superstitions eradicated, and to supervise the collection of tithes, a tax paid to the Church. The churchmen involved in this work must have reported back to their superiors about conditions in their new island homes. Sadly little of this correspondence has survived — indeed, much of the reporting may have been verbal — but some indication of the ecclesiastical traffic conversion generated is given in the *History of the Archbishops of Hamburg-Bremen* that Adam of Bremen wrote just after the Norman Conquest. We have already come across his picture of Scandinavian religion and politics in Chapter 5, but his interest extended to all parts of the Viking world (indeed, he even briefly mentioned Iceland and Greenland) because the church of Hamburg-Bremen claimed to have the sole rights to undertake missionary activity in areas under Scandinavian control as well as in Scandinavia.

According to Adam, Orkney Islanders (and Icelanders and Greenlanders too) came to Archbishop Adalbert of Hamburg-Bremen and 'begged that he send preachers thither.' Adalbert is said to 'have appointed a certain Turolf to the Orkneys', as well as sending 'John, who had been consecrated in Scotland, and a certain other who bore his own name Adalbart.' Later on, Adam mentions Turolf again (this time calling him Throlf), adding that he was appointed 'bishop for the city of Birsay' (the designation of the remote tidal island of Birsay as a *civitas* 'city' betrays Adam's lack of familiarity with the Orkneys) and that Hamburg-Bremen's authority superseded that of English and Scottish bishops who had previously had jurisdiction over the islands.[10] However, Adam's purpose was to emphasize the power of Adalbert and Hamburg-Bremen in the North, and he may therefore be claiming more legitimate authority for Adalbert than the archbishop actually had. Indeed, in 1072-73, Earl Paul Thorfinnsson received a York appointee, Ralph, as bishop of Orkney. Ecclesiastical authority was clearly complicated in the Scandinavian colonies of the west, and in 1103, with the establishment of an archbishopric in Lund (now southwest Sweden), responsibility for the North was transferred again. Another realignment took place in 1153 with the appointment of an archbishop of Trondheim, whose cathedral was built in that town on the west coast of Norway. Trondheim (or Nidaros, to give it its medieval name) retained ecclesiastical authority in the Scandinavian colonies of the west right up until the mid-thirteenth century in the case of the Hebrides and the Isle of Man (transferred first to York and then Canterbury) and until 1472 in Orkney and Shetland, when they were transferred to the jurisdiction of St Andrews.

Scandinavian Kings and Their Kingdoms in the West

We have already seen how the Danish king Svein Estrithsson and his son, Knut II, both launched unsuccessful campaigns against newly conquered England. The failure of these attempts tell us as much about their own kingdoms as about the new order that they found in England. Less well known is the fact that a few years later, in 1098, the Norwegian king, Magnus Bare-Foot, sailed into British waters on an ambitious campaign to assert his power in the Northern and Western Isles, the Isle of Man, and the Norse colonies in Ireland. Even more amazingly, he apparently enjoyed considerable short-term success, installing his son Sigurd as ruler of Orkney, plundering the Hebrides, and capturing the king of Man. A treaty was made with Edgar, the king of Scotland, which conceded the islands of Bute, Arran, the Cumbraes and Gigha to Norway. Perhaps surprisingly, Magnus appears to have been the first Norwegian king to attempt to enforce his sovereignty over the Norwegian colonies in Britain and Ireland. However, his death in Ireland in 1103 brought an end to this short-lived royal control, as Norwegian kings were too preoccupied with domestic politics to keep a close eye on what was happening in the western colonies. It was not until the middle of the thirteenth century that another Norwegian king, Hákon Hákonarson, was strong enough at home to attempt to exercise his control over the Scottish islands. Unfortunately for him, the 150-year gap between his and Magnus Bare-Foot's expeditions (d. 1263) had seen considerable changes in the political landscape of western Britain and Ireland, as well as in Scandinavia.

Civil War in Scandinavia

What were the circumstances that so engrossed successive rulers of Denmark and Norway from the latter years of the eleventh century, and how did these affect their relationship with the Scandinavian and non-Scandinavian communities in the British Isles? As has been hinted at above, Scandinavian kings obviously needed to be secure enough at home in order to launch foreign adventures, but the medieval period saw prolonged conflict and civil war in both Norway and Denmark over the question of royal succession. The idea of hereditary right to the throne was established to some degree in the Viking Age: Cnut the Great was the son of Svein Forkbeard who was the son of Harald Blue-Tooth. But it was not always that simple: for example, Cnut only became king of Denmark after his older brother had died, a couple of years after he became king of England. In fact, conflict seems to have been the rule rather than the exception, as there were no strict rules about succession in Viking-Age or medieval Scandinavia and, in particular, no tradition of primogeniture, where the eldest son succeeded his father. There were frequently rival claims to the throne, such as that between two sons of Harald Fine-Hair of Norway, Erik Blood-Axe and Hákon the Good. Harald himself had stipulated that Erik should be his successor, but Hákon used military force to dislodge him from the throne of Norway. The rule of force was very much a part of Viking-Age Scandinavia, and it remained so in the early medieval period, leading to significant domestic conflict and civil wars in both Norway and Denmark.

Denmark

In Denmark, the first signs of the civil war to come were seen in the murder of King Knut II in Odense in 1086. The last of Svein Estrithsson's many sons to succeed to the Danish throne was Niels, who exploited his brother Knut's canonization and significantly included the Latin phrase *rex gratia Dei* in his title: 'king by the grace of God'. But this divine support did not prevent over twenty-five years of bitter civil war breaking out between his own sons and those of brother, Erik Ejegod. During this period, too, weak kings attempted to bolster their positions by paying homage to German emperors and using German mercenaries to fight Danish battles. Open conflict began when Magnus, son of Niels, murdered his cousin, Knut Lavard, who was the son of Erik, near Ringsted in January 1130. Knut Lavard's family, especially his brother Erik, were determined to take their revenge for this murder — and Magnus was shortly afterwards killed in a battle at Fotevik. Magnus's father, Niels, who was still actually king at this point, fled Denmark, but was killed in Schleswig not long afterwards. He was succeeded by Erik Emune, the brother of the murdered Knut Lavard. But a couple of years later he too was murdered, and his successor and nephew, another Erik (Lam), decided that life as king was too risky and retired to a monastery.

At this point, there were three separate contenders to the Danish throne: Knut Magnusson, son of Magnus Nielson; Valdemar, son of Knut Lavard; and Svein Eriksson, son of Erik Emune. They came to a deal in 1157, to divide the kingdom of Denmark between them, and met in Roskilde to celebrate this new compromise. The celebrations did not, however, go quite as planned: Knut was murdered and Valdemar badly wounded, leaving Svein to assume sole control of Denmark. But Valdemar was not yet ready to concede defeat, and with the support of the so-called sons of Skjalm, a powerful family from the Danish island of Zealand, he raised an army and fought a battle at Grathe (just south of Viborg) on 23 October 1157, in which he defeated Svein's army and killed Svein. This victory made Valdemar, usually called Valdemar the Great, the sole king of Denmark, a position he enjoyed until 1182. He showed his gratitude to the sons of Skjalm, making one of his strongest supporters, Absalon, bishop of Roskilde. Absalon went on to become archbishop of Lund, and it was he who commissioned the Danish historian, Saxo, to write a history of Denmark, which glorified the family of Valdemar. Valdemar's father, Knut Lavard, was made a saint in 1170. Valdemar's son, called Knut, succeeded to the throne with the minimum of opposition, and ruled for about twenty years, before his brother, Valdemar II the Victorious, succeeded to the throne, again with no real fuss, in 1202.

The peaceful years between Valdemar's victory at Grathe and the death of Valdemar II in 1241 were marked by a blossoming of diplomatic and trading relations with England, clearly illustrating the link between domestic harmony and foreign policy. For example, there are many royal letters of English rolls relating to trade during the reign of Valdemar II. Matthew Paris, monk and historian of St Albans Abbey, recounts an extraordinary episode during the abbacy of Wulfnoð (mid-ninth century) concerning the theft of St Alban's relics by Danes, a story that he attributes to three men of St Albans, who were in the service of King Valdemar II of Denmark: Odo, the royal treasurer; Master Nicholas, treasurer of Denmark; and Edward the Clerk, later Privy Councillor to Henry III. There is a letter from Thomas à Becket to Valdemar II, appealing for help against Henry II, and interestingly Matthew Paris also records that Valdemar II's death cut short his plans for an invasion of England. However, now properly integrated into western Christendom, the Danes seem instead to have looked eastward to expand their influence, launching a crusade against their Baltic neighbours, the pagan Wends, who had repeatedly attacked Denmark during the civil war years, and later Estonia. Politically and religiously, Denmark's gaze was now, at the beginning of the thirteenth century, very much directed eastwards, with a cautious eye on the German empire to the south.

Norway

In the sixty years or so that followed the death of Harald Hard-Ruler at Stamford Bridge in 1066, the kingdom of Norway was often ruled by two or more kings, who were, until 1130, descendants of Harald Hard-Ruler. These kings often had their power bases in different parts of Norway, in one of the country's two richest regions: the district in and around the present-day capital, Oslo, in south-east Norway; and in the area surrounding the seat of the archbishops in Trondheim, midway

201

along Norway's North Sea coast, where the earls of Lade had wielded considerable power during the Viking Age. This division of power was a clear indication that the political unification of this huge country was far from complete, despite Harald Fair-Hair's claim to have united the kingdom in the Battle of Hafrsfjord at the end of the ninth century. In the years 1067-69 Olaf and Magnus, sons of Harald Hard-Ruler, shared the throne. Olaf, nicknamed the Peaceful, survived his brother and went on to rule Norway single-handed until 1093.

William the Conqueror made early attempts to establish good relations with Olaf the Peaceful, sending an embassy to secure special trading privileges for English traders in Bergen. This is a clear illustration of the importance of Norwegian trade to England, also reflected in the fact that there are ten times more documents relating to Norway than to Denmark in the National Archives. But this was not a one-way relationship. The English town of Grimsby in northeast Lincolnshire was the most important port for Norwegian trade in the period before the thirteenth century, when it was eclipsed by King's Lynn. *Orkneyinga Saga* records the visit of Kali, later Earl of Orkney, to Grimsby in around 1120, and paints a vivid picture of a bustling port, full of northern merchants: 'he [Kali] met a great number of people from Norway, the Orkneys, Scotland and the Sudreys [the Hebrides],' as well as Harald Gille, who later became king of Norway. Kali sailed from Grimsby back to Bergen, and there is a skaldic verse about his trip:

> *Unpleasantly we have been wading*
> *In the mud of a weary five weeks.*
> *Dirt we had indeed in plenty,*
> *While we lay in Grimsby harbour;*
> *But now on the moor of sea-gulls*
> *Ride we o'er the crests of billows,*
> *Gaily as the elk of bowsprits*
> *Eastwards ploughs its way to Bergen.*[11]

One historian of Grimsby has written that in many instances 'post-Conquest Lincolnshire appears as a kind of remoter suburb of Norway.'[12] An Augustinian abbey founded in Grimsby in the early twelfth century was dedicated to St Olaf, the Norwegian king who had been killed in battle in 1030, as well as to St Augustine, and a seal of the Abbey was found on the coast of Norway in 1911. One abbot of Grimsby accompanied Stephen, the legate of Pope Alexander III, to Norway in the second half of the twelfth century. There are documents, such as Henry II's writ enforcing the right of the reeves of Lincoln to a toll from Scandinavian merchants (1155-75), which refer to Norse merchants visiting Grimsby and 'other ports of Lincolnshire'.[13] In 1162, William de Grimesbi was in Norway to buy hawks and gerfalcons (large falcons) for the king. Indeed, birds of prey seem to have been an important export and diplomatic commodity for Norway — in 1228 the king of Norway sent falcons and gerfalcons to Henry III, along with two clerical envoys who were allowed to take up to 400 quarters of grain from Grimbsy.[14] Timber was also imported from Norway — in 1230, ten Norwegian ships with timber were recorded in port at Grimsby. There were clearly other links between the two countries as well: Geoffrey of Monmouth's *History of the Kings of England*, written in 1135, shows the interest of the English in Norway, attributing its conquest to Arthur; while Bjarni Erlingsson of Bjarköy took back to Norway with him in 1286 a Middle English romance (now lost, *Lady Olive and Landres her Son*) and had it translated into Norwegian.[15]

After the death of Olaf the Peaceful in 1093, the Norwegian kingship was split once more — between Magnus 'Bare-Foot', son of Olaf, and Hákon, Olaf's nephew. Again this arrangement was relatively short-lived, as Magnus survived his cousin, and ruled alone until 1103. That Magnus was secure is illustrated by his prolonged absences in the British Isles (see above). Following his death in Ireland, Magnus was succeeded by his three sons: Øystein, Sigurd and Olaf. Sigurd, known as Sigurd the Crusader, had spent three years abroad, taking part in the First Crusade — a clear illustration of the process of Scandinavian integration into the Christian community. He spent the winter of 1107 as a guest at the court of Henry I, an event again recorded in skaldic verse by the Icelandic poet Einar Skúlason:

> *The king is on the waves!*
> *The storm he boldly braves.*
> *His ocean steed,*
> *With winged speed,*
> *O'er the white-flashing surges,*
> *To England's coast he urges;*
> *And there he stays the winter o'er:*
> *More gallant king ne'er trod that shore.*[16]

All these joint kingships were not always entirely lacking in friction, but it was not really until Sigurd the Crusader's death in 1130 that what is known as the *Borgerkrig* or 'civil war' period began in Norway, lasting for a hundred years. The civil war did not rage continually over this hundred-year long period: it flared up on several occasions, and was most intense in the last two decades of the twelfth century, but there were often quite long periods of relative peace. As in Denmark, the old Germanic rules of equal succession among brothers and half-brothers were the source of the problem. Another reason why the old policy of joint kings was finally abandoned was that joint kings also had to share the resources of the kingdom, and this limited their ability to recruit armies and to dispense wealth to keep their followers sweet. These limitations became increasingly problematic as imported ideals of kingship started to change expectations and aspirations of kings and nobles alike. However, the immediate cause of the civil war was the arrival on the Norwegian scene of a man from Ireland called Harald Gilchrist or, as he was known in Scandinavian sources, Harald Gille, together with his mother. He claimed to be the son of Magnus Bare-Foot, and therefore King Sigurd's half-brother, and said he was prepared to walk over nine red-hot plough-shares to prove his right to the throne. His claim was apparently proven by this ordeal, but neither Harald nor Sigurd's son, Magnus, really wanted to share the Norwegian throne, and Magnus gathered together a large army to secure his sole right to the throne in 1134. His subsequent capture, imprisonment, mutilation (he was castrated and his feet were chopped off) and blinding by Harald's men marked the beginning of a bloody and a bitter conflict.

Of course if you live by the sword, you have to be prepared to die by the sword, and that is precisely what happened to Harald the following year (1136), when he refused to acknowledge the rights of another illegitimate son of Magnus Bare-Foot, called Sigurd. Sigurd rescued the mutilated King Magnus from his prison, and together they tried to establish their rule over Norway. Theirs was however not a particularly successful or long-lived rule (ending in 1139), and three sons of Harald Gille (Inge Krokrygge, Sigurd Munn, Øystein) shared power for the next twenty years or so. Following the death of two of these, Inge Krokrygge's rule was challenged by a ten-year-old illegitimate son of Sigurd Munn called Hákon Herdebrei. Despite his age, Hákon had the advantage of support from the big noble families of Trøndelag (the region around Trondheim), and with their help he defeated Inge in battle. The case of Hákon demonstrates another important feature of the civil wars in Scandinavia in general: that often the heir to the throne was a mere child, who served as a convenient front for power-hungry nobles, hoping to use the kingship as a tool for gaining their own political demands.

Power-hungry churchmen soon realized the advantage of this idea also. As early as the end of the eleventh century, there had been a European-wide movement towards reform in the Church, led by the

Pope, which in practice meant reforming the Church so that it would be economically self-governing and free from royal control in legal matters and when it came to appointing bishops. In Norway, the Church got its own archbishop in the 1150s, based in Trondheim, and this also marked the beginning of the Norwegian Church's attempt to win independence for itself from the king of Norway at a time when the king was weakened by civil war. Archbishop Øystein Erlendsson (1161-88) of Trondheim formed an alliance with the powerful Erling Skakke, a nobleman married to Sigurd the Crusader's daughter, and the father of a boy, called Magnus Erlingsson. Together the archbishop and Erling plotted to have Magnus made king, even though he had no real claim to the throne. The archbishop was able to salve his conscience by consoling himself with the fact that at least Magnus was the son of a married couple — most of the contenders to the throne during the civil wars were not. All of the country apart from Trøndelag was won over or coerced and Magnus, at the grand old age of seven, was crowned king of Norway in Bergen in 1163. Part of the deal was to give the Church more freedom than it had previously had, and a new law of succession was passed at the same time, which laid down that Norway should only have one king at a time, not joint kings. It also stipulated that the king should be the oldest son of the old king, born within marriage. The new king would be confirmed in his kingdom by a council of bishops, farmers and king's followers, and crucially the bishops had the right of veto if they did not like the decision. In spite of all this legal ceremony, there was still opposition — in Trøndelag, and also from a series of rival kings who had to be defeated by Erling Skakke.

One of these was a man called Sverri, a priest from the Faroes, who claimed to be son of a king, but who probably was not. He defeated and killed Erling in battle at Kalvskinnet, just outside Trondheim, in 1179, and defeated and killed Magnus five years later in a sea-battle off Norway's west coast at Fimreite. The name given to Sverri's followers was the Birchlegs (*Birkibeinar*) — they were poor and their nickname refers to the fact that they wore shoes made out of birch-bark. He had a reputation for being a good military tactician, and fought about sixty battles in Norway — a good indication of the political unrest. While he had support in Trondheim and the surrounding area, he failed to win control over the whole of Norway. The Norwegian Church was also opposed to him as he had killed Magnus and also fiercely disputed the validity of the concessions that Magnus had allowed the Church on becoming king. He was excommunicated from the Church by the pope, and an alliance between some of the powerful aristocratic families and the Church, called the 'Croziers' (*Baglar*), led to his downfall. Following his death in 1202, Norway was effectively divided into a Birchleg stronghold, around Trondheim and in western Norway, and a Crozier stronghold around Oslo and to the north of Oslo. During this turbulent period, Norwegians sought outside support to strengthen their positions. In 1186, King Sverri had thanked the Englishmen who came to Bergen, bringing wheat, honey, flour and cloth, and an English clerk, called Martin, served as the king's chaplain.[17] After Sverri's death, the Birchleg and Crozier factions competed for the support of King John of England, and in October 1216 John issued a letter at Grimsby giving safe conduct to two ships that had arrived from Norway. The civil war also affected other parts of the British Isles: in 1195, Sverri of Norway took Shetland with all its taxes and dues from the Orkney earl Harald Maddadarson as punishment for his support of the rebellion against Sverri in 1193-94. This led to closer relations between Shetland and Norway, while Orkney moved increasingly into the orbit of Scottish politics. In 1208, when peace was finally negotiated between the *Birkibeinar* and *Baglar* in Norway, there was a plundering expedition in the Hebrides and the Isle of

Man, followed by the visit of the islands' kings to the Norwegian court to renew their oath of fealty to the new king and to pay the long overdue tribute they owed him.

In 1217 the rival parties sank their differences and supported the crowning of a unity candidate, Hákon IV Hákonarson (d. 1263), who was Sverri's grandson. However, Hákon was only thirteen years old, and so his uncle, Earl Skúli Bárðarson, shared power with him. It is no coincidence that peace at home during Hákon's reign also saw a blossoming of economic and diplomatic relations with the English. Trade between England and Norway thrived: there were many letters issued by the English king to protect the interests of Norwegian merchants and 'our dear friend, the King of Norway', and a formal trade agreement between Hákon and Edward III was confirmed in August 1223. The importance of this trade has also been illustrated archaeologically, by excavations at Bryggen in Bergen, where large quantities of English pottery, mainly from East Anglia and Lincolnshire, have been uncovered in layers from the thirteenth and fourteenth centuries — easily outnumbering the amount of continental pottery. Diplomatically, too, there is much evidence for extremely amicable relations: for example, *Petrus de Norwey* was the English king's representative in Limerick in 1272; Matthew Paris, the St Albans monk, visited Norway during the reign of King Hákon Hákonarson, in 1248, and served as a financial agent of the Benedictine monastery of Nidarholm, off the coast near Trondheim. Another monk of St Albans, Richard, also served as an envoy of Hákon four times between 1234 and 1241.

While relations with England were strengthened, there was trouble between Norway and Scotland over Norwegian colonies in the west. Hákon took advantage of peace at home to embark upon a new period of Norwegian expansion. The king intervened in Icelandic politics, where the previous century had seen the growing power of a few significant families who accumulated more and more land, result-ing in the formation of miniature kingdoms called *ríki*. By 1220 five families, the Ásbirningar, Sturlungar, Oddaverjar, Haukdælir and Svínfellingar, controlled virtually all of the 39 administrative districts (*goðorð*) into which Iceland was divided. The most famous casualty of Hákon's involvement in Iceland was the nobleman, historian and politician Snorri Sturluson, a member of the Sturlungar family, who had sworn loyalty to the Norwegian king. In 1218, Snorri visited the court of the 14-year-old Norwegian king, Hákon Hákonarson, who was then ruling with his uncle, Earl Skúli Bárðarson. Snorri was well received and when he returned to Iceland some two years later, he was given a ship and other splendid gifts by the earl, and he became a royal retainer. He also promised to persuade the Iceland-ers to accept Norwegian rule. Yet although Hákon's reign was later remembered as ushering in a so-called 'Age of Greatness', ending the turmoil of the years of civil war, there was in fact considerable conflict between the young king and his uncle in the 1230s. Snorri returned to Norway in 1237, following his expulsion from his home at Reykholt by his nephew Sturla Sighvatsson, and he became caught in the crossfire of Hákon's and Skúli's fight for the Norwegian throne. Snorri stayed with the earl and with the earl's son during his two-year stay in Norway, and was apparently made an earl himself by Skúli. This earned Snorri Hákon's enmity, and the Norwegian king forbade Snorri to leave the country. But Snorri ignored Hákon's command and returned to Iceland and his estate at Reykholt as soon as he heard that Sturla Sighvatsson had been killed in battle. Civil war broke out in Norway at the same time, and was only resolved in 1240 when Hákon won a victory over Skúli in the Battle of Oslo. Hákon then instructed the Icelander Gissur Thorvaldsson, his newly appointed earl and Snorri's son-in-law, to ensure that the 'traitor' Snorri returned to Norway or else to kill him. Snorri was executed in the cellar of his home in Reykholt on 22 September 1241. Hákon then very conveniently claimed all of Snorri's *ríki*, and this marked the beginning of a process whereby the Norwegian king, now that his energies were no longer focused on civil war at home, was able to subject Iceland to Norway by 1262.

Hákon's Western Expedition

Shortly after his Icelandic successes, Hákon set off for Scotland, determined to bring all of Norway's colonies around the Scottish coast very firmly under his control, as Magnus Bare-Foot had done some 160 years previously. An isolated cave, where St Maolisa had once lived as a hermit, can still be found in sandstone cliffs on the west side of Holy Island. This small island lies just off the east coast of the Scottish Isle of Arran, forming the excellent harbour of Lamlash Bay. It was here that King Hákon Hákonarson's fleet sheltered in Arran Sound (between Arran and Holy Island) before confronting the Scots in an inconclusive battle at Largs in 1263. Later the Norwegians rested on the island, known to the Norse as *Melansey*. Eight runic inscriptions, scratched by Scandinavians on the walls of the cave, can still be read today. These inscriptions are runic graffiti, probably recording the names of some of the men who took refuge on the island in 1263: Olaf, John, Onund, Svein, Amund, Nicholas of Hæn and Vigleik the steward, whose role in the battle is detailed by *Hákon's Saga*. Hákon's fleet slowly limped northwards before putting in at Orkney, where the king died of illness. His son and successor, Magnus known as 'Law-Mender', recognized that he could not realistically maintain Norwegian control of the western colonies and formally ceded them to the Scottish king by the Treaty of Perth in 1266 for a payment of 4,000 marks over the next four years, with an annual sum of 100 marks to be paid in perpetuity. The treaty also required the Scots to acknowledge Norwegian sovereignty over the Northern Islands.

Deterioration of Relations

At the end of the thirteenth century, Scandinavia's economic and diplomatic relations with her British neighbours were undergoing important changes. The main catalyst in this realignment of interests was the growing power of the Hanseatic League, a trading organization centred on the ports of northern Germany, which by the early years of the fourteenth century had come to totally dominate the trade of northern Europe. The Hansa established an office or *kontor* in Bergen that became one of their most important trading bases and which came to control totally the export of Norwegian herring and stockfish. At the *kontor*'s peak in 1450-1550, around 1,000 Germans lived in Bergen all year round, and the same number again came there in the summer to trade, making the merchants a significant proportion of the town's population of about 6,000. The Hansa also traded from Oslo and Tønsberg in Norway, and came to control the important Scanian fair (in present-day south Sweden, but part of Denmark in the medieval period) — an internationally significant market that had grown up around the herring fisheries in the Sound, the sea passage between Jutland and Sweden and the entrance to the Baltic Sea. The rise of the Hansa naturally affected Denmark's, but more importantly, Norway's economic links with England — and once economic ties were weakened, diplomatic ties became less important. The result was a marked cooling of relations, which ultimately saw Norway strengthen its ties with Scotland in an attempt to rebalance the political scales in northern Europe.

In 1290, Edward I's son was betrothed to the Scottish queen Margaret, known as the Maid of Norway as she was the daughter of Eric, king of Norway. But she died, and Edward I's rejection of the

211

Norwegian political and financial claims on Scotland at Berwick in 1292 must have bred disappointment in Norway. The Norwegians turned their diplomatic attention to the Bruce family in Scotland and France, in clear opposition to England. Following 1290, more and more Norwegian trade passed into German hands. In 1310, one of a certain William Toller's ships, carrying grain from East Prussia to England, was wrecked in the Norwegian port of Malestronde. Although the ship's master came to an agreement with the king's bailiff for removing and storing the grain safely, the bailiff seized the cargo and imprisoned the crew for a year and a half, and when a Grimsby man, Geoffrey le Taverner, was sent with a letter from Edward II to the Norwegian king, he too was imprisoned. In 1312, English fishermen killed a tax-collector off the Norwegian coast, an incident that was followed by arrests and the exclusion of English merchants from Bergen. By the time the Black Death hit Europe, it has been said that 'English and Norwegian merchants almost ceased to cross the North Sea.'[18]

The End of the Scandinavian Period

At what point relations with Scandinavia stopped being a significant part of the British and Irish political, economic, and social landscape is not an easy question to answer. Of course, some parts of the British Isles retained their links with Norway, Denmark and Iceland longer than others — indeed, contact of one kind or another across the North Sea can be traced right down to the present day. However, all the evidence points to an important dislocation in the fourteenth century. This was a time of economic depression throughout Europe, during what is called the Little Ice Age. There was a significant drop in temperatures, and this obviously affected harvests. Trading relations between England and Scandinavia seriously deteriorated as the German-based Hanseatic League extended its control of Scandinavian trade. Economic disputes in turn affected political relations between England and Scandinavia, and the situation was made considerably worse by the devastation wrought by the Black Death, which arrived in Scandinavia in 1349, as well as by Scandinavia's increasing preoccupation with internal affairs.

Norway, which had been England's most important trading partner, and which was the country with the closest links to the Scandinavian colonies in the west, suffered the most from the Black Death: it has been estimated that the country's population may have dropped as much as 64 per cent, from about 350,000 to about 125,000. The result of this reduction was, of course, massive depopulation — villages and farms were abandoned, as their inhabitants either died or fled — but Norwegian historians also consider the plague as the principal cause of the decline and fall of the sovereign Norwegian state, a fall represented in the Union of Kalmar. In the years after the Black Death the Danish kings, financed and backed by the Hansa, moved to assert their own control of their northern neighbour. In an agreement made at Kalmar (Sweden) in 1397, Norway, with her colonies (the Faroes, Iceland, Orkney and Shetland), Sweden and Denmark all agreed to be ruled by one monarch, Erik of Pomerania (in present-day north Germany). The agreement made at Kalmar was of lasting influence in Scandinavian politics, and bound Norway and Denmark together right up until 1814. Sweden, never happy with the Union, left in 1523, when Gustav Vasa was elected to the Swedish throne. While it lasted, the Union was in effect a Danish empire, with some direct control over Norway, and a looser type of overlordship over Sweden. Following the formation of the Danish dominated Union of Kalmar in 1397, Norway did not become an independent political entity again until 1905. Of course, the rulers of Norway and Denmark did not cut themselves completely off from their English neighbours: the first king of the Union of Kalmar, Erik

(VII) of Pomerania, married Philippa of England (daughter of Henry IV) in 1406. But Erik himself hailed from northern Germany, signalling the new economic and political direction that Scandinavia took in the Middle Ages. The Scandinavian languages contain massive numbers of German loan-words, relating to all spheres of everyday life, that were borrowed during this period, and this is clear evidence that Scandinavia's long period of outward expansion was most definitely over. The pawning of the islands of Orkney and Shetland to Scotland in 1465-66 is the final episode in this chapter — the king of Denmark did not have enough money to provide an adequate dowry for his daughter Margaret's marriage to James III of Scotland. This deal marks the end of a long-term dispute between Scotland and Norway/Denmark over the status of the islands. Indeed, the Northern Isles had come near to being bargained away as early as 1281. The islands themselves, particularly Orkney, had also been subject to increasing 'Scottification', politically, economically, linguistically and culturally. As William Thomson has said of fourteenth-century Orkney: 'the whole medieval structure of North Atlantic society was in a state of disintegration.'[19] What followed here, as elsewhere in the British Isles, was the cementing of a significant political, economic, and cultural realignment, with England and Scotland dominant, and with Scandinavian kings in no position to negotiate.

8
LEGACY OF THE VIKINGS

It should be clear by now that the Viking impact on the British Isles was much more far-reaching than the destruction that their raids and campaigns wrought upon communities from Shetland in the north to Portland in the south, from the monasteries of Ireland in the west to the towns along England's east coast. As earls, kings and local leaders they shaped the political history of these islands, and as farmers and traders they contributed to the development of a thriving economy. Throughout the British Isles, the Vikings' language and culture left their mark, and the Viking history of the British Isles can still be traced in their stone monuments, their inscriptions, their burials, their houses and even in the genes of their ancestors. Yet there are clearly great differences in the extent to which this Viking legacy is evident: in the Irish countryside, in Wales and in Cornwall, the Vikings appear to have left comparatively little trace of their activities; while Shetland is so Scandinavian in character that it seems like an accident of history that it is now part of the British Isles rather than part of the Norse world like its northern neighbour, the Faroes.

By the middle of the fourteenth century, when the Black Death devastated Europe, the Scandinavians in the British Isles were no longer, strictly speaking, Vikings: the 'classic' period of raiding that had so terrorized Europe was some four or five hundred years in the past by then — roughly the same amount of time that separates us from our Tudor and Stuart predecessors. Nor, in some cases, were the Scandinavians in the British Isles really Scandinavian — in Scotland and Ireland, the 'Scandinavians' had long since settled down and married into local families: Scandinavian names can be found alongside Celtic names, Scandinavian genes alongside Celtic genes. Politically, the power of the Scandinavian kings in the British Isles, never strong in the independent communities of the Irish Sea and the North Atlantic, was always doomed, overshadowed by the growing centralization and strength of national monarchies in England and Scotland. Moreover, in Scandinavia itself there was an intense struggle for political dominance. Norway, the country with the closest links to Britain and Ireland, ultimately lost in this struggle — in 1397 it fell under the control of the king of Denmark, a period of domination that lasted some five hundred years. Denmark itself was by this time, economically and politically, in the hands of the Hanseatic League, a trading association of the towns of northern Germany. Politically, economically and culturally, the Middle Ages in Scandinavia were the antithesis of the Viking Age — and in the British Isles, memories of the Vikings receded until a new generation of scholars reawakened interest in their exploits, an interest that peaked in the Victorian period.

A comparatively new strand of research has opened up in recent years — the evidence that genes provide for the Viking contribution to the population of the British Isles. This idea of shared blood was in fact something that many Victorian writers had romantically dwelt upon. Following the discovery of the ABO system of blood groups in 1901, there have been many studies of their geographical distribution, reflecting differences in national and regional populations that may, in some cases, be linked to population migrations. In 1971, the second edition of Peter Sawyer's *The Age of the Vikings* included a fairly lengthy footnote discussing studies that link Scandinavia and the British Isles, such as that by J.A. Donegani, N. Dungal, E.W. Akin and A.E. Mourant on 'The blood groups of the Icelanders'.[1] This revealed that the distribution of blood groups in Iceland was quite unlike that found in Norway, but was very similar to that of northern and western Britain. Even more recently, studies conducted by Agnar Helgason suggest that perhaps a quarter of Icelandic men have some Gaelic ancestry, but perhaps most remarkably, his study of mitochondrial DNA, passed directly from mother to baby, suggests that around half of Icelanders' female ancestors were Gaelic.[2]

As DNA sampling techniques and analysis have improved, scientists have conducted a programme of DNA sampling across the British Isles to try and establish whether or not there is in fact any biological evidence for large-scale Scandinavian immigration. The ambitious 'Blood of the Vikings' programme headed by David Goldstein at University College, London in connection with the BBC series took DNA samples from modern Danish and Norwegian men, allowing scientists to identify distinctly 'Viking' Y-chromosome signatures in their DNA. These were then compared with samples taken from men living in former Viking colonies throughout the British Isles and having family links in that area for at least three generations. Unfortunately, the results did not help to resolve the debate about numbers of Viking settlers in eastern England, mainly because the Anglo-Saxons who settled there in the fifth century came from Denmark and northern Germany: the genetic signatures of Viking and Anglo-Saxon are therefore too close. In Ireland and Anglesey in northern Wales, samples revealed a 'Celtic' marker on the Y chromosome very similar to that found in the DNA of men from the Basque region in northern Spain. However, in other parts of the British Isles, Scandinavian influence could be clearly seen — and not surprisingly, this was most evident in Orkney. This is clear proof, if it was needed, of the island's thorough Scandinavianization, and gives some scientific credibility to the Victorian view that:

Still in our race the Norse king reigns;
His best blood beats along our veins;[3]

It has taken over 150 years of research and the development of increasingly sophisticated scientific and archaeological techniques to reassess and reshape the legacy of the Vikings in the British Isles. How will new finds change our views of the Vikings, and what will be considered the legacy of the Vikings in the British Isles in another 150 years' time?

NOTES AND SUGGESTIONS
FOR FURTHER READING

INTRODUCTION
1. Terry Deary, *The Vicious Vikings*, London: Scholastic, 1994, p. 126.

1. UNCOVERING THE VIKING PAST

SUGGESTIONS FOR FURTHER READING

Adam of Bremen, *History of the Archbishops of Hamburg-Bremen*. Translated with introduction and notes by Francis J. Tschan; with new introduction and selected bibliography by Timothy Reuter. New York: Columbia University Press, 2002.

Alfred the Great: Asser's Life of King Alfred *and Other Contemporary Sources*. Translated by Simon Keynes and Michael Lapidge. London: Penguin, 1983.

The Anglo-Saxon Chronicle. Translated and edited by Michael J. Swanton. London: J.M. Dent, 1996.

The Annals of Ulster (to AD 1131). Translated and edited by Seán Mac Airt and Gearóid Mac Niocaill. Dublin: Dublin Institute of Advanced Studies, 1983.

Ashdown, Margaret, *English and Norse Documents Relating to the Reign of Ethelred the Unready*. Cambridge University Press, 1930.

Cronica Regum Mannie et Insularum: Chronicles of the Kings of Man and the Isles. B. L. Cotton Julius A vii. Transcribed and translated with an introduction by George Broderick. The Manx Museum and National Trust, Douglas 1979. 1991 reprint by Copy Shop, Douglas.

Domesday Book: A Complete Translation. Edited by Ann Williams and the Alecto Domesday Editorial Board. London: Penguin, 2002. (Useful single volume containing all the counties covered by the Domesday survey, with an index of modern place-names.)

Douglas, D.C. and G.W. Greenaway, *English Historical Documents II 1042-1189*. 2nd edition. London: Eyre & Spottiswoode, 1981.

Early Sources of Scottish History A.D. 500-1286. 2 vols. Collected and translated by Alan Orr Anderson. Edinburgh: Oliver & Boyd, 1922. Available in reprint by Paul Watkins, Stamford, 1990.

Egil's Saga. Translated by Herman Pálsson and Paul Edwards. Harmondsworth: Penguin, 1976. A new translation by Bernard Scudder was published by Penguin in 2004.

Encomium Emmae Reginae. Edited and translated by Alistair Campbell, with new introduction by Simon Keynes. Camden Classic Reprints, 4. Cambridge University Press, 1998.

Hall, Richard A., *Viking Age Archaeology in Britain and Ireland*. Princes Risborough: Shire, 1990. (A short readable survey (about 60 pages) of Viking activity with details of archaeological finds, including coins, graves, and stone sculpture.)

Jesch, Judith, *Ships and Men in the Late Viking Age*. Woodbridge: Boydell & Brewer, 2001. (Critical and detailed survey of the vocabulary of skaldic poems and runic inscriptions, which offers many useful insights into Viking activity.)

Njal's Saga. Translated by Magnus Magnusson and Hermann Pálsson. Harmondsworth: Penguin, 1960. A new translation by Robert Cook was published by Penguin in 2001.

Ohthere and Wulfstan. Two Voyagers at the Court of King Alfred. Edited by Niels Lund and translated by Christine E. Fell. York: William Sessions, 1984.

Orkneyinga Saga. Translated by Hermann Pálsson and Paul Edwards. London: Penguin, 1981.

Page, R.I., 'Rune-masters and Skalds', in James Graham-Campbell, ed., *The Viking World*. London 1980 (2nd ed. 1989), pp. 154-71. (Nicely-illustrated introduction for the general reader.)

Page, R.I., *Chronicles of the Vikings*. London: British Museum, 1995.

Rollason, David, with Derek Gore and Gillian Fellows-Jensen. *Sources for York History to AD 1100. The Archaeology of York, 1*. York: York Archaeological Trust, 1998.

Snorri Sturluson, *Heimskringla: Sagas of the Norse Kings*. 3 vols. Translated by Samuel Laing. London: Dent, 1961-64. Another good translation of *Heimskringla*, by Lee M. Hollander (Austin: University of Texas, 1971) is still in print.

War of the Gaedhil with the Gaill, or The Invasion of Ireland by the Danes and other Norsemen. Translated and introduced by J.H. Todd. *Rerum Britannicarum medii ævi scriptores*, 48. London: Rolls Series, 1867.

Whitelock, Dorothy, ed., *English Historical Documents c. 500-1042*. 2nd edition. London: Eyre & Spottiswoode, 1979.

NOTES

1. Quoted in *Gerald Durrell: The Authorised Biography* by Douglas Botting, London: HarperCollins, 1999, p. 199.

2. Unless otherwise stated, all references to the *Chronicle* are taken from Michael Swanton's excellent translation and edition of *The Anglo-Saxon Chronicle*, London: Dent, 1996.

3. Winston Churchill, *A History of the English-Speaking Peoples 1: The Birth of Britain*, London: Cassell, 1974, p. 70.

4. English spoken and written between around 1100 and 1500 is known as Middle English, to distinguish it from its predecessor, Old English, and its successor, Modern English.

5. Barbara Crawford, *Scandinavian Scotland*. Leicester University Press 1987, p. 6.

6. Arne Kruse, 'Norse Topographical Settlement Names on the Western Littoral of Scotland', in Jonathan Adams and Katherine Holman, eds,

Contact, Conflict, and Coexistence: Scandinavia and Europe 800-1350. Turnhout: Brepols, 2004, pp. 97-107.

2. RAIDERS FROM THE NORTH

SUGGESTIONS FOR FURTHER READING

Doherty, Charles, 'The Viking Impact upon Ireland.' In Anne-Christine Larsen, ed., *The Vikings in Ireland,* pp. 29-35. Roskilde: The Viking Ship Museum, 2001 (Short survey of Ireland at the time of the first Viking raids — and a brief assessment of the Vikings role in changing Irish society.)

Etchingham, Colmán, *Viking Raids on Irish Church Settlements in the Ninth Century.* Maynooth Monographs, Series Minor, 1. Maynooth: The Department of Old and Middle Irish, St Patrick's College, 1996. (Short and useful study that compares the numbers of Viking and Irish attacks on monasteries.)

Keynes, Simon, 'The Vikings in England, c. 790-1016.' In Peter Sawyer, ed., *The Oxford Illustrated History of the Vikings*, pp. 48-82. Oxford University Press, 1997. (Excellent short introduction to the Viking impact on England from the early raids to the conquest of England by Svein Forkbeard, which discusses place-names, coins and sculpture, as well as written evidence.)

Ó Corráin, Donnchadh, 'Ireland, Wales, Man, and the Hebrides.' In Peter Sawyer, ed., *The Oxford Illustrated History of the Vikings*, Oxford University Press, 1997, pp. 83-109. (Short essay that provides an excellent introduction to the main events of the period and the Viking impact on the Irish Sea region. A welcome attempt to look at Viking activity beyond the limits of modern national borders.)

Pedersen, Anne, 'Anglo-Danish Contact across the North Sea in the Eleventh Century'. In *Scandinavia and Europe 800-1350: Contact, Conflict and Coexistence*, edited by Jonathan Adams and Katherine Holman, pp. 43-67. Brepols: Turnhout 2004. (Very useful survey of archaeological finds from Denmark that demonstrate contact with England, from the period of the early raids to the more sustained links evident during the reign of Cnut. Much of this material has not been available in English before.)

Wamers, Egon, 'Insular Finds in Viking Age Scandinavia and the State Formation of Norway'. In H.B. Clarke *et al., eds, Ireland and Scandinavia in the Early Viking Age,* pp. 37-72. Four Courts, Dublin, 1998. (Technical survey of the archaeological finds from Scandinavia, examining their type, distribution and date, with an interesting attempt to link it to the development of royal power in Norway, where the finds are concentrated.)

NOTES

1. John Hines, *The Scandinavian Character of Anglian England in the pre-Viking period.* 1984, pp. 293-94, quoted in Bjørn Myhre, 'The Beginning of the Viking Age — Some Current Archaeological Problems', in Anthony Faulkes and Richard Perkins, eds, *Viking Revaluations.* London: Viking Society, 1993, pp. 182-204 (quotation on p. 188).

2. Bjørn Myhre, 'The Beginning of the Viking Age — Some Current Archaeological Problems', in Anthony Faulkes and Richard Perkins, eds, *Viking Revaluations.* London: Viking Society, 1993, p. 198.

3. Letter from Alcuin, quoted in R.I. Page, *Chronicles of the Vikings.* London: British Musuem, 1995, p. 79.

4. Adam of Bremen, *History of the Archbishops of Hamburg-Bremen,* translated by Francis J. Tschan, New York: Columbia University Press, 2002, Book 4, 31, p. 211.

5. Myhre (note 1), pp. 196-7.

6. Justin Pollard, *Alfred the Great: The Man Who Made England.* London: John Murray, 2005.

7. *The Annals of St-Bertin,* translated by Janet L. Nelson, Manchester University Press, 1991.

8. Quotation taken from Donnchadh Ó Corráin, 'The Vikings in Ireland', in Anne-Christine Larsen, ed., *The Vikings in Ireland*, p. 20, Roskilde: Viking Ship Museum, 2001, p. 20.

9. Lochlann is likely to have been somewhere in the Western Isles of Scotland, but it may have been as far afield as the district of Rogaland in south-west Norway.

10. Quotation taken from Ó Corráin (note 8), pp. 21-22.

11. The *Annals of Ulster* record that Norsemen in 798 burned *Inis Padraig*, sometimes identified as St Patrick's Holm off the west coast of Man, but it is probably a reference to St Patrick's Island in Dublin Bay.

12. The name 'Pict' was an umbrella term, given by the Romans to the various tribes that inhabited Scotland north of the Antonine Wall, and it means 'painted', apparently referring to the local custom of painting their bodies. The Picts remain an enigmatic group, known primarily through symbol stones and ogham inscriptions, and may have consisted of various Celtic and non-Celtic populations.

13. The location of *Brunanburh* is unknown, although many commentators favour a location in northern England. Place-name evidence suggests that it may well have been in Cheshire (present-day Bromborough), but this cannot be proven. Athelstan's victory renewed his authority in northern England.

14. In *Egil's Saga*, the battle is said to have taken place at Vin Moor (ch. 52-54).

15. Richard Hall, *Viking Age York*, London: Batsford 1994, p. 19.

3. COLONISTS

SUGGESTIONS FOR FURTHER READING

Abrams, Lesley and David Parsons, 'Place-names and the History of Scandinavian Settlement in England', in John Hines, Alan Lane and Mark Redknap, eds, *Land, Sea and Home*, pp. 379-431. Leeds: Maney, 2004. (An invaluable survey of scholarship on Scandinavian place-names by a linguist and historian, that raises many interesting and intriguing questions and underlines the importance of place-names to historians of the Viking period. An essential starting point for those seeking an in-depth assessment of place-name evidence.)

Barnes, Michael P., 'The Scandinavian Languages in the British Isles: The Runic Evidence', in Jonathan Adams and Katherine Holman, eds, *Scandinavia and Europe 800-1350: Contact, Conflict, and Coexistence*, pp. 121-36, Brepols: Turnhout, 2004. (Authoritative, sometimes technical, survey of the evidence that Scandinavian runic inscriptions provide for the use and survival of Scandinavian speech in the British Isles. Includes an appendix of transliterated inscriptions (not translated into modern English).)

Barnes, Michael P. *The Norn Language of Orkney and Shetland.* Lerwick: Shetland Times, 1998. (Short but comprehensive book that surveys the Scandinavian language spoken in the Northern Isles for some 800-900 years. There is also a useful bibliography and several examples of spoken and written Norn, with English translations and commentary.)

Cameron, Kenneth, ed., *Place-name Evidence for the Anglo-Saxon Invasion and Scandinavian Settlements.* Nottingham: English Place-Name Society, 1977. (Classic and influential piece of scholarship that discusses the chronological and geological relationship between Scandinavian place-names in *by*, *thorp*, as well as the Grimston hybrids.)

Crawford, Barbara E., ed., *Scandinavian Settlement in Northern Britain.* London: Leicester University Press, 1995. (Collection of 13 articles by internationally recognized historians, geographers and linguists, which examines Scandinavian place-names from Shetland to northern England. Includes over forty maps.)

Fellows-Jensen, Gillian, 'In the Steps of the Vikings.' In James Graham-Campbell *et al.*, eds, *Vikings and the Danelaw: Select Papers from the Proceedings of the Thirteenth Viking Congress,* pp. 279-88. Oxford: Oxbow, 2001. (Recent overview of the type and significance of Scandinavian names in the Danelaw by the most influential recent scholar of Scandinavian place-names in the British Isles. Gillian Fellows-Jensen is continually revising and refining her theories in light of new research, and this is a welcome summary of her position.)

Fellows-Jensen, Gillian, 'Nordic Names and Loan-words in Ireland.' In Anne-Christine Larsen, ed., *The Vikings in Ireland*, pp. 107-13. Roskilde: The Viking Ship Museum, 2001. (Valuable survey of the place-name and linguistic evidence with a discussion of their significance.)

Fellows-Jensen, Gillian. 'Scandinavian Settlement in Yorkshire: Through the Rear-view Mirror.' In Barbara E. Crawford, ed., *Scandinavian Settlement in Northern Britain*, pp. 170-86. London: Leicester University Press, 1995. (Important reassessment of the significance of Scandinavian place-names in this region by this renowned scholar.)

Fellows-Jensen, Gillian, 'Scandinavian Settlement in the Isle of Man and North-west England: The Place-name Evidence.' In Christine E. Fell *et al.*, eds, *The Viking Age in the Isle of Man*, pp. 37-52. London: Viking Society for Northern Research, 1983. (Examines the evidence for Gaelic survival on Man during the Viking Age, and draws attention to links between the island's place-names and those of the Wirral.)

Geipel, John, *The Viking Legacy: The Scandinavian Influence on the English and Gaelic Languages*. Newton Abbot: David & Charles, 1971. (Accessible and useful book that looks at all the linguistic evidence from the British Isles.)

Gelling, Margaret, 'Norse and Gaelic in Medieval Man: The Place-name Evidence.' In Thorsten Andersson and Karl Inge Sandred, eds, *The Vikings: Proceedings of the Symposium of the Faculty of Arts of Uppsala University; June 6-9, 1977*, pp. 107-18. Stockholm: Almqvist & Wiksell, 1978. (Puts forward her controversial view that Gaelic died out on the Isle of Man during the Viking Age.)

Greene, David, 'The Influence of Scandinavian on Irish.' In Bo Almqvist and David Greene, eds, *Proceedings of the Seventh Viking Congress, Dublin, 15-21 August 1973*, pp. 75-82. Dublin: Royal Irish Academy, 1976. (Survey of loan-words in Irish and their meaning, which concludes that Norse was spoken in Dublin and some other settlements until the Anglo-Norman invasion of 1169.)

Kruse, Arne, 'Norse Topographical Settlement Names on the Western Littoral of Scotland.' In Jonathan Adams and Katherine Holman, eds, *Scandinavia and Europe 800-1350: Contact, Conflict, and Co-Existence,* pp. 97-107. Turnhout: Brepols, 2004. (Recent and important reassessment of the significance of these place-names that challenges the orthodox view that they were given by Norse seamen passing by the area rather than settlers.)

Lund, Niels, 'The Settlers: Where do we Get them from - and do we Need them?' In Hans Bekker Nielsen, Peter Foote, and Olaf Olsen, eds, *Proceedings of the Eighth Viking Congress Århus 24-31 August 1977,* pp. 147-71. Odense University Press, 1981. (Examines the evidence for an unrecorded secondary migration of Scandinavians into eastern England, and concludes that Scandinavian place-names may reflect changes in landownership rather than large-scale migration. The debate is still ongoing — see Abrams and Parsons above.)

Oftedal, Magne, 'Scandinavian Place-names in Ireland.' In Bo Almqvist and David Greene, eds, *Proceedings of the Seventh Viking Congress, Dublin, 15-21 August 1973,* pp. 125-33. Dublin: Royal Irish Academy, 1976. (Discusses the meaning of some of the Scandinavian place-names.)

Page, R.I., 'How Long did the Scandinavian Language Survive in England? The Epigraphical Evidence.' In Peter Clemoes and Kathleen Hughes, eds, *England before the Conquest: Studies in Primary Sources Presented to Dorothy Whitelock,* pp. 165-81. Cambridge University Press. (Important survey of inscriptions that may provide evidence for the survival of Old Norse speech in England. Suggests that some examples of Norse in post-Conquest England may reflect recent contact with Norse-speaking Isle of Man, rather than the survival of the language among communities that settled there in the tenth century.)

Parsons, David N., 'How Long did the Scandinavian Language Survive in England? Again.' In James Graham-Campbell *et al.,* eds, *Vikings and the Danelaw: Select Papers from the Proceedings of the Thirteenth Viking Congress,* pp. 299-312. Oxford: Oxbow, 2001. (Thorough and interesting reassessment of this question, which examines place-names, inscriptions

227

and other linguistic evidence. Definite conclusions cannot be reached because of the nature of the evidence that has survived, but it seems that some pockets of Norse speakers may have survived in areas of northern England into the eleventh century and possibly beyond.)

Stenton, F.M., *Anglo-Saxon England*. 3rd edition. Oxford: Clarendon Press, 1971. (Classic and massive scholarly tome that examines every aspect of English history during the period 500-1087, in which Stenton sets out his views of the Scandinavian settlement of England.)

Townend, Matthew, *Language and History in Viking Age England: Linguistic Relations between Speakers of Old Norse and Old English*. Turnhout: Brepols, 2002. (Often technical, but important as this is the first ever book to study the linguistic contact between speakers of Old Norse and Old English in Viking-Age England. Surveys the place-names and written evidence, as well as discussing possible models of intelligibility.)

Townend, Matthew, 'Viking Age England as a Bilingual Society.' In Dawn M. Hadley and Julian D. Richards, eds, *Cultures in Contact: Scandinavian Settlement in England in the Ninth and Tenth Centuries*, pp. 89-105. Turnhout: Brepols, 2000. (A shorter presentation of the evidence for contact between speakers of Old Norse and Old English, summarizing some of the main points in the author's book (see above). Proposes that speakers of each language could understand each other without the need for translators.)

NOTES

1. P. H. Sawyer, *The Age of the Vikings*, 2nd edition, London: Arnold, 1971, pp. 172-3.

2. *The Annals of Ulster (to AD 1131)*, translated by Seán Mac Airt and Gearóid Mac Niocaill, Dublin: Dublin Institute of Advanced Studies, 1983.

3. *Orkneyinga Saga*, translated by Hermann Pálsson and Paul Edwards, London: Penguin, 1981, ch. 4.

4. Christopher D. Morris quoted in Alan King, 'Post-Roman Upland Architecture in the Craven Dales and the Dating Evidence', in John

Hines, Alan Lane and Mark Redknap, eds, *Land, Sea and Home*, Leeds: Maney, 2004, p. 335.

5. *Orkneyinga Saga* (note 3), ch. 31.

6. *Orkneyinga Saga* (note 3), ch. 66.

7. Although at the end of the Cheshire folios, some estates 'between the Ribble and the Mersey' are detailed.

8. Winston Churchill, *A History of the English-Speaking Peoples 1: The Birth of Britain*, London: Cassell, 1974, p. 76.

9. Sawyer (note 1), p. 128.

10. There are twenty-eight personal names of continental origin compounded with *-by* in the area around Carlisle and along the coastal plain of Cumbria. These names are probably connected with William Rufus's and Henry I's settlement of the area with peasants from the south and Bretons, Flemings and Normans (See Gillian Fellows Jensen, *Scandinavian Settlement Names in the North-West*. Copenhagen: C.A. Reitzel 1985, p. 22).

11. This term, Old Scandinavian, is used to differentiate the language used during the Viking Age from Old Norse, which is the name given to the classical North Germanic language used from roughly 1150 to 1350, most notably in Icelandic sagas, histories and skaldic poetry.

12. *Ohthere and Wulfstan: Two Voyagers at the Court of King Alfred*, edited by Niels Lund, York: William Sessions, 1984, pp. 56-7.

13. Matthew Townend, *Language and History in Viking Age England*, Turnhout: Brepols, 2002, see pp. 181-5 for a summary.

14. For an explanation of these grammatical terms, see Michael Barnes, *A New Introduction to Old Norse: Part 1 Grammar*, London: Viking Society for Northern Research, 1999, esp. pp. 22-7.

15. Discussed by Townend (note 13), pp. 208-10.

16. Dudo of St Quentin, *History of the Normans*, translated by Eric Christiansen, Woodbridge: Boydell, 1998, pp. xvii, 97. Dudo's account is, however, not an objective history in our sense of the word and, as Christiansen writes, this is 'not reliable evidence of the linguistic map of tenth-century Normandy', note 326 on p. 210.

17. James Lang, ed., *Corpus of Anglo-Saxon Stone Sculpture III: York and Eastern Yorkshire*, London: The British Academy, 1991, pp. 163-66.
18. H. Loyn, *The Vikings in Britain*, London: BCA, 1977, p. 115.
19. Anna Ritchie, *Viking Scotland*, London: Batsford, 1993, p. 28.
20. Michael Dolley, 'The Palimpsest of Viking Settlement on Man' in Hans Bekker-Nielsen *et al.*, eds, *Proceedings of the Eighth Viking Congress Århus 24-31 August 1977*, pp. 173-81, Odense University Press, 1981 (quotation on p. 177).
21. Barbara Crawford, *Scandinavian Scotland*, Leicester University Press, 1987, p. 102.

4. VIKING KINGS

SUGGESTIONS FOR FURTHER READING

Barrow, G.W.S., *Kingship and Unity: Scotland 1000-1306*. Edinburgh University Press, 1981. (Readable and comprehensive, this helps to put the actions of Scandinavian rulers — in the British Isles and in Scandinavia — in their wider context, demonstrating how the formation of a strong Scottish monarchy affected its neighbours.)

Crawford, Barbara E., ed., *St Magnus Cathedral and Orkney's Twelfth Century Renaissance*. Aberdeen University Press, 1988. (Collection of 16 articles that mark the 850th anniversary of St Magnus Cathedral in Orkney by examining its architectural, artistic, ecclesiastical and historical background at the centre of the Norse earldom.)

Dolley, Michael, *Viking Coins of the Danelaw and of Dublin*. London: British Museum, 1965. (Classic British Museum pamphlet, with illustrations, that links coins and politics to outline the history of the Viking kings of Dublin and the Danelaw.)

Hudson, Benjamin, *Viking Pirates and Christian Princes. Dynasty, Religion, and Empire in the North Atlantic*. New York: Oxford University Press, 2005. (The stories of two families — the Olafssons and Haraldssons — who dominated politics in Dublin, the Hebrides and the Isle of Man during the tenth and twelfth centuries. An unusual and welcome attempt to move away from scholarship that follows national borders and the limits of historical periods, such as the Viking Age. Hudson also shows how these Viking families soon abandoned piracy and established themselves as Christian rulers in the Scandinavian and Celtic worlds.)

M.K. Lawson, *Cnut*. London: Longman, 1993. A new edition, published by Tempus (Stroud, 2004) is also available (Detailed study of the Danish king's career in England, Scandinavia and elsewhere, which is essential reading for those wanting to understand Cnut's reign and achievements.)

Rollason, D., with D. Gore and G. Fellows-Jensen, *Sources for York History to AD 1100*. York: York Archaeological Trust, 1998. (Collection of primary sources that contains, amongst other things, a very useful outline of the kings of York and the main events during the period.)

Rumble, Alexander R., ed., *The Reign of Cnut: King of England, Denmark and Norway*. London: Leicester University Press, 1994. (Extremely useful collection of twelve papers that covers all aspects of Cnut's reign, including his earls, his laws, his coins, and the Scandinavian poetry composed at his court.)

Smyth, Alfred P., *Scandinavian York and Dublin: The History and Archaeology of Two Related Viking Kingdoms*. Dublin: Irish Academic Press, 1987. (Classic, sometimes controversial, account of the extremely complex web of politics that linked York and Dublin. Essential reading.)

NOTES

1. *Anglo-Saxon Chronicle*, 1051.
2. Letter of 1019-20; see Dorothy Whitelock, *English Historical Documents c. 500-1042*. 2nd ed. London: Eyre & Spottiswoode, 1979, p. 415.
3. Letter of 1027; see Whitelock (note 2), pp. 416-18.
4. Rather confusingly, Emma took the English name Ælfgifu on becoming queen.
5. Dorothy Whitelock (note 2), p. 245.

6. Michael Dolley, *Viking Coins of the Danelaw and of Dublin*, London: British Museum, 1965, p. 21.

7. The medieval Icelandic *Egil's Saga*, translated by Herman Pálsson and Paul Edwards, Harmondsworth: Penguin, 1976, claims that Erik was given York by Athelstan to protect the north against the Scots and the Irish Norse (ch. 59).

8. Snorri Sturluson, *Heimskringla: Saga of Harald Finehair*, translated by Samuel Laing, London: Dent, 1961-64, ch. 43.

9. Sigtrygg was murdered on his second journey to Rome.

10. Michael Dolley, 'The Palimpsest of Viking Settlement on Man' in Hans Bekker-Nielsen *et al*, eds, *Proceedings of the Eighth Viking Congress Århus 24-31 August 1977*, Odense University Press, 1981, p. 176.

11. This Norse name for the Hebrides means 'the Southern Isles' and reflects a Norwegian geographical perspective — the present name, the Western Isles, derives instead from a Scottish point of view.

12. All translations are taken from *Cronica Regum Mannie et Insularum: Chronicles of the Kings of Man and the Isles*. B.L. Cotton Julius A vii, translated by George Broderick, Douglas: The Manx Museum and National Trust, 1979. 1991 reprint by Copy Shop, Douglas.

13. G.W.S. Barrow, *Kingship and Unity: Scotland 1000-1306*, Edinburgh University Press, 1981, p. 26.

14. F.T. Wainwright, ed., *The Northern Isles*, Edinburgh: Nelson, 1962, pp. 189-90.

5. PAGAN MEETS CHRISTIAN

SUGGESTIONS FOR FURTHER READING

Abrams, Lesley, 'The conversion of the Danelaw.' In James Graham-Campbell *et al.*, eds, *Vikings and the Danelaw: Select Papers from the Proceedings of the Thirteenth Viking Congress*, pp. 31-44. Oxford: Oxbow, 2001. (Scholarly survey of what is known about the Christianization of Scandinavians that settled in northern and eastern England, which raises many interesting questions.)

Abrams, Lesley, 'The Conversion of the Scandinavians of Dublin,' *Anglo-Norman Studies* 20 (1998), pp. 1-29. (Scholars differ widely in their dating of the conversion of the Vikings in Ireland. Abrams examines why this is so by looking at the evidence — mainly from chronicles — that refers to the religion of the Scandinavians. She concludes that the picture seems quite different from Anglo-Saxon England, where defeated Vikings were forced to convert.)

Adam of Bremen, *History of the Archbishops of Hamburg-Bremen*. Translated with introduction and notes by Francis J. Tschan; with new introduction and selected bibliography by Timothy Reuter. New York: Columbia University Press, 2002. (Important eleventh-century source for religious and political history of Scandinavia, written by a German monk, who consulted, among others, King Svein Estrithsson of Denmark (d. 1076).)

Biddle, Martin and Birthe Kjølbye-Biddle, 'Repton and the Great Heathen Army, 873-4.' In James Graham-Campbell *et al.*, eds, *Vikings and the Danelaw*, pp. 45-96. Oxford: Oxbow, 2001. (Summary of research and interpretation of this important archaeological site.)

Crawford, Barbara E., ed., *Conversion and Christianity in the North Sea World*. St John's House Publications, 8. St Andrews: Committee for Dark Ages Studies, University of St Andrews, 1998. (Collection of seven essays that examine the archaeology and politics of conversion along northern Britain's North Sea coast (Scotland and Northumbria) and in Scandinavia between 500 and 1100 AD.)

Ellis Davidson, H.R., *Gods and Myths of Northern Europe*. Harmondsworth: Penguin, 1964. (Classic and readable account of what is known about Scandinavian paganism from literary accounts).

Fell, Christine E., 'Anglo-Saxon Saints in Old Norse Sources and vice versa.' In Hans Bekker-Nielsen, Peter Foote and Olaf Olsen, eds, *Proceedings of the Eighth Viking Congress, Århus, 24-31 August 1977*, pp. 95-106. Odense University Press, 1981. (Short conference paper that outlines evidence for the cult of Scandinavian saints, such as St Olaf, in the British Isles, and for Icelandic interest in English saints and religious figures, such as Edward the Confessor.)

Gräslund, Anne-Sofie, 'Religion, Art, and Runes.' In William W. Fitzhugh and Elisabeth I. Ward, eds, *Vikings: The North Atlantic Saga*, pp. 55-69. Washington, DC: Smithsonian Institution, 2000. (A short introductory essay, accompanied by colour illustrations, that includes sections on the major gods and goddesses, burial practices, cult places, art, and conversion.)

Halsall, Guy, 'The Viking Presence in England? The Burial Evidence Reconsidered.' In Dawn M. Hadley and Julian D. Richards, eds, *Cultures in Contact: Scandinavian Settlement in England in the Ninth and Tenth Centuries*, pp. 259-76. Turnhout: Brepols, 2000. (Useful survey and re-evaluation of the significance of Viking graves.)

Lindow, John, *Norse Mythology: A Guide to the Gods, Heroes, Rituals, and Beliefs*. Oxford University Press, 2001. (Excellent account of all aspects of Norse mythology, with an extensive dictionary-like chapter explaining the meaning of names and terms, alongside chapters that put Scandinavian mythology in its historical context and explain the meaning of mythic time. Particularly useful is the detailed bibliography with notes to help readers.)

Orchard, Andy, *Cassell's Dictionary of Norse Myth and Legend*. London: Cassell, 1997. (Extremely useful alphabetical catalogue of supernatural beings, heroes, monsters, and myths, supported by an extensive bibliography and suggestions for further reading. It also deals with the social and historical background to the myths, and with topics such as burial and sacrifice.)

Page, R.I., *Norse Myths*. London: British Museum, 1990. (General introduction to Scandinavians gods and heroes, and the legends about them. The best starting point for beginners, but also with much food for thought for other readers, and a reliable introduction to some of the complexities of these often contradictory myths.)

The Poetic Edda. Translated by Carolyne Larrington. Oxford University Press, 1996. (Most recent translation in English of this collection of poems about Norse mythology, with introduction, notes and suggestions for further reading.)

Snorri Sturluson, *Edda.* Translated by Anthony Faulkes. London: J. M. Dent, 1987 (Excellent English translation of this vital source for Norse mythology, with a useful and reliable introduction.)

NOTES

1. See translation and commentary in R.I. Page, *Chronicles of the Vikings*, London: British Museum, 1995, p. 79.

2. See *Alfred the Great: Asser's* Life of King Alfred *and other Contemporary Sources*, translated by Simon Keynes and Michael Lapidge, London: Penguin, 1983, p. 85.

3. Adam of Bremen, *History of the Archbishops of Hamburg-Bremen*, translated by Francis J. Tschan. New York: Columbia University Press, 2002, Book 4, ch. 27.

4. The best available English translation of Ibn Fadlan's account of can be found in H.M. Smyser, 'Ibn Fadlan's Account of the Rus with some Commentary and Some Allusions to Beowulf.' In Jess B. Bessinger Jr and Robert P. Creed, eds, *Medieval and Linguistic Studies in Honor of Francis Peabody Magoun, Jr*, pp. 92-119, London: Allen & Unwin, 1965.

5. Snorri Sturluson, *Heimskringla: Olaf's Saga*, translated by Samuel Laing. London: Dent, 1961-64, ch. 244.

6. Olwyn Owen, 'The Scar Boat Burial — and the Missing Decades of the Early Viking Age in Orkney and Shetland', in Jonathan Adams and Katherine Holman, eds, *Scandinavia and Europe 800-1350*, p. 14, Turnhout: Brepols 2004.

7. Julian D. Richards, *Viking Age England*, Stroud: Tempus, 2004, pp. 195-201.

8. Barbara Crawford, *Scandinavian Scotland.* Leicester University Press, 1987, pp. 118, 125-7.

6. SCANDINAVIAN SOCIETY

SUGGESTIONS FOR FURTHER READING

Bailey, Richard N., *Viking Age Sculpture in Northern England*. London: Collins, 1980. (Classic introduction to this fascinating evidence for Scandinavian influence in England that can be enjoyed by beginner and academic alike.)

Crawford, Barbara E., *Scandinavian Scotland*. Leicester University Press, 1987. (This book has an excellent section on the 'establishment of administrative structures' in Scotland, the Northern and Western Isles and the Isle of Man.)

Dumville, D.N., 'The Treaty of Alfred and Guthrum.' In David N. Dumville, ed., *Wessex and England from Alfred to Edgar*, pp. 1-27, Woodbridge: Boydell, 1992. (Useful summary of research on the treaty which emphasizes its limitations — and the fact that it seems to have lasted for only a few years.)

Fenger, Ole, 'The Danelaw and the Danish Law: Anglo-Scandinavian Legal Relations during the Viking Period', *Scandinavian Studies in Law* 16 (1972), pp. 85-96. (Summary of research on the question of whether Scandinavian influence in the law of the Danelaw is simply linguistic.)

Fuglesang, Signe Horn, 'Art', in Else Roesdahl and David M. Wilson, eds, *From Viking to Crusader: Scandinavia and Europe 800–1200*, pp. 176-84. The 22nd Council of Europe Exhibition. Copenhagen: Nordic Council of Ministers and The Council of Europe, 1992.

Graham-Campbell, James, 'Viking Art', in James Graham-Campbell, ed., *The Viking World*. London: Frances Lincoln, 1980 (2nd ed. 1989), pp. 130-53. (Short, nicely illustrated introduction for the general reader, which discusses each style with examples.)

Holman, Katherine, *Scandinavian Runic Inscriptions in the British Isles: Their Historical Context*. Tronehim: Tapir, 1996. (In-depth study of the 135 inscriptions in Scandinavian runes that have been found in England, Scotland and the Isles, and the Isle of Man, which links them to other evidence of Viking activity in these places and analyses the historical evidence they provide.)

Jesch, Judith, *Women in the Viking Age*. Woodbridge: Boydell, 1991. (First book-length study in English to examine women's lives in Viking-Age Scandinavia and in Viking colonies from Greenland to Russia. This book offers a new perspective on Viking society that is refreshingly different from the traditional image of a violent and male-dominated world, and is highly recommended for general and academic readers.)

Klindt-Jensen, Ole and David M. Wilson, *Viking Art*, London: George Allen & Unwin, 1966. (Classic introduction to the different styles of Viking art, although new finds have since altered the date ranges of the styles and their distribution.)

Lang, James, *Anglo-Saxon Sculpture*. Princes Risborough: Shire, 1988. (Short book, ideal for beginners, that surveys the form, iconography and function of sculpture from England, and includes a short anthology of particularly interesting pieces.)

'Laws' in Phillip Pulsiano, ed., *Medieval Scandinavia: An Encyclopedia*, New York: Garland, 1993. (With contributions summarizing the current state of knowledge by Ole Fenger on Denmark, Hans Fix on Iceland, Magnus Rindal on Norway, and Elsa Sjöholm on Sweden.)

Leahy, Kevin and Caroline Paterson, 'New Light on the Viking Presence in Lincolnshire: The Artefactual Evidence.' In James Graham-Campbell *et al.*, eds, *Vikings and the Danelaw*, pp. 181-202, Oxford: Oxbow, 2001. (Important article that, as well as including an introduction to the impact of the Vikings on Lincolnshire, examines new finds of metalwork, suggesting that the Scandinavian settlement of the region was considerable.)

Neff, Charlotte, 'Scandinavian Elements in the Wantage Code of Æthelred II', *Journal of Legal History* 10 (1989), pp. 285-316. (Extremely detailed examination of this law-code, discussing possible evidence of Scandinavian legal practice.)

Ó Floinn, Raghnall, 'Irish and Scandinavian Art in the Early Medieval Period.' In Anne-Christine Larsen, ed., *The Vikings in Ireland*, pp. 87-97. Roskilde: The Viking Ship Museum, 2001.

Page, R.I., *Runes*. London: British Museum, 1987. (Short introductory book that surveys the variety of runic inscriptions and alphabets, including those from Scandinavia and Anglo-Saxon England. Written by an acknowledged authority, this is an excellent starting point for those seeking a sensible and reliable introduction to runes and how they were used).

Page, R.I., 'The Manx Rune-stones', in Christine E. Fell *et al.*, eds, *The Viking Age in the Isle of Man*, pp. 133-46, London: Viking Society for Northern Research, 1983 (In-depth discussion of the readings and significance of these runic inscriptions.)

Page, R. I., 'Rune-masters and Skalds', in James Graham-Campbell, ed., *The Viking World*, pp. 154-71, London 1980 (2nd ed. 1989). (Nicely-illustrated introduction for the general reader.)

The Poetic Edda, translated by Carolyne Larrington, Oxford University Press, 1996. (Complete translation of the poems *Hávamál* and *Rigspula* can be found under 'Sayings of the High One' and 'The List of Rig' respectively.)

Sawyer, Birgit, *The Viking-Age Rune-Stones: Custom and Commemoration in Early Medieval Scandinavia*. Oxford University Press, 2000. (This brings together a number of Sawyer's theories about the historical significance of 2,307 Viking-Age rune-stones from Scandinavia, and centres on her main argument that the entire corpus can be viewed as the result of concern for inheritance and property.)

Stocker, David, 'Monuments and Merchants: Irregularities in the Distribution of Stone Sculpture in Lincolnshire and Yorkshire in the Tenth Century.' In Dawn M. Hadley and Julian D. Richards, eds, *Cultures in Contact: Scandinavian Settlement in England in the Ninth and Tenth Centuries*, pp. 179-212. Turnhout: Brepols, 2000. (Scholarly article.)

Stocker, David and Paul Everson, 'Five Towns Funerals: Decoding Diversity in Danelaw Stone Sculpture.' In James Graham-Campbell *et al.*

(eds), *Vikings and the Danelaw,* , pp. 223-243, Oxford: Oxbow, 2001. (In-depth examination of sculpture from Lincolnshire, 'Stamfordshire' and Derbyshire, relating its distribution and decoration to Viking-Age history in these areas).

NOTES

1. Winston Churchill, *A History of the English-Speaking Peoples 1: The Birth of Britain,* London: Cassell, 1974, p. 82.
2. See R.I. Page, *Chronicles of the Vikings,* London: British Museum, 1995 for a selection of verses from this poem (quotation from p. 138).
3. Judith Jesch, *Women in the Viking Age,* Woodbridge: Boydell, 1991, p. 74.
4. R.I. Page, *Chronicles of the Vikings,* London: British Museum, 1995, pp. 225-6.
5. H. Loyn, *The Vikings in Britain,* London: BCA, 1977, p.125.
6. Sir Frank Stenton himself was particularly careful to differentiate the Danelaw from the areas which were colonized by Danes: 'The prevalence of Danish custom within a particular district does not mean that it had been colonized in force by Danish settlers. The establishment of a Danish aristocracy which controlled the course of business in the local courts would hardly be less effective than the settlement of an army in imprinting a Danish character on the law of a shire. The eleventh-century writers who described the greater part of eastern England as the Danelaw were not theorizing about the racial composition of its inhabitants.' (*Anglo-Saxon England,* Oxford: Clarendon, 1971, pp. 506-7.)
7. F.L. Attenborough, *The Laws of the Earliest English Kings,* Cambridge, 1922, pp. 106-7.
8. A.J. Robertson, T*he Laws of the Kings of England from Edmund to Henry I,* Cambridge, 1925, pp. 102-3.
9. Dorothy Whitelock, ed., *English Historical Documents c. 500-1042,* 2nd ed., London: Eyre & Spottiswoode, 1979, p. 436.
10. Whitelock, ed. (note 9), p. 435.
11. Attenborough (note 7), pp. 120-21.

12. Charlotte Neff, 'Scandinavian Elements in the Wantage Code of Æthelred II', *Journal of Legal History* 10 (1989), p. 311.

13. Niels Lund, 'King Edgar and the Danelaw', *Mediaeval Scandinavia* 9 (1976), pp. 181-95 (quotation on p. 195).

14. Ole Fenger, 'The Danelaw and the Danish Law: Anglo-Scandinavian Legal Relations during the Viking Period', *Scandinavian Studies in Law* 16 (1972), p. 94

15. F.W. Maitland, *Domesday Book and Beyond*, Cambridge University Press, 1897, p. 139.

16. The Oseberg ship was in fact not a warship but a pleasure yacht, designed for cruising along the coast. Its wide hull would have made it unstable in the open seas.

17. The so-called Broa style is frequently mentioned in conjunction with the Oseberg style: this is extremely similar to the Oseberg style and is named after a grave find from Broa on the Swedish island of Gotland.

18. Kevin Leahy and Caroline Paterson, 'New Light on the Viking Presence in Lincolnshire: The Artefactual Evidence.' In James Graham-Campbell *et al.*, eds, *Vikings and the Danelaw*, Oxford: Oxbow, 2001, p. 189.

19. Richard N. Bailey, *Viking Age Sculpture*, London: Collins, 1980, p. 80.

20. David Stocker and Paul Everson, 'Five Towns Funerals: Decoding Diversity in Danelaw Stone Sculpture.' In James Graham-Campbell *et al.*, eds, *Vikings and the Danelaw*, Oxford: Oxbow, 2001, p. 225.

7. AFTER THE NORMAN CONQUEST

SUGGESTIONS FOR FURTHER READING

Childs, Wendy, *The Trade and Shipping of Hull 1300-1500*. East Yorkshire Local History Society (No. 43), 1990. (Pamphlet with detailed account of the commodities and shipping coming into this important port, as well as voyages made by Hull fishermen and traders.)

Forte, Angelo, Richard Oram and Frederik Pedersen, *Viking Empires*. Cambridge University Press, 2005. (New survey of Scandinavia and

the westward expansion of the Vikings. Chapter 13 is particularly useful for those wishing to find out about events in Scandinavia after 1066
— one of the very few books in English to cover this period.)

Helle, Knut, 'Anglo-Norwegian Relations in the Reign of Håkon Håkonsson (1217-63)', *Mediaeval Scandinavia 1*, 1968, pp. 101-14. (Scholarly
but readable article, covering a topic that is largely neglected.)

Leach, Henry Goddard, *Angevin Britain and Scandinavia*. Cambridge,
MA: Harvard University Press, 1921. (Now over eighty years old, but
still the only book examining this topic. The author is mainly concerned with the evidence of literary links, and his treatment of the
evidence is anecdotal and uncritical, as well as being coloured by his
rather romantic attitudes: that England and Scandinavia were linked
by ancient ties of blood, and that the heroic feats of the Vikings rein-
vigorated the English.)

Rigby, S.H., *Medieval Grimsby: Growth and Decline*, Hull: University of
Hull, 1993. (A detailed account of the trade of this important east-
coast town, which had close connections with Scandinavia.)

Roesdahl, Else and David M. Wilson, eds, *From Viking to Crusader: Scandinavia and Europe 800-1200.* The 22nd Council of Europe Exhibition.
Copenhagen: Nordic Council of Ministers and The Council of Europe,
1992. (Catalogue of the exhibits, containing masses of illustrations and
a large number of short introductions into topics such as art, runes,
Scandinavian paganism, churches, weapons, dress, coins, and pilgrimages and crusades. Includes a very useful chronological table up until
1200, and the longer timespan also helps to illustrate the impact of
Christian European culture on the Scandinavian countries.)

Tuck, Anthony, 'Some Evidence for Anglo-Scandinavian Relations at the
End of the Fourteenth Century', *Mediaeval Scandinavia 5*, 1972, pp.
75-88. (Detailed and useful article that examines the diplomatic and
commercial ties linking England and Scandinavia, set in the context
of European politics. A topic that is generally neglected in general
accounts of this period of English history.)

NOTES

1. *Anglo-Saxon Chronicle*, version C, 1066.

2. Winston Churchill, *A History of the English-Speaking Peoples 1: The Birth of Britain*, London: Cassell, 1974, p. 117.

3. Andrew Bridgeford, *1066: The Hidden History of the Bayeux Tapestry*. London: Harper Perennial, 2004, p. 14.

4. Adam of Bremen, *History of the Archbishops of Hamburg-Bremen*, translated by Francis J. Tschan, New York: Columbia University Press, 2002, p. 128.

5. Svein was succeeded by five of these sons in turn: Harald Hén 'Soft Whetstone' (d. 1080), Knut II Sveinsson (d. 1086), Olaf Hunger (d. 1095), Erik Ejegod 'Ever-Good' (d. 1103), and Niels (d. 1134).

6. Thorlac Turville-Petre, *England the Nation: Language, Literature and National Consciousness 1290-1340*, Oxford University Press, 1996. A short summary of his discussion of Havelock is found in 'Representations of the Danelaw in Middle English Literature', in James Graham-Campbell *et al.*, eds, *Vikings and the Danelaw*, Oxford: Oxbow, 2001, pp. 345-55.

7. See Judith Jesch, 'Skaldic Verse in Scandinavian England', in James Graham-Campbell *et al.*, eds, *Vikings and the Danelaw*. Oxford: Oxbow, 2001, pp. 313-25.

8. The manuscript (BM, Addit. MS 10, 374) is discussed by Thomas Dunham Whitaker, *An History of the Original Parish of Whalley, and Honor of Clitheroe*. Vol. 1. 4th edition by John Gough Nichols and Ponsonby A. Lyons. London: Routledge, 1872.

9. The traditional order of the Scandinavian 16-rune alphabet is: fuþark hniast tbmlR, with later additions to this, such as e, d, and p, being tagged on to the end.

10. Adam of Bremen, *History of the Archbishops of Hamburg-Bremen*, translated by Francis J. Tschan, New York: Columbia University Press, 2002, pp. 134, 183.

11. *Orkneyinga Saga*, translated by Hermann Pálsson and Paul Edwards. London: Penguin, 1981, ch. 60.

12. E. Gillett, *A History of Grimsby*, Oxford University Press, 1970, p. 8.
13. D.C. Douglas and G.W. Greenaway, eds, *English Historical Documents II 1042-1189*, 2nd ed., London: Eyre and Spottiswoode, 1981, p. 970.
14. Gillett (note 12), p. 15.
15. Henry Goddard Leach, *Angevin Britain and Scandinavia*. Cambridge, MA: Harvard University Press, 1921, pp. 47, 68-72; 241-45.
16. Snorri Sturluson, *Heimskringla: The Saga of the Sons of Magnus*, transl. by Samuel Laing, London: Dent. 1961-64, ch. 3.
17. Knut Helle, 'Anglo-Norwegian Relations in the reign of Håkon Håkonsson (1217-63)', *Mediaeval Scandinavia* 1, 1968, p. 103.
18. Leach (note 15), p. 61.
19. W.P.L. Thomson, *History of Orkney*, Edinburgh: Mercat, 1987, p. 111.

8. LEGACY OF THE VIKINGS

NOTES

1. P. H. Sawyer, *The Age of the Vikings*, 2nd ed., London: Arnold, 1971, pp. 255-6.
2. See Julian Richards, *Blood of the Vikings*, London: Hodder & Stoughton, 2001, pp. 126-7.
3. Gerald Massey, 'The Norseman' (1861), quoted in Andrew Wawn, 'Hereward, the Danelaw and the Victorians', in James Graham-Campbell *et al.,* eds, *Vikings and the Danelaw,* Oxford: Oxbow, 2001, pp. 357-68.

SELECTED BIBLIOGRAPHY

There are a huge number of books about the Vikings in general, and numerous articles and books about the impact of the Vikings on different parts of the British Isles. This reflects both the diversity of the Viking experience in different parts of Britain and Ireland and the continued interest of academics and the general public in this exciting and important period of our past. As a result, this bibliography is extremely selective and simply provides an introduction to the most important and recent work published in English.

Until Julian Richards' *Blood of the Vikings*, no book reviewing the Viking impact on the British Isles had been published since Henry Loyn's *The Vikings in Britain* (1977), so for more recent accounts, incorporating new archaeological evidence in particular, readers are instead referred to surveys of the individual countries, such as James Graham-Campbell and Colleen Batey's *Vikings in Scotland: An Archaeological Survey*, Mark Redknap's *Vikings in Wales: An Archaeological Quest*, and Julian Richards' *Viking Age England*. To help the reader, I have subdivided the bibliography into books and articles relevant to the British Isles in general, to England, to Ireland, to Scotland and the Isles, and to Wales. Readers looking for a more general survey of Viking activity at home and abroad are referred to one of the many overviews available in the final section of this bibliography.

For those seeking more in-depth analysis, there are several recently published collections of papers about the Vikings in Britain and Ireland: *Land, Sea and Home. Proceedings of a Conference on Viking-period Settlement* (edited by John Hines and others (Leeds: Maney, 2004)), *Vikings and the Danelaw* (edited by James Graham-Campbell and others (see below under England)), *Scandinavia and Europe 800-1350: Contact, Conflict, and Coexistence* (edited by Jonathan Adams and Katherine Holman (Turnhout: Brepols, 2004), *Cultures in Contact: Scandinavian Settlement in England in the Ninth and Tenth Centuries* (edited by Dawn Hadley and Julian D. Richards (see below under England)), *The Vikings in Ireland* (edited by Anne-Christine Larsen (see below under Ireland), and *Ireland and Scandinavia in the Viking Age* (edited by H.B. Clarke and others (see below under Ireland). All of these books contain introductory surveys alongside more detailed articles about the impact of the Vikings in these regions.

Those interested in finding out more about the Vikings might also be interested in the journal *Saga-Book*, published by the Viking Society for Northern Research. This has in-depth reviews of books and detailed articles on the history, literature, language and archaeology of Scandinavia in the Middle Ages. The Viking Society also holds meetings twice a year and organizes an annual conference in England for those new to the subject, as well as producing editions and translations of sagas, poetry and histories. Those interested in subscribing should write to the Society at vsnr@ucl.ac.uk or visit their website www.shef.ac.uk/viking-society/.

Surveys of Viking Activity in the British Isles

Davies, Wendy, ed., *From the Vikings to the Normans*. Oxford University Press, 2003 (particularly Barbara Crawford's article 'The Vikings', pp. 41-71, which provides a survey of Viking activity in the British Isles from the ninth to the mid-eleventh century.)

Hall, Richard A., *Viking Age Archaeology in Britain and Ireland.* Princes Risborough: Shire, 1990. (A short readable survey (about 60 pages) of Viking activity with details of archaeological finds, including coins, graves, and stone sculpture.)

Loyn, H.R., *The Vikings in Britain.* London: BCA, 1977. (Classic survey. See introduction for further details.)

Richards, Julian, *Blood of the Vikings.* London: Hodder and Stoughton, 2001. (Readable and nicely illustrated book produced to accompany the BBC TV series. See introduction for further details.)

England

Baldwin, John R. and Ian D. Whyte, eds, *The Scandinavians in Cumbria.* Edinburgh: Scottish Society for Northern Studies, 1985. (Collection of articles about different types of evidence for Vikings: archaeology, history, sculpture, place-names and language.)

Barlow, Frank, *The Godwins: The Rise and Fall of a Noble Dynasty.* London: Pearson, 2002. (Excellent account of late Anglo-Saxon England, from Cnut's reign to the Norman Conquest, seen through the fortunes of the Anglo-Danish Godwin family.)

Campbell, James, ed., *The Anglo-Saxons.* London: Penguin, 1991. (Best general introduction to the period, with many illustrations.)

Cavill, Paul, Stephen E. Harding and Judith Jesch, *Wirral and its Viking Heritage.* Nottingham: English Place-Name Society, 2000. (Collection of articles by modern scholars published alongside classic essays by F.T. Wainwright, J. McN. Dodgson, and J.D. Bu'lock on the place-names and history of the region.)

Clanchy, M.T., *England and its Rulers 1066-1272.* 2nd edition. Oxford: Blackwell, 1998 (Good survey of the political history of this period.)

DeVries, Kelly, *The Norwegian Invasion of England in 1066*. Woodbridge: Boydell, 1999 (The only modern in-depth treatment of the Battle of Stamford Bridge.)

Edwards, B.J.N., Vik*ings in North West England: The Artifacts*. Lancaster: Centre for North-West Regional Studies, University of Lancaster, 1998. (Comprehensive survey of the archaeological evidence for the Vikings, divided into chapters on burials, weapons and loot, sculpture and the Cuerdale hoard.)

Fletcher, Richard, *Bloodfeud: Murder and Revenge in Anglo-Saxon England*. London: BCA, 2002. (Fascinating account of northern politics that runs from the period of Scandinavian political dominance to the aftermath of the Norman Conquest.)

Gore, Derek, *The Vikings and Devon*. Exeter: Mint, 2001. (Short but useful introduction that focuses on a region that is often neglected in mainstream accounts of the Vikings.)

Graham-Campbell, James *et al.*, eds, *Vikings and the Danelaw: Select Papers from the Proceedings of the Thirteenth Viking Congress*. Oxford: Oxbow, 2001 (21 separate articles by experts examining the nature of the Viking impact through archaeological, historical, sculptural, place-name, literary and coin evidence.)

Hadley, Dawn, *The Northern Danelaw: Its Social Structure, c. 800–1100*. London: Leicester University Press, 2000. (Extremely detailed analysis.)

Hadley, Dawn and Julian D. Richards, eds, *Cultures in Contact: Scandinavian Settlement in England in the Ninth and Tenth Centuries*. Turnhout: Brepols, 2000. (15 articles by experts that examine the gradual assimilation of Viking settlers and the new regional identities that followed.)

Hall, Richard A., *Viking York*. London: B.T. Batsford, 1994. (With over 100 illustrations, this is the standard account of Viking Jorvik written by the director of the Coppergate excavations in the city. Focusing on archaeological evidence, the book examines the development of the city, the people, their houses and their lifestyles.)

Harding, Stephen, *Viking Mersey: Scandinavian Wirral, West Lancashire and Chester*. Birkenhead: Countyvise, 2002. (Popular and comprehensive account of a range of evidence for the Scandinavians in this part of north-west England. Written by a Wirralonian, this book is particularly interesting for its sections of local landmarks with Scandinavian names, local surnames, and the account of how modern genetic science is being used to track down the descendants of Vikings. Invaluable for interested locals, this also has a useful listing of websites and details of the author's own archive of newspaper articles, and TV and radio broadcasts.)

Hart, Cyril, *The Danelaw*. London: Hambledon, 1992. (Exhaustive survey of Danelaw institutions and administrations, using the evidence of Domesday Book, charters and wills. Also includes essays on problematic points regarding Battles of the Holme, *Brunanburh*, Ringmere, Maldon, and *Assandun*, and a discussion of Hereward the Wake.)

Hill, David, *An Atlas of Anglo-Saxon England*. Oxford: Blackwell, 1981. (Useful survey of all aspects of Anglo-Saxon England presented in map form with short text summaries. Includes maps showing the locations of Viking attacks and the movements of the Viking armies.)

Higham, N.J., and D.H. Hill, eds, *Edward the Elder 899-924*. London: Routledge, 2001. (Collection of 22 articles by experts examining the neglected 24-year reign of King Alfred's son, during which Edward campaigned successfully against the Vikings in northern and eastern England.)

Huscroft, Richard, *Ruling England 1042-1217*. Harlow: Pearson, 2005. (Clear introduction to the main political events in England between the end of Scandinavian rule and the Magna Carta, including chronology of main events (from 978) and useful suggestions for further reading.)

Kapelle, William E., *The Norman Conquest of the North: The Region and its Transformation, 1000-1135*. London: Croom Helm, 1979. (Authoritative and detailed account of the complex politics of the Anglo-Scandinavian north of England before and after 1066.)

Keynes, Simon, 'The Vikings in England, c. 790-1016.' In Peter Sawyer, ed., *The Oxford Illustrated History of the Vikings*, pp. 48-82, Oxford University Press, 1997, pp. 48-82. (Excellent short introduction to the Viking impact on England from the early raids to the conquest of England by Svein Forkbeard, which discusses place-names, coins and sculpture, as well as written evidence.)

Lawson, M.K., *Cnut: The Danes in England in the Early Eleventh Century*. London: Longman, 1993. (Definitive and detailed historical account of Cnut's reign, and the collapse of Danish rule in England.)

Margeson, Sue, *The Vikings in Norfolk*. Norwich: Norfolk Museums Service, 1997. (Illustrated booklet that provides a brief introduction to the Vikings in this region, playing particular attention to their impact on the region as seen through archaeological evidence.)

Page, R.I., *'A Most Vile People'; English Historians on the Vikings*. The Dorothea Coke Memorial Lecture in Northern Studies, University College London, 19 March 1986. London: Viking Society for Northern Research, 1987. (Short, authoritative account of different attitudes to the Vikings by contemporaries and early medieval historians. Full of thought-provoking insights.)

Richards, Julian D., *Viking Age England*. 2nd ed. Stroud: Tempus, 2001. (Using the latest archaeological evidence, this book provides a clear overview of the Viking contribution to Anglo-Saxon

England, and includes many useful suggestions for further reading.)

Sawyer, Peter H., *From Roman Britain to Norman England.* 2nd ed. London: Routledge, 1998. (Classic and comprehensive analysis of English history, tracing the Anglo-Saxon, Viking, and Norman conquests, by influential author. An essential introduction for anyone interested in placing the Viking raids on England in a wider historical context.)

Stafford, Pauline, *Unification and Conquest: A Political and Social History of England in the Tenth and Eleventh Centuries.* London: Edward Arnold, 1989. (Excellent analysis of this turbulent period of English history.)

Stenton, F.M., *Anglo-Saxon England.* 3rd ed. Oxford: Clarendon Press, 1971. (Classic work of scholarship that shaped views of the Anglo-Saxons and Vikings for generations.)

Ireland

Clarke, Howard B., Máire Ní Mhaonaigh and Raghnall Ó Floinn, eds, *Ireland and Scandinavia in the Early Viking Age.* Dublin: Four Courts, 1998. (Collection of 16 articles by experts on relations between Ireland and Scandinavia up until around 1000, which includes useful surveys of archaeological evidence and overviews from both Irish and Scandinavian perspectives.)

Larsen, Anne-Christine, ed., *The Vikings in Ireland.* Roskilde: The Viking Ship Museum, 2001. (Compilation of 14 articles by scholars from Ireland, England and Denmark that examines the meeting of Irish and Viking cultures through place-names, archaeology, history, literature, religion, and the history of art. Produced in conjunction with an exhibition, including a summary article surveying the exhibits.)

Ó Corráin, Donnchadh, 'Ireland, Wales, Man, and the Hebrides.' In Peter Sawyer, ed., *The Oxford Illustrated History of the Vikings*, pp. 83-109, Oxford University Press, 1997. (Short essay that provides an excellent introduction to the main events of the period and the Viking impact on the Irish Sea region. A welcome attempt to look at Viking activity beyond the limits of modern national borders.)

Ó Cróinín, Dáibhí, *Early Medieval Ireland 400–1200*. London: Longman, 1995. (Standard text-book for this period.)

Smyth, Alfred P., *Scandinavian York and Dublin: The History and Archaeology of Two Related Viking Kingdoms*. Dublin: Irish Academic Press, 1987. (Classic, sometimes controversial, starting point for those wishing to understand the complexities of this obscure period of Irish and Northumbrian history and trace the close links between Viking activity in Ireland and northern England.)

Scotland, Including Orkney, Shetland, the Hebrides and the Isle of Man

Batey, Colleen E., Judith Jesch and Christopher D. Morris, eds, *The Viking Age in Caithness, Orkney and the North Atlantic*. Edinburgh University Press, 1993. (Authoritative collection of 35 essays on the Vikings and their immediate successors in northern Scotland, the Northern Isles, Greenland, Iceland and the Faroe Islands. Some articles are general surveys, while others are rather specialist.)

Crawford, Barbara E., *Scandinavian Scotland*. Leicester University Press, 1987. (Essential starting point for anyone wishing to know more about the impact of the Vikings on Scotland, the Northern and Western Isles, and the Isle of Man between around 800 and 1066. This book covers historical, archaeological, place-name, and literary evidence, and also includes useful sections on sources and the geography of this area.)

Fell, Christine E. *et al.*, eds, *The Viking Age in the Isle of Man*. London: Viking Society for Northern Research, 1983. (Important collection of 12 articles by experts, surveying Norse influence on archaeology, place-names, coins, runic inscriptions, sculpture and language of the island.)

Graham-Campbell, James and Colleen E. Batey, *Vikings in Scotland: An Archaeological Survey*. Edinburgh University Press, 1998. (Comprehensive survey, which includes sections on Scotland before the Vikings, the Norwegian background, and sources, as well as regional overviews and chapters on graves, settlements, coins and silver.)

Hudson, Benjamin, *Viking Pirates and Christian Princes. Dynasty, Religion, and Empire in the North Atlantic*. New York: Oxford University Press, 2005. (The stories of two families — the Olafssons and Haraldssons — that dominated politics in Dublin, the Hebrides, and the Isle of Man from the tenth to the twelfth century. An unusual and welcome attempt to move away from scholarship that follows national borders and the limits of historical periods, such as the Viking Age. Hudson also shows how these Viking families soon abandoned piracy and established themselves as Christian rulers in the Scandinavian and Celtic worlds.)

McDonald, R. Andrew, *The Kingdom of the Isles: Scotland's Western Seaboard, c.1100–c.1336*. East Linton: Tuckwell, 1997. (An essentially political history from the mighty Somerled to the first Lord of the Isles, John MacDonald, which saw the rise and fall of this island kingdom and the emergence of a new form of lordship.)

Ó Corráin, Donnchadh, 'Ireland, Wales, Man, and the Hebrides.' In Peter Sawyer, ed., *The Oxford Illustrated History of the Vikings*, pp. 83-109, Oxford University Press, 1997. (See above, under Ireland.)

Owen, Olwyn, *The Sea Road: A Viking Voyage Through Scotland*. Edinburgh: Canongate books with Historic Scotland, 1999. (Lively and accessible survey of sites and finds from Scotland and the Isles, with many illustrations and maps.)

Power, Rosemary, 'Meeting in Norway: Norse-Gaelic Relations in the Kingdom of Man and the Isles, 1090-1270', *Saga-Book* 29, 2005, pp. 5-66. (A valuable survey of events and personalities in this obscure but important time, which is often neglected as it postdates the Viking Age. Also a welcome attempt to tackle the complexities of this region's history, where English, Irish, Norwegian, Scottish and Welsh politics intersect.)

Ritchie, Anna, *Viking Scotland*. London: B.T. Batsford and Historic Scotland, 1993 (Popular survey of Viking impact, focusing on archaeological legacy. Also includes short chapters on period 1100-1300 and Scotland's Viking inheritance.)

Thomson, William P.L., *History of Orkney*. Edinburgh: Mercat Press, 1987. (2nd edition, 2001). (Authoritative and readable survey from the Picts to the twentieth century. This is particularly useful for its extensive treatment of the period between 1066 and 1466 that is generally neglected or skimmed over in many books.)

Wales

Davies, Wendy, *Wales in the Early Middle Ages*. Leicester University Press, 1982. (Excellent survey of the entire period.)

Loyn, Henry, *The Vikings in Wales*. The Dorothea Coke Memorial Lecture in Northern Studies, University College, London, 1976. London: University College, London, 1977. (Short pamphlet that is a classic account of Viking activity and impact, by an eminent historian.)

Ó Corráin, Donnchadh, 'Ireland, Wales, Man, and the Hebrides.' In Peter Sawyer, ed., *The Oxford Illustrated History of the Vikings*, pp. 83-109 Oxford University Press, 1997 (see above, under Ireland).

Redknap, Mark, *Vikings in Wales: An Archaeological Quest.* Cardiff: National Museums and Galleries of Wales, 2000. (Popular and lavishly illustrated account that provides an up-to-date account of archaeological finds, alongside summaries of place-names and sculpture. Useful appendices include suggestions for further reading, a glossary, museums and monuments to visit, and a summary list of silver hoards found in Wales.)

General Accounts of the Vikings

Graham-Campbell, James, ed., *The Viking World.* 2nd ed. London: Windward and Frances Lincoln, 1989. (Lavishly illustrated account for the general reader.)

Graham-Campbell, James, ed., *Cultural Atlas of the Viking World.* Oxford: Andromeda, 1994. (Another illustrated account for the general reader; similar to *The Viking World* but with more detailed text.)

Helle, Knut, ed., *The Cambridge History of Scandinavia: Vol. 1: Prehistory to 15.* Cambridge University Press, 2003. (Massive scholarly tome containing over 20 articles relating to all aspects of Scandinavian history during this period.)

Holman, Katherine, *Historical Dictionary of the Vikings.* Lanham, MD: Scarecrow, 2004. (Alphabetical catalogue of people, events, and finds from the Viking Age, with a chronology of events and introductory essay. Useful reference tool, rather than a read.)

Richards, Julian D., *The Vikings: A Very Short Introduction.* Oxford University Press, 2005. (Brief, readable survey of Vikings at home and abroad, as well as interesting chapter on the Romantic revival of the Vikings, Nazi propaganda and contemporary views of the Vikings.)

Roesdahl, Else, *The Vikings*. Rev. ed. London: Penguin, 1998. (Written by an eminent Danish archaeologist, this is a readable introduction with slightly more emphasis on Scandinavians at home than abroad.)

Roesdahl, Else and David M. Wilson, eds, *From Viking to Crusader: Scandinavia and Europe 800-1200*. The 22nd Council of Europe Exhibition. Copenhagen: Nordic Council of Ministers and The Council of Europe, 1992. (Catalogue of the exhibits, containing masses of illustrations and a large number of short introductions into topics such as art, runes, Scandinavian paganism, churches, weapons, dress, coins, pilgrimages and crusades.)

Sawyer, Birgit and Peter, *Medieval Scandinavia: From Conversion to Reformation circa 800-1500*. Minneapolis: University of Minnesota, 1993. (Extremely useful survey of Scandinavian history, that looks at developments with Denmark, Norway and Sweden rather than focusing on the Viking attacks. The longer time period also allows the authors to show how Scandinavia was fully integrated into the European political and cultural mainstream.)

Sawyer, P.H., *The Age of the Vikings*. 2nd ed. London: Edward Arnold, 1971. (Influential re-evaluation of the impact of the Vikings, with its main focus on Western Europe. Essential starting point for anyone interested in understanding modern debates.)

Sawyer, P.H., *Kings and Vikings*. London: Methuen, 1982. (Important account of internal developments in Scandinavia, alongside Viking activity.)

Sawyer, Peter, ed., *The Oxford Illustrated History of the Vikings*. Oxford University Press, 1997. (Useful collection of articles by acknowledged experts, surveying Viking activity abroad and Scandinavian society at home. More in-depth articles than some introductions, with the emphasis on history and literature, rather than archaeology.)

KEY DATES

786-802 Reign of King Beorhtric of Wessex; *Anglo-Saxon Chronicle* recorded attack on Portland, Dorset, England by men from Hordaland, Norway.

793   Monastery of St Cuthbert on Lindisfarne, Northumbria, England attacked by Vikings on 8 June.

795   Viking attacks on *Rechru* (probably Rathlin Island off northern Irish coast) and Scottish Hebridean island of Skye recorded by *Annals of Ulster*.

802   Monastery on Hebridean island of Iona attacked by Vikings.

806   Another Viking attack on Iona left 68 monks dead.

825   Vikings attacked Hebridean island of Iona again, killing its prior, Blathmac.

835   Isle of Sheppey in Thames estuary attacked by Vikings.

836   Viking victory over the West Saxons at Carhampton, Somerset, England. Viking fleets moved inland in Ireland.

839   Viking attack on the Picts.

840   First overwintering of Vikings in Ireland, on Lough Neagh.

841   Vikings established settlement (*longphort*) in Dublin, Ireland.

844   Viking fleet on Lough Ree plundered surrounding area.

849   New Viking fleet arrived in Ireland.

851   First overwintering of Vikings in England, on Isle of Thanet in Thames Estuary. London and Canterbury attacked. Vikings defeated at Aclea by West Saxons. Clash between incoming 'dark' (=Danes?) and established 'fair' (=Norwegians?) Vikings in Dublin.

852	Viking raids on the Welsh coast.
853	All Vikings in Ireland submitted to Olaf the White.
865	Great Army arrived in East Anglia, England, commencing long campaign that resulted in first Scandinavian settlements of England.
866	English town of York captured by Great Army. Picts paid tribute to the Vikings.
867	Kings Ælla and Osberht of Northumbria killed during attempt to recapture York from Vikings.
869	Edmund, king of English East Anglia, killed by Vikings.
870	Dublin Vikings besieged and captured Scottish stronghold of Dumbarton, Strathclyde, south-west Scotland.
871	Alfred became king of English kingdom of Wessex.
873	Death of King Ivar of Dublin. Great Army wintered in Repton, Derbyshire, England.
874	Ceolwulf established as puppet ruler of Mercia. Split in Great Army. One part of Great Army, led by Halfdan, headed north, while other, under three kings, moved south and wintered in Cambridge.
876	Halfdan's Vikings settled in English kingdom of Northumbria.
877	North-eastern half of Mercia settled by Scandinavians.
878	Following surprise Viking attack on Chippenham, Alfred the Great of Wessex forced to take refuge in marshes of Athelney, Somerset. Vikings defeated by English under Alfred of Wessex at Edington. Treaty of Wedmore established border between Wessex and Scandinavian army in East Anglia; treaty included conversion of Viking leader, Guthrum. First overwintering of Vikings in Wales (in Dyfed).
880	English kingdom of East Anglia settled by Great Army under Guthrum.
886	Terms of Treaty of Wedmore reconfirmed by King Alfred and Guthrum.

c. 890   Death of Guthrum of East Anglia.

893-96   Viking army under Hastein attempted further conquests in England, but was unsuccessful.

893   Battle of Buttington (probably the village near Welshpool, Powys, Wales). English and Welsh forces besieged and then defeated Hastein's Vikings.

896   Sihtric, son of Ivar, killed during dispute between rival Scandinavian factions in Dublin.

899   Death of King Alfred of Wessex. Succeeded by son, Edward the Elder.

902   Vikings expelled from Dublin by Irish.

903   Ingimund and his Vikings expelled from Anglesey.

910   English victory over Danish settlers at Battle of Tettenhall, Staffordshire, England on 5 August. Three Danish kings — Eowils, Halfdan, and Ivar — killed, along with eleven *jarls*.

912-20   English reconquest of Danelaw.

914   Viking fleet from Brittany raided in south Wales.

917   Norse settlement of Dublin reestablished by Sigtrygg Cáech.

919   Ragnald recognized as king of York.

924   Death of Edward the Elder. Succeeded by Athelstan.

927   Athelstan reconquered York from Guthfrith, brother of Sigtrygg Cáech.

937   Battle of Brunanburh fought by English king, Athelstan, against Hiberno-Norse alliance. English victory recorded in poem in *Anglo-Saxon Chronicle*.

954   Erik Blood-Axe, last Viking king of York, killed at Stainmore in Yorkshire, England.

978   Æthelred II crowned king of England.

980   Vikings of Dublin defeated in Battle of Tara in Ireland.

985   Sigurd the Stout became earl of Orkney.

989   Sigtrygg Silk-Beard became king of Dublin.

991   Battle of Maldon in Essex, England. First Danegeld paid after Olaf Tryggvason's Viking army defeated English under Ealdorman Byrthnoth.

1002   King Æthelred II of England ordered massacre of all Danes in England on St Brice's Day (13 November).

1009-12 Viking army of Thorkell the Tall harried southern England.

1013   Svein Forkbeard of Denmark received submission of English.

1014   Death of Svein Forkbeard. Æthelred II returned from exile in Normandy, and Cnut left for Denmark. Battle of Clontarf fought near Dublin, Ireland, on Good Friday. Irish high-king, Brian Boru, killed. Death of Sigurd the Stout. His son, Thorfinn the Mighty, became earl of Orkney.

1015   Cnut returned with army to England.

1016   Death of Æthelred II. Succeeded by his son, Edmund Ironside. Edmund defeated by Cnut at Ashingdon. England partitioned between Cnut and Edmund at Olney. Death of Edmund.

1017   Cnut, son of Svein Forkbeard of Denmark, crowned king of England. Cnut married Emma of Normandy, widow of Æthelred II.

1019   Cnut became king of Denmark after death of brother, Harald.

1028   Cnut installed son, Svein, and Svein's English mother, Ælfgifu, as representatives in Norway.

1035   Death of Cnut, king of England, Denmark and Norway. In England, Cnut succeeded by son, Harold Harefoot; in Denmark, by son, Harthacnut; and in Norway, by Olaf Haraldsson's son, Magnus the Good.

1040   Harthacnut became king of England following death of Harold Harefoot on 17 March.

1042   Death of Harthacnut marked end of Danish rule in England. English royal line restored with coronation of Edward the Confessor, son of Æthelred II and Emma of Normandy.

1052   Diarmait, king of Leinster, seized control of Dublin.

1065   Death of Thorfinn the Mighty.

1066   King Harald Hard-Ruler of Norway killed in Battle of Stamford Bridge, Yorkshire, England. William the Conqueror defeated English king, Harold Godwinesson, in Battle of Hastings.

1069-70 Svein Estrithsson, king of Denmark, invaded England.

1072   Diarmait, 'king of Wales and the Isles and Dublin' died. Muirchertach, great-grandson of Brian Boru, became king of Dublin.

1073   Vikings attacked St David's, Wales.

1075   Last Danish invasion of England by Knut II Sveinsson and Earl Hákon of Denmark in support of an uprising against William the Conqueror. York was plundered, but the Danes then left England.

1079   Godred Crovan became king of the Isle of Man after victory at Battle of Skyhill.

1080   Vikings attacked St David's, Wales.

1085   Knut II of Denmark abandoned plans for invasion of England following domestic unrest.

1086   Knut II of Denmark murdered in Odense. Domesday Book presented to William the Conqueror.

1089   Vikings attacked St David's, Wales again.

1091   New Viking attack on St David's, Wales. Godred Crovan became king of Dublin.

1094   Godred Crovan expelled from Dublin; Domnall mac Muirchertaig became king of Dublin.

1095-96 Death of Godred Crovan; succeeded by his son, Lagman, who then abdicated in favour of Domnall mac Muirchertaig of Dublin.

1098   King Magnus Bare-Foot of Norway's first expedition to Norse colonies in the west. He deposed earl of Orkney and put his son, Sigurd, in charge of the islands; captured king of Isle of Man; defeated the Norman earls of Chester and Shrewsbury off Anglesey (Battle of the Menai Straits); his overlordship of the Isles was recognized by Edgar, king of Scotland.

1102 Magnus Bare-Foot's second western expedition. He spent the winter with Muirchertach II, Irish high-king, and made a marriage alliance with him.

1103 Death of Magnus Bare-Foot in Ulster, Northern Ireland. Olaf I, son of Godred Crovan, became king of the Isle of Man.

1117 Earl Magnus of Orkney murdered on island of Egilsay by his cousin, Hákon Paulsson.

1118 Domnall mac Muirchertaig of Dublin deposed.

1136 St Magnus's nephew, Rognvald Kali, became earl of Orkney. Work on a cathedral dedicated to St Magnus of Orkney begun at Kirkwall.

1156 Somerled of Argyll won control of the southern Hebrides (south of the Ardnamurchan Point) from his brother-in-law, Godred II of Man.

1158 Death of Earl Rognvald Kali of Orkney.

1170-71 Anglo-Norman conquest of Dublin; the town's last Norse king was executed.

1195 Norway took Shetland with all its taxes and dues from the Orkney earls as punishment for their part in the rebellion against King Sverri of Norway.

1231 First Scottish earl of Orkney.

1263 King Hákon IV Hákonarson of Norway fought the Scots in the Battle of Largs off Scotland's west coast. Inconclusive, but Hákon forced to retreat to Orkney, where he died.

1266 Treaty of Perth signed by Norway and Scotland; Scotland purchased the Norwegian colonies of the Hebrides, including the Isle of Man. Although technically under the Scottish crown after the Treaty of Perth (1266), descendants of Somerled (MacDougalls and later MacDonalds) remained as Lord of the Isles until 1493.

1468-69 Orkney and Shetland pawned to Scotland by Christian I, king of Denmark and Norway, in payment of the dowry of his daughter, Margaret, on her marriage to James III of Scotland.

iNDEX

CPSIA information can be obtained
at www.ICGtesting.com
Printed in the USA
LVHW110604060821
694642LV00003B/33